/ATMOSPHERE/
THE ORIGIN OF AIR GRID

VICTORIA WATSON

Based on my original thesis submitted for the degree of Doctor of Philosophy,
University College London, 2004

An AIR Grid Publication

ISBN: 9780995589384

INTRODUCTION

The thesis begins with an observation by the art historian Rosalind Krauss about the modernist architect Ludwig Mies van der Rohe. In 1992 Krauss had been invited to speak at a symposium. It was a celebration of the twenty fifth anniversary of the Toronto Dominion Centre, a building designed by Mies between 1963 and 1969, towards the end of his life (Mies dies in 1969). The symposium papers were published in The Presence of Mies, a book edited by the art historian Detlef Mertins. In the introduction to her paper, appearing under the title The Grid, the /Cloud/ and the Detail, Krauss expressed some surprise because as she was researching the topic she came across a strange new phenomenon, an anti-modernist Mies, she wrote:

As I was reading some of the recent literature on Mies van der Rohe, I encountered a phenomenon I had not known of until then: I came across the politically correct Mies, the poststructuralist Mies, almost, we could say, the postmodernist Mies. Which also means that I began to understand what I had not before, namely, why I had been invited to a conference on the 'presence of Mies.'[1]

To understand why Krauss was bemused it is necessary to know something of the history of the old Mies. Unlike Le Corbusier, Walter Gropius and other representatives of the Modern Movement it was not until late in his career that Mies came to be considered a leading contributor to that movement. It was in the 1950s and '60s that Mies, then in his 70s, began to enjoy a wealth of commissions and publications about his work. However, just as Mies' career was rising to a pinnacle of success so, within the institution of architecture, a growing critique of the tenets of the Modern Movement was beginning to form. The critique, broadly labelled 'post-modernism' could be aimed as easily at the mythic figure of Mies as it could be aimed at the Modern Movement in general. During the 1970s the positive response and reception of Miesian architecture began to diminish. In the face of a burgeoning post-modern critique that called for a plurality of architectures, supposedly responsive to the complexity of social structures and institutions, Mies' architecture came to look anaemic and boring.[2] Interest in Mies lay dormant for several years, but in 1986 an important event took place that was to initiate a reawakening of interest; that event was the reconstruction of the Barcelona Pavilion.

The Barcelona Pavilion had been designed by Mies and erected to serve as a showcase exhibit, its purpose being to represent the German Weimar Republic at the Barcelona International Exposition of 1929. Despite its temporary status, the pavilion was written into the histories of Modern Movement Architecture as a key structural feature, it became an icon of that history. However, because it had been dismantled shortly after the exposition, so the pavilion's reputation was built on the evidence of photography, reproductions of drawings and textual descriptions but on little, if any, direct, first hand experience of the building itself.

The reconstruction of the pavilion was organised by Ignasi de Solà Morales, Christian Cirici and Fernando Ramos. The value of the reconstruction was that it facilitated embodied, real-time encounters with an actual built structure. Such encounters triggered novel, even spooky experiences because it was not only the physical presence of the pavilion, the materials, the disposition of space, the quality of light and air as it permeated and mediated the pavilion's surfaces that visitors encountered but also the pavilion's mythic status within the canonical history of the Modern Movement, which seemed to bring with it the curious feeling that something from the past had returned to haunt the present!

The novelty of the pavilion had a curious effect on the appreciation of Miesian architecture, a kind of forgetfulness set in, as if the pavilion had leapfrogged over all Mies' other works, causing them to disappear. If the pavilion came to be seen as the focal point of Mies' career then it is hardly surprising the large tower and single-span structures he developed in the 1950s and 60s receeded into the background.

Seen as the focus of Mies' career, the pavilion was made to endure a superfluity of critical attention, perhaps more than any small, temporary structure can reasonably be expected to sustain! In her Toronto paper Krauss observed that much of this attention was being framed in terms of a critical strategy, originally developed by herself and others, for understanding Minimalist sculpture:

For it seems that a certain reading of Minimalism - let us call it phenomenological - had been imported into the field of architectural criticism to attack received opinion about Mies' purported classicism, his formalism, his aloofness. If Minimalist sculpture was initially understood - indeed in certain circles continues to be understood - through a set of classicist and idealist terms, understood, that is, as projecting timeless, unchanging geometries, what we might refer to in shorthand as Platonic solids, this reading was challenged (by myself and others) as entirely inappropriate to work that immersed itself in the actual, contingent particularities of its moment of being experienced, insisting that its very point was to focus its viewer's attention on how it changed from moment to moment of its perception in real time.[3]

Krauss then went on to state that while she was interested in the arguments laid out in favour of the new Mies the old one was for her much more interesting, she wrote:

Now, while I was very interested in the arguments laid out on behalf of this anti-classical Mies, I must say that I was far more riveted by another Mies, to whom I was re-introduced by Franz Schulz's critical biography, the Mies who, in perfect International Style manner continued to insist on architecture and the production of truth as generated by a set of a priori and universalizing laws, and who was caught up in the entirely modernist obsession of repeating a very small repertory of structural ideas - namely the prismatic tower and the universal space of the clear-span pavilion - and was, throughout his career, committed to the use of the grid. It was this Mies who, one chilly day in April 1967, presided over the nine-hour procedure of slowly jacking up the 1,000-ton plate of the gridded roof of the Berlin National Gallery so that it could be lowered onto the pin-joint connections of the eight columns that were to support it - making it seem therefore to float slightly above the columns and the glass of the pavilion's walls like a strangely weightless and buoyant cloud. [4]

The Mies who features in this thesis is the one whom Krauss was referring to here, i.e., the old Mies of the Modern Movement in Architecture, not the new Mies of the reconstructed pavilion.

The first part of the thesis, entitled Specters of Mies, examines the Modern Movement characterization of Mies, it aims to question and to clarify some of the assumptions upon which that characterization was based. Section 1.1: A Modern Movement Mies, introduces Mies' work in relation to the critical writing of authors who saw the Modern Movement in a positive light and sought to promote it. But it concludes by introducing a critic who was not so positive about the Modern Movement. His name was Henri Lefebvre, a social theorist and philosopher who, in the 1960s, was responsible for formulating a convincing and highly influential critique of the Modern Movement in Architecture and of modernist architects such as Mies. Lefebvre blamed the Modern Movement for having:

...outlined formulated and helped realize the space characteristic of capitalism - that is characteristic of that society which is run and dominated by the bourgeoisie.[5]

This quotation is taken from Lefebvre's book The Production of Space that he wrote between 1968 and 1972. The book presented a fascinating theory of architecture, which, amongst other things, included a convincing critique of the post war reconstruction then taking place in Europe. Throughout the book Lefebvre portrayed the new architecture of the emerging post war world as little more than the reification of the capitalist economy.

At the time Lefebvre was writing The Production of Space Mies was rising to a prestigious position, with a growing reputation as a leading proponent of Modern Movement principles and attitudes. Lefebvre's hostility towards Mies is only one instance of the general hostility he often expressed towards architects of the Modern Movement. Section 1.1 concludes by introducing the specter of Lefebvre to the specter of Mies; it is set in 1960, where Lefebvre was expressing grave reservations about the new architecture of the post war world.

Section 1.2: Miesian Architecture & Lefebvrian Space, breaks with the analysis of Section 1.1 and is more speculative. Having concluded Section 1.1 by introducing Lefebvre to the Modern Movement Mies, Section 1.2 attempts to apply Lefebvre's ideas about architecture, as opposed to his criticism of the Modern Movement, to the architecture of Mies. The reason for engaging with Mies' work through a body of ideas that, at least superficially, seems hostile to it is because many of Lefebvre's ideas about architecture are derived from philosophical and theoretical sources that were also important influences for Mies. By turning the lens of Lefebvrian theory onto the architecture of Mies it is the intention of this section of the thesis to produce a new reading of Mies, hopefully a useful one with which to confront the Minimalist readings that Krauss objected to at the Toronto conference.

The body of research that first began to reveal the extent of Mies' philosophical and theoretical preoccupations and influences was conducted by the architectural historian Fritz Neumeyer. It was published under the title Mies van der Rohe, Das Kunstlose Wort: Gedanken zur Baukunst. Neumeyer's book was first published in the same year as the opening of the newly reconstructed Barcelona Pavilion, 1986.

Neumeyer's book was translated into English and republished in 1991 as The Artless Word, Mies van der Rohe on the Building Art. It was an ingenious work of archival research. Through meticulous analysis and knowledgeable interpretation of the Mies archives, Neumeyer put together an astonishing intellectual biography. The book presented Mies as an avid reader in the fields of architectural theory, nineteenth century German aesthetics, Modern and Medieval philosophy and science, particularly life-sciences. Neumeyer located Mies' work in a tradition of thinking about architecture that could be traced back to Alberti, taking as its fundamental premise the concept of concinnitas.[6] This aspect of Neumeyer's reading is left as a tantalising yet peripheral aside in the thesis work.[7]

Neumeyer's research has been an invaluable resource for this thesis, affording valuable and exciting insights into Mies' intellectual life and supplying much of the scholarship necessary to connect Mies' thinking to Lefebvre's.

The second part of the thesis, Making and Using AIR (nee Cotton) Grid, arises from the second part of Krauss' Toronto paper. In the first part of her paper Krauss drew attention to two key aspects of Mies' modernism, the first was the problem of the grid and the second was the question of autonomy. She then declared herself inadequate to the task of discussing these topics through reflection upon works of architecture and so, in the second part of the paper, turned to the work of the painter Agnes Martin.

Krauss introduced Martin as a painter who, since 1960, had been obsessed with producing paintings, always measuring six foot square and constructed with pencilled lines on a lightly gessoed canvas surface (figure 1). The lines were arranged either as grids or as bands. Although for Krauss Martin's paintings were unflinchingly abstract she complained of a general tendency amongst critics to read them as analogues of nature. Such readings, complained Krauss, were made despite the insistence of Martin herself that her paintings were not about nature:

It is this covert allusion to nature that the category 'abstract sublime' has come to imply, with the abstract work always able to be decoded by its romantic double: Mark Rothko read out through Casper David Friedrich; Jackson Pollock by J.M.W. Turner's storms; Martin by Turner's skies.[8]

Krauss was not convinced by the romantic readings of Martin's work, to make her point she drew attention to Martin's own insistence on the work's abstraction and the fact of its lacking a subject. With great approval Krauss cited a reading made by a critic called Kasha Linville, focusing on Linville's reading of a painting entitled *Red Bird*. Linville's reading included a description of what it is actually like to be in the presence of the painting. It described the painting as a sequence of optical textures that change as the viewing distance changes and it identified three key moments in the sequence of change. In her Toronto paper Krauss used quotations from Linville to describe those three moments:

First there is the close-to reading, in which one is engaged in the work's facture and drawing, in the details of its materiality in all their sparse precision: the irregular weave of the linen, the thickness and uniformity of the gesso, the touch of the application of the pencilled lines.[9]

The second moment of the painting occurs when the viewer steps back from the canvas, moving away from the tactile immediacy of the painting's materiality and mode of making. Linville observed how, as the viewer moves away, the painting changes, it becomes ambiguous. She used the expression 'going atmospheric' to evoke what it was like to experience the transition, as if the painting dissolves.

FIGURE 1

Agnes Martin, Night Sea, 1963, oil and gold leaf on canvas, 182.9 x 182.9 cm

Reflecting on Linville's account, Krauss wrote:

Linville's description of this effect is elegant and precise. 'I don't mean 'atmosphere' in the spatially illusionistic sense I associate with color field painting," she writes. 'Rather it is a non-radiating, impermeable....mist. It feels like, rather than looks like atmosphere. Somehow the red lines (she is writing here of a work called Red Bird) dematerialize the canvas, making it hazy, velvety.' [10]

The third moment of the painting involves a further stepping back from the canvas, in this transition the feeling of atmosphere dissipates and the painting becomes flat and opaque. As Krauss explained:

Wall-like and impenetrable, this view now disperses the earlier atmosphere. And this final result, as Linville again writes on Martin, is 'to make her paintings impermeable, immovable as stone.' [11]

Having introduced painterly atmospherics into her discussion, Krauss then went on to make an important distinction between the notion of 'atmosphere' involved in the abstract sublime readings of Martin's paintings and the notion of 'going atmospheric' that came out of Linville's reading. She explained how the abstract sublime readings posited atmosphere as the subject of the painting, wherein, just like any other landscape subject, such as clouds, sea or light, atmosphere is signified as the content of an image. On the other hand, Krauss explained, in Linville's reading atmosphere is presented as an affect of the painting, the painting does not look like atmosphere, it feels like atmosphere, it induces the perception of atmosphere in the viewer. Krauss uses inverted commas and forward slashes respectively to mark the distinction between atmosphere-as-signified and atmosphere-as-signifier:

Linville's three distances, that is, transform the experience from an intuition into a system, and convert 'atmosphere' from a signified (the content of an image) into a signifier - /atmosphere/ [12]

When language is theorised as a system for the production of meaning the signifier is considered to be a signal. In any linguistic system the significance of the signifier depends on everything else within that system which the signifier is not. The implication of Krauss' reading of Linville's three distances is that the signifier /atmosphere/ belongs to the system of signifiers with only one member. Because there are no other signifiers to relate to, so the atmospheric signifier cannot produce meaning, it is a system without difference, thus in a sense it is a pure signifier.

Another word that might be used instead of atmosphere is cloud. The actual experience of being engulfed by a cloud can be alarming, certainly it is visually challenging and can induce blindness, which can in turn give rise to loss of nerve, breathlessness and panic. However to a person standing outside, looking in, a cloud can be quite exhilarating because, as they gaze upon the nebulous volume, they are free to enjoy the curious bifurcation between sense and sensation at play in the process, as their perceptual apparatuses try to fathom the cloud's resistant depths.

In her Toronto paper Krauss implied that what she had to say about Martin's painterly grids had some bearing on the architectural grids of Mies; but she offered little if any guidance as to how to make the connection. There are two obvious differences between Martin's grids and Mies.' First, the marks of a pencil on a stretched and gessoed canvas produce hers, while his are produced by constructing out of steel, concrete, stone and glass. Second, Martin's paintings are produced at a scale that corresponds, approximately, to the size of the human body; Mies constructions are produced at the scale of the medium or large building.

The second part of this thesis is a design project, it aims to test out the thesis that Mies' grids too can be understood as /atmosphere/ and thus, in a certain sense, as messages from the forever unknown, i.e., pure signifiers.

The first section of the second part of this thesis, Genesis & Evolution, is a record of the research and development of AIR Grid. AIR Grid is a device for the production of /atmosphere/. As an artifact it occupies a region somewhere between Martin's painting and Mies' architecture. Air Grid is unlike Martin's painting in that it is, like Mies' architecture, constructed, not drawn. On the other hand, AIR Grid is unlike Mies' architecture in that it is, like Martin's painting, produced at a scale corresponding, approximately, to that of the human body, not that of the medium or large building.

The second section of the second part of this thesis, The Cotton Caves addresses the question of programme, that is the question of how the /atmosphere/ generated by AIR Grid, might be utilised, as a signifier, to trigger feelings of the unknown and yet, perhaps, necessary and valuable? In this section the thesis returns to address Lefebvre's critique of Modern Movement attitudes in architecture.

PART ONE
SPECTERS OF MIES

This part of the thesis is an analysis of a number of theoretical ideas about architecture that can be associated with Mies' work. It consists of two sections:

1.1: A Modern Movement Mies
1.2: Miesian Architecture & Lefebvrian Space.

In the first section the analysis is anchored in the study of that body of criticism which was instrumental in elevating Mies to the position where he was deemed to be a leading practitioner of the Modern Movement in Architecture. In the second section the argument is based upon the application of Henri Lefebvre's ideas about architecture (as opposed to his criticism of the Modern Movement) to the architecture of Mies. The reason for engaging with Mies' work in this way is because many of Lefebvre's ideas about architecture were derived from philosophical and theoretical sources that were also important for Mies' intellectual development. Thus Lefebvre's presuppositions about the intellectual lacuna of Modern Movement theory needs qualification if it is to be applied to Mies.

1.1: A MODERN MOVEMENT MIES

This section begins by exploring a body of literature that features Mies' architecture as its subject. The texts of study were produced between 1920 and 1960, i.e., the period of Mies' slow rise to fame. During the 1920s Mies began to participate in the activities of the Berlin avant-garde. His participation took a number of forms including theoretical and realised architectural projects, designing and organising exhibitions, organising and contributing to publications, membership of committees and institutions. By 1960 the name of Mies was almost synonymous with the Modern Movement in Architecture, he was considered a leading exponent of that movement. Mies was the director of the school of architecture at the Illinois Institute of Technology, he was conducting a successful practice in Chicago that was receiving commissions for prestigious projects in the United States, Canada, South America and Europe.

The texts selected and examined in this section are interesting in three respects, two of them positive, the third problematic. Since the 1960s there has been a tendency to refer to the Modern Movement as if it were a single entity, driven by a homogenous set of interests, aims and objectives. The texts examined in this section evidence a diversity of critical interests, developed through engagement with Mies work. Between them the texts demonstrate some of the quite considerable diversity of interests hidden beneath the rubric of the Modern Movement. Second, each text presents Mies' architecture from within a specific critical framework. Taken together the selection of critical positions offers a provocative, if by no means exhaustive, array of concepts for understanding Mies work. Third, there is a tendency among the texts to revere Mies' work. Reverence is problematic because it places a barrier around the work and reduces its usefulness as a cultural model, closing it to new lines of inquiry and to further critical attention.

The concluding pages of this section introduce two texts by Lefebvre. The first, Notes on a New Town, published in 1960, did not refer directly to Mies. However it was concerned with the Modern Movement in Architecture because Lefebvre saw evidence of that movement in the post-war reconstruction and development taking place in Europe at the time. Lefebvre was particularly critical of the attitudes to architecture and planning presupposed in the development of new towns, he doubted if those developments were capable of producing authentic architecture (we will consider later what Lefebvre meant by authentic). It was these concerns that led Lefebvre, between 1968 and 1972, to write The Production of Space. It was in that book that Lefebvre explicitly located the origins of Modern Movement attitudes to space in the activities of the historic Bauhaus.

The Bauhaus was the state school of architecture and design of the German Weimar republic, it ran from 1919 to 1933. Mies was associated with the activities of the Bauhaus and between 1930 and 1933 was the school's director. Because of his association with the Bauhaus Lefebvre blamed Mies for having *'outlined formulated and helped realize the space characteristic of capitalism - that is characteristic of that society which is run and dominated by the bourgeoisie.'*[1] This section concludes with a discussion of those aspects of Bauhaus theory to which Lefebvre objected.

Theo van Doesburg: Pure Surface

Between 1925 and 1927 the de Stijl artist and theorist Theo van Doesburg wrote a series of articles about developments within contemporary architecture in Germany; these were published in the magazine Het Boubedrijf. Van Doesburg wanted to chart the development of what he understood to be a new kind of architecture. In order to theorise the new architecture Van Doesburg posited a binary structure of material and spirit, which, by attending to the functional needs of the dwelling, the new architecture would unify. Van Doesburg posited the functional needs of the dwelling as being of two types: physico-functional and psycho-functional. Each type corresponded to one term of the material/spatial binary. Physico-functional to material and psycho-functional to spirit, or sur-material needs as Doesburg sometimes referred to them:

In order to clarify the possibility of the unity of so-called 'spiritual' and material-constructive elements in architecture, one should imagine a dwelling laid out practically and logically in all respects. Everything in it caters to our material needs in the most comprehensive sense. Living in this dwelling, we will feel satisfied in only one sense, this dwelling will be in harmony with ourselves in only one aspect - the physico-functional. However, architecture may be expected to give all round satisfaction. Architecture will be the expression of the complete human being. That is to say: beside the physico-functional needs there are others (although inseparable from the one mentioned): psycho-functional ones, optic, phonetic, tactile ones etc. If these sur-material needs are not satisfied in our living quarters, we look for them outside, in museums, the concert hall etc. Because of architecture's deficiency we have wanted to escape this dualism by hanging paintings on our walls, by making furniture 'artistic', yes - by turning our homes into museums.[2]

Van Doesburg looked upon Mies as an architect who had made considerable innovations in the field of material-constructive design and who had thereby contributed toward the creation of a new appearance for architecture. He was especially impressed by Mies theoretical projects for urban towers made from glass.

In the early 1920s Mies produced two projects for glass

towers, these were the Project for an Office Building for Friedrichstrasse, Berlin, 1921, and the Project for a Glass Skyscraper, 1922 (Figure 2). These were theoretical projects represented in drawings and models, they were exhibited and published in magazines in Europe and in America, but were never built. In Mies' glass tower designs Van Doesburg saw lightness, clarity and impermanence, qualities which he took to be in accordance with the life tempo of modern times. As he explained:

The life tempo changes constantly according to inner cultural motivation, and architecture is only genuine when it is an expression of the cultivated awareness of time.[3]

For Van Doesburg the 'nervous' life tempo of modern times contrasted with the slow rhythm of the times directly preceding:

In contrast to modern, nervous man, who looks downward (to which fact we owe, among other things, the so-called footlight advertisements), people from the seventeenth and eighteenth century moved slowly, their gaze directed upwards. As we owe the modern footlight signs to the gait of modern man, so we owe the carefully applied ornamentation on the facades of houses to the gait of mankind of those times. The human being 'mit modernen Nerven' does not need, nor has the time to enjoy such ornaments.[4]

Van Doesburg admired Mies' glass tower designs because they demonstrated the constructive-material idea of a light, clear and transparent architecture with no need for applied ornamentation. However, he could not give his unqualified approval because of the curvaceous and diamantine shapes of the towers (figure 3). Van Doesburg read the curves and splayed angles of Mies' towers as evidence that they had been developed from a purely physico-functionalist approach to design. Although Van Doesburg thought the approach preferable to merely copying forms of the past, he was concerned that alone a physico-functionalist approach was insufficient and needed to be complimented by a psycho-functional approach.

Van Doesburg gave two reasons for his objections, first, he was anxious that architecture should not be confused with fine art - we have already seen something of this attitude in his objection to the house becoming like a museum. The confusion led to what Van Doesburg termed 'individual typification,' he gave the example of baroque and rococo architecture to illustrate what he meant, specifically it was the excessive ornament of baroque and rococo that Van Doesburg read as symptomatic of disciplinary confusion. Van Doesburg saw the danger of a different kind of formal excess in the case of contemporary, functionalist, approaches.

FIGURE 2

Mies van der Rohe, five seminal projects:
1. Office Building, Friedrichstrasse, Berlin, 1921, 2. Project for a Glass Skyscraper, 1922, 3. Concrete Office Block, 1922, 4. Brick Country House, 1922, 5. Concrete Country House, 1923

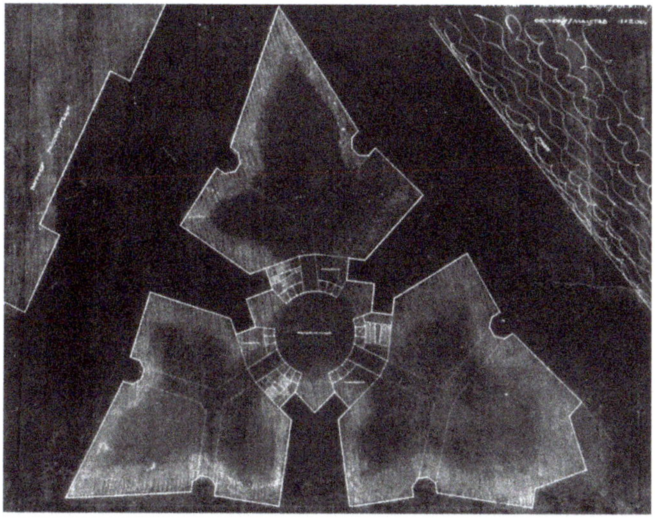

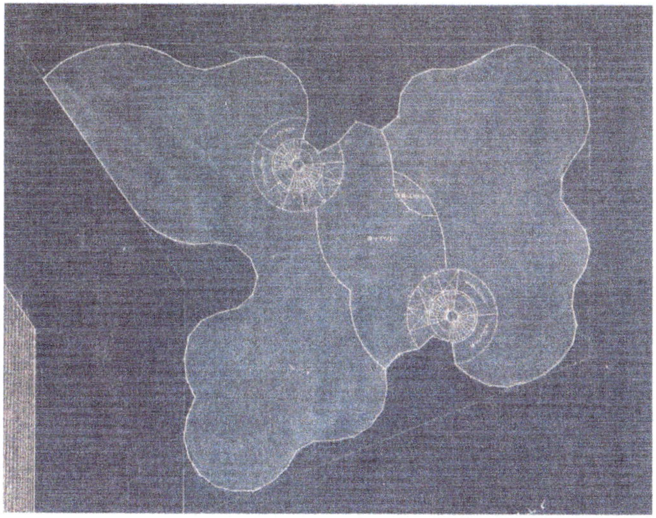

FIGURE 3

Above: Mies van der Rohe, Office Building, Friedrichstrasse, Berlin, 1921, typical floor plan
Below: Mies van der Rohe, Project for a Glass Skyscraper, 1922, typical floor plan

However, with the contemporary functional approach the formal excess could no longer be attributed to a fascination for applied ornament, rather it was due to the tendency of architects to design within a strict and highly particular definition of the building's material function. In adopting a strict, physico-functionalist approach to design, Van Doesburg claimed, the design process inevitably led to an over individualization of the built form. He wrote:

The so-called functionalists have, by a so very strict definition of the material function of the business enterprise in its ground plan and elevation, returned architecture again to the stage of individual typification of shape. What originated in decorative architecture as a result of esthetic speculation, emerges in the so called functionalist architecture out of purely economic and practical reasons. Thus, two essentially completely opposite view points can lead to one and the same result.[5]

Second, Van Doesburg objected to a strictly physico-functionalist approach to design because he believed the nervous modern individual required generous, rectangular spaces and not, as he saw it, fussily over determined spaces arrived at by mean-minded considerations of economy and practicality only:

The functionalists are adversaries of the rectangular layout of space, because in their eyes it is a waste of space.[6]

Van Doesburg evidenced his arguments against functionalist design by quoting from Adolf Behne's book *The Modern Functional Building* (1926):

The rectangular space, the straight line are not functional, but mechanical creations. When I consistently take biological function as a starting point, then the rectangular space is well-nigh nonsensical, for its four corners are dead space, unusable. If I would outline the actually used, trodden space of, for instance, a room, then I would definitely end up with a curve. The course of organic life does not know right angles nor straight lines.[7]

Having quoted him, Van Doesburg proceeded to attack Behne's biological argument by suggesting the excess cubic capacity of space laid out according to a rectilinear schema was indispensable for the psychological and mental well-being of the modern nervous system:

Our modern nervous system could not endure for long in a space functionally economized to the extreme, we need, in addition, freedom of movement. I would almost be so bold as to say a space for our mind.[8]

Van Doesburg's suspicions that Mies' glass towers were

based on a functionalist approach to design was not entirely convincing. The projects were first published as illustrated articles in the magazine Frülicht, 1, no.4, 1922. In the text Mies explained his deployment of curvaceous and diamantine forms without mentioning function, explaining how he had derived the forms from experiments with large glass models and how he had been particularly struck by the way light played upon the glass surfaces. In fairness to Van Doesburg it is important out point out the difficulty of conveying the phenomenon of light playing upon glass through the medium of the published article. Although transparency could have been conveyed through photographs it is difficult for a photograph to convey the shifts and constant transformations of reflections as light plays with glass.

In 1927 Van Doesburg was able to experience for himself a glass space designed by Mies. The German Werkbund exhibition, held in Stuttgart to explore the theme of dwelling (Mies was the director), included a special section on industry and craft. The special section was held in the Gewerbehalle Stadtgarten, in the centre of Stuttgart, with Mies responsible for one large installation. Mies divided a single hall into three areas, separated by fixed but freestanding walls of glass. The glass walls were made by mounting large sheets of glass in flat frames on nickel coated steel. A ceiling, consisting of strips of stretched fabric, ran above the tops of the freestanding glass walls and served to unify the three sub-spaces. The floor finish, in linoleum, picked out in zones of white, grey and red, almost, but not quite, coinciding with the spatial schema of the glass walls. Each of the three sub-spaces was sparsely but sufficiently furnished to indicate a particular mode of occupancy: living room, dining room, work room (figure 4).

Van Doesburg was at least as impressed, if not more so, by the exhibit in the Gewerbehalle Stadtgarten as he was by the exhibition of 'live' housing, which was to become famous as the Weißenhof Siedlung. Referring to Mies' design as 'the glass hall,' Van Doesburg especially appreciated the way Mies had solved the problem of displaying delicate materials in a public exhibition:

The glass hall, also executed after a design of Mies van der Rohe, owes its creation to the unequivocal task of displaying fragile materials (semi-transparent and opaque glass of different colors) in such a way that it would be shown to full advantage.[9]

In trying to articulate what it was about the design of the glass hall that so impressed him, Van Doesburg introduced the notion of materials having what he termed an 'energy force.' He suggested the best designers were able to work with the energy force of the material,

FIGURE 4

Mies van der Rohe, Glass Hall, exhibit of the Glass Industry, Werkbund Exhibition, Stuttgart, 1927 rather than against it, he wrote:

Every material has its own energy force and the challenge is to enhance this energy force to its maximum by proper application. The opposite is: violation of the material by wrong application, whereby a relatively large percentage of the energy force is lost. Weighing one material against another in respect to their energy and character, and proportioning them well, most certainly belongs to the essence of the new architecture. Only in this way can modern architecture bring to realization what it has to offer in involuntary beauty.[10]

By working with the energy force of a particular material Van Doesburg suggested it was possible to reveal a particular kind of beauty. He called it involuntary beauty and he understood it arose as a consequence of working with the character of the material itself, rather than imposing a preconceived aesthetic idea. The notion of materials possessing their own character endowed them with a kind of vitality and in those terms the art of the architect, or designer, who worked the materials could be understood as a mixture of charm and affection.

For Van Doesburg the work of the architect is a kind of seduction, leading to an involuntary disclosure of beauty. It appears, not in the construction, but by means of the construction. The energy force of the material is material is revealed as an 'ultimate surface,' he wrote:

The ultimate surface is in itself the result of the construction. The latter expresses itself in the ultimate surface. Bad construction leads to a bad surface. Good construction produces a sound surface with tension. Indeed, the finishing touch of architecture is in the finish of the surface, interior as well as exterior. The development of the ultimate surface is essential, from the first stone to the last stroke of paint. Every architect having a visual sense for construction knows this, and with this glass display Mies van der Rohe proved to be on top of this new problem.[11]

Notice the 'ultimate surface,' is a very particular surface, a surface with tension. Glass is somewhere between a solid and a liquid and does not always give the effect of being in tension, but the glass that Mies experimented with in his architecture, thin sheets of plate glass of enormous dimensions, did have a taut, membrane-like feeling.

Although Van Doesburg had not been able to detect surface tension in Mies' theoretical projects for towers of glass, reading only transparency, lightness and clarity, it seems that in the glass hall at Stuttgart he found himself feeling, not reading. What he felt was something radiant and fragile, he equated it with the *'new ideal of an empty space and a pure surface.'*[12]

Metaphysical Architecture: Alice Through the Looking Glass

The first reference to Mies to appear in print in Great Britain was an article by the architect Raymond McGrath. It was published in The Architectural Review in January 1932 and entitled Looking into Glass. The article was primarily about plate glass and about the potential for its use in the construction of architectural interiors. It introduced Mies as an architect known *'particularly by his interiors at the Plateglass Exhibition at Stuttgart, by his German Pavilion at the Barcelona Exhibition and by his Haus Tugendhat in Brünn.'*[13] Looking into Glass was illustrated with photographic images of Mies' projects. McGrath admired the projects for the perceptual effects they gave rise to, which he understood as a consequence of the deployment of large, unbroken surfaces of toned glass in black, grey and opal white. The effects he admired most were:

1) the illusion of depth and of space
2) reflections of the surrounding gardens or landscape

For McGrath, Mies' surfaces were not the taught, plasma-like boundaries enjoyed by Van Doesburg but a species of looking-glass mirror.

McGrath was interested in the potential for using glass in architecture more generally, he believed it had soothing qualities that could calm psychological distress. For him the beauty and value of the Miesian interiors was their potential for encounters of a mystical, magical kind, which he referred to as a *'sudden encounter with metaphysical architecture.'*[14] By metaphysical McGrath seems to have meant the opening up of an imaginary, magical world on the other side of the mirror, he wrote:

But more than any other synthetic material glass administers to our psychology and is, for that reason, such a softening influence upon the minds of journalists and their readers, 'professor lives in Glasshouse,' and 'Crystal Walls in London' are headlines capable of conjuring up as much magic as 'Alice through Looking Glass'.[15]

To enter into McGrath's feeling for glass it is worth following-up his reference to Alice's passage through the looking-glass. As it is narrated by Lewis Carroll, Alice to begin with, just looks into the glass, it is not a narcissistic gaze, she is not gazing at her own image but looking into the mirror filled with wonder and curiosity. Alice wants to see what lies beyond the limits of her own field of vision, to know if the world beyond continues as a mirror image of her own world, or is the mirroring effect only an illusion that will run out as she delves deeper into the mirror world. Scrutinizing he field of vision, Alice reports what she sees to Kitty the Kitten:

...now we come to the passage. You can just see a little peep of the passage in Looking-glass House, if you leave the door of our drawing-room wide open: and it is very like our passage as far as you can see, only you know it may be quite different on beyond.[16]

Alice's curiosity and determination lead her to clamber up onto the chimney-piece (the looking-glass is hanging above the fire-place), all the while carrying on the conversation with Kitty:

Let's pretend the glass has got all soft like gauze, so that we can get through. Why its turning into a sort of mist now, I declare! It'll be easy enough to get through.[17]

Sure enough the glass melts away into a bright silvery mist and Alice passes through and into the world on the other side. In passing through the mirror one of two things must have happened to Alice, either the mirror has dissolved or she has. Perhaps it was the hint of a similar kind of dissolution that McGrath felt in the Miesian interior, leading him to associate Mies' glass architecture with softness and metaphysical beauty.

In Mies' sparse writings it is hard to find any references that indicate Mies shared the same notion of metaphysics as McGrath's. The closest was a short text on the subject of mirrorglass, written as a contribution to a prospectus of the Verein Deutscher Spiegalglas Fabriken of March 13, 1933, but remained unpublished. In his text Mies used the notion of a 'luminous,' and 'original beauty,' which he claimed could be revealed through the deployment of glass in building:

Only now can we articulate space freely, open it up and connect it to the landscape. Now it becomes clear again what a wall is, what an opening, what is floor and what ceiling. Simplicity of construction, clarity of tectonic means, and purity of material reflect the luminosity of original beauty.[18]

Mies' desire for beauty, linked to his evident interest in glass, did seem to imply some kind of metaphysical curiosity. And there does seem to have been some similarity to McGrath's insofar as both saw glass as a means of challenging the limits of vision and thereby effecting the dissolution of spatial divisions, but notice there is an important difference. Mies was looking from the inside out into the natural environment. He was interested in the way glass might be used to create a transparent boundary between interior space and the surrounding landscape; he was not interested in seeing some other world beyond that boundary. Mies considered glass as an important factor in the form-giving process, he thought by using it he would be able to make the constructive elements of the building clear and unequivocal.

Mies' concern for clarity would seem to imply an interest in the transparency of glass, rather than its mirroring potential. In the context of his mirror-glass article the original beauty to which he referred seemed to lie much closer to Van Doesburg's notion of involuntary beauty, which was to be arrived at by working sympathetically with the material properties of glass, than to McGrath's magical kind of beauty.

There are other instances in which Mies referred to beauty in his writing. In 1930 he wrote an article entitled Build Beautifully and Practically! Stop this Cold Functionality, published in The Duisberger Generalanzeiger, 49, January 26. Here Mies claimed it was an anthropomorphic desire to search-out beauty and for this reason architecture could never be merely a matter of finding rational or technically perfect solutions to problems, he wrote:

It is a natural, human characteristic to consider not only the purposeful but also to search out and love beauty. Due to the powerful advance of technology this self-evident awareness seems to be somewhat repressed. It often appears as if our time would content itself with technical perfection. But this will not remain so. Our time has enormously many means for form-giving at its disposal. It just has not learned how to master them, perhaps because the mastery of the means, the technical difficulties alone, already requires so much energy that nothing is left over to apply these means also in a form-giving way.[19]

Here Mies directly associated beauty with form-giving. The term form-giving (formgebung) had been widely used in discussions of architecture since Goethe. In his article Mies relied on familiarity with the term to discuss his own work, but he qualified what form-giving meant to him by telling his readers a little more about what he meant by beauty. First he explained that *'beauty does not float around in the air, it is attached to things and irrevocably connected to the forms of the real world.'*[20] This statement would seem to cancel once and for all any suspicions that Mies' understanding of beauty was founded on a transcendental metaphysics. He went on to confirm his realist sense of beauty by describing it as a relational property, he wrote:

And what finally is beauty? Certainly nothing that can be calculated or measured. It is always something imponderable, something that lies in between things.[21]

One implication of Mies' comments on beauty is that beauty, by the nature of its being 'between things,' was in the air. However, for all its pervasiveness, beauty was not an unbounded expanse, like light. Beauty was drawn into the air as the immaterial trace of those formal relationships human subjects are aware of in perception.

Although Mies remarks on beauty are somewhat cryptic they nevertheless make it clear that Mies' understanding of beauty was not metaphysical in same transcendent sense of McGrath's understanding of beauty. Mies' interest in beauty was linked to a concern for the way that extensions, boundaries and thresholds are perceived in embodied, anthropological experience, in other words to an interest in space.

The International Style: The Rule of Function

In the same year as McGrath's article appeared the Museum of Modern Art in New York staged its first architectural exhibition. As an accompaniment to the exhibition the architect Philip Johnson and the architectural historian Henry-Russell Hitchcock prepared a book bearing the same name as the exhibition: The International Style. Jointly, the purpose of the exhibition and book was to identify and to make known to the American public the emergence of a new style of architecture.[22]

Although the new Style was presented as a mode of formal expression transcending national boundaries, it was endowed with a predominantly European heritage. The basic idea underpinning Johnson and Hitchcock's argument was that architecture is 'scientific building, infused with the aesthetic intelligence of genius.' The International Style listed four European architects as leading exponents of the new style, they were: Le Corbusier, Walter Gropius, JJP Oud and Mies, whom they praised as innovators in the fields of technology and aesthetics:

Whether or not the contemporary style should produce architecture as well as building, it certainly does so. Indeed many developments in structure and in articulation of function now incorporated in minimal building were first evolved in expensive constructions. All the leading modern architects of the international style have been technical as well as aesthetic innovators. The European functionalists who now disown Le Corbusier and Oud, and Gropius and Mies van der Rohe first learned the science of building from them. Most American functionalists have much to learn from the leaders of the international style, even if they cannot accept sincerely the aesthetic discipline those leaders have brought into being.[23]

In yoking architecture to the notion of technical innovation, The International Style linked it to the twin notions of progress and efficiency.

As a mode of expression *The International Style* was said to be characterised by three formal tendencies:

1) an emphasis on volume and transparency over solidity and mass.
2) the elaboration of surfaces, not through applied

ornamentation, but through a selective choice of material finishes and constructional detail

3) asymmetrical spatial composition born out of the contending demands of structural regularity and of functional specificity.

In order to demonstrate how the characteristics of the new style translated into actually buildings and projects a variety of examples by European architects were adduced and illustrated. These included but were by no means restricted to works by Corbusier, Gropius, Oud and Mies. In identifying the new style in this way, the authors of The International Style made it seem as if the history and theory of the buildings and projects to which they referred was secondary to the development of the new style. Presented as if the actual buildings and projects were exemplars of its stylistic principles, the new style was made to seem like a self-determining, autopoietic phenomenon that had arisen spontaneously, causing works such as the Barcelona Pavilion and the Tugendhat House to come into being. Presented as exemplary expressions of the new style, Mies' buildings became available to the American public as instances of 'scientific building infused with the aesthetic intelligence of genius.'

One telling omission from the pages of The International Style was the post-revolutionary works of the Soviet avant-garde. The buildings and projects of these architects were aimed at total social reconstruction. These architects believed there was an intimate link between a society and the physical environment it inhabits and as a consequence they believed the Communist revolution would be ineffective unless it totally transformed the Soviet environment. Through experimentation in urban design and architecture the Soviet architects aimed to evolve revolutionary structures that could reorientate the social totality. So far as formal expression was concerned it is hard to see why Soviet buildings and projects were left out of The International Style. Buildings such as Moisei Ginzburg and Ignatii Milinis' Narkomfin Building, Moscow, 1928-29; Ilija Golosov's Zuyev Club, Moscow, 1928; Konstantin Melnikov's Krivoarbatskil Pereulok residence, Moscow, 1929; Konstantin Melnikov's Soviet Pavilion for the Paris Exposition, 1925; all featured the characteristic modes of expression of the new style: emphasis on volume and transparency over solidity and mass; elaboration of surfaces through a selective choice of material finishes and constructional detail; asymmetrical spatial composition (figure 5). The omission of the Soviet work was symptomatic of a more general reduction present amongst the pages of The International Style, which was the tendency to promote the new style in the name of 'function.'

The authors of The International Style had a particular sense of function in mind that they explained in the final

FIGURE 5

top left: Moisei Ginzburg and Ignatii Milinis, Narkomfin Building, Moscow, 1928-29
top right: Ilija Golosov, Zuyev Club, Moscow, 1928,
bottom left: Konstantin Melnikov, Krivoarbatskil Pereulok Residence, Moscow, 1929
bottom right: Konstantin Melnikov, Soviet Pavilion, Paris Exposition,1925

chapter of the book, in a discussion of the 'Siedlung' housing typology, they wrote:

The modern Siedlung raises the question of what is meant by function in architecture more pertinently than does any other type of building. The general function is clear both in Europe and in America: to provide a large number of dwellings outside the city but still not too distant from the place of work of the inhabitants. Problems of communications, of retail merchandising and of entertainment are various, but they offer no field for architectural controversy. The more of such communal functions that can be incorporated in the same general plan, the more interesting and architectural will be the resultant Siedlung.[24]

The authors of The International Style regarded uncontroversial functions to be the principle dictate of contemporary building economics and the role of architecture in that economy was to formerly celebrate the variety of functions in new building settlements (Siedlung). By contrasting one uncontroversial function in relation to another, the role of the architect was to compose a safe, picturesque scenario for people to live in. This politically correct, reductive understanding of function would explain why the authors of the International Style excluded the Soviet works from their book, because these architects did not want to follow function, they wanted architecture to take charge!

In insisting that architecture was subordinate to function the authors of The International Style stood in direct opposition to the aims of the Soviet avant-garde. For The International Style uncontroversial function was sovereign and the place of architecture in functions' absolute rule was to simply draw attention to the variability of functions, to contrast one uncontroversial function against another, thereby creating an optically stimulating yet politically soporific environment. Unlike the Soviet architects, whose aims and objectives encouraged them to practise architecture as something experimental and new, The International Style used the concept of function as a limiting authority placed over and above architectural invention and imagination.

Philip Johnson's Monograph on Mies: Structural Honesty

The first monograph on Mies was written by one of the authors of The International Style, Philip Johnson. It was published in 1947 and, like The International Style, Johnson wrote it to coincide with an exhibition, a solo exhibition of Mies' work that was staged by the Museum of Modern Art in New York and ran from September 16 to November 23, 1947. What was effective about Johnson's monograph was the way it made the diversity of Mies' work seem to cohere in a single, seamless development.

Mies' early work bears little resemblance to the work he

was producing by 1947. Compare, for example, the Urbig House, Berlin-Neubabelsberg, of 1914 (figure 6) with The Farnsworth House, Fox River Valley, Plano, which Mies began work on in 1945 (figure 7). While the former displays the characteristic features of a traditional house, with walls, windows, door and roof, the latter does not look like a house at all. The Farnsworth House looks like an open frame with a number of horizontal slabs and large sheets of glass suspended within it. Or, compare the Project for an Office Building, Friedrichstrasse, Berlin, 1921 (figure 2) with The Promontory Apartments, Chicago, 1949 (figure 8); both are sky-scraper type structures but whereas the former rises abruptly from the pavement of the city street and is clad in a sheath of rippling glass, striated by sharp vertical incisions of dark and light, the latter rises up through a haze of foliage, appearing as a grid of vertical columns striated by alternate bands of horizontal glass and opaque cladding panels. Johnson's monograph made differences like these seem as if they belonged to a continuous and unbroken chain of development. It did so by dividing the text into four parts, denoting each part as corresponding to a distinct phase in Mies' developmental history. In order to make his history convincing Johnson had to show how works of the later phases could be read in terms of formative principles already apparent in works of the earlier phases.

In the first section of the monograph Johnson explained how, in his earliest phase, Mies had been influenced by two leading architects of the older generation, namely Peter Behrens and Hendrik Petrus Berlage, he wrote:

While in The Hague, Mies was impressed by the buildings of the Dutch architect, Hendrik Petrus Berlage (1859-1934) who, with Behrens, was an important forerunner of modern architecture. Behrens approached architecture from the point of view of form, Berlage from the point of view of structure. Thus the former contributed the reduction of Neoclassic shapes to simple rectangular blocks, the latter, the practice of structural honesty derived from the theories of Ruskin and Morris: namely that those parts of a building resembling supports should actually support and, conversely, that all the supporting elements should be evident.[25]

In associating 'reductive, Neoclassical shape' with Behrens and 'structural honesty' with Berlage, Johnson used Mies' early influences to establish a field of tension between two differing attitudes to form, which he then used to structure his history. The direction of Mies' history, as argued by Johnson, results in a synthesis of the two differing attitudes that are at odds in the early work but reconciled later.

In the second section of his monograph Johnson wrote about Mies' involvement in the intellectual climate of inter-war Berlin. Here Johnson has to convert Mies' evident

FIGURE 6

Mies van der Rohe, Urbig House, Neubabelsberg, Berlin, 1914, exterior view

FIGURE 7

Mies van der Rohe, Farnsworth House, Plano, Illinois, 1945 -'50, exterior view

FIGURE 8

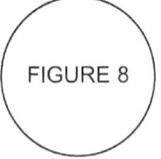

Mies van der Rohe, with Pace Associates & Holsman, Holsman, Klekamp and Taylor, Promontory Apartments, Chicago, 1949, exterior view interest in the avant-garde movements of the time into the terms that structure his history. To do so Johnson reduced the interests of the Berlin avant-garde to just two rival attitudes, 'painting' on the one hand and 'technolatry' on the other, he wrote:

Painting as an influence was rivalled by technolatry, which swept over post-war europe proclaiming the machine as the deus ex machina of the plastic arts. In Germany, as elsewhere, architects stripped their buildings of superfluous detail and made their surfaces smooth and plain; they exploited the esthetic effects of machine-made materials such as steel and glass; and like Le Corbusier, they began to think of their houses as 'machines for living'. Curiously enough, in re-examining the function of architecture they were extending the nineteenth-century philosophy of structural honesty, which had led its advocates to denounce the machine in favour of handicraft and Gothic revivalism.[26]

By linking technolatry with structural honesty Johnson connected Mies' second phase with his first, but notice, where structural honesty shunned the machine, technolatry did not.

Most of the second section was taken up with an account of five speculative projects from the early 1920s, that were presented as generative forms from which the buildings of the future would grow. These were, first, the Office Building, Friedrichstrasse, Berlin, 1921, second, The Glass Skyscraper, Berlin 1922, third, The Concrete Office Block, 1922, fourth, The Brick Country House, 1922, fifth, The Concrete Country House, 1923 (figure 2). Johnson's account of the first two projects concentrated on the interaction of light with large surfaces of glass, he was most impressed by Mies' large hand-drawn renderings of the glass towers. With the third project it was the system of concrete beams and floor slabs that interested Johnson, he was most impressed by the strong horizontal rhythm of solid and void that striates the office block. The description of the fourth project focused on the plan configuration. What struck him was the way space was defined, not by cellular rooms but by a disposition of free-standing walls. He admired the fifth project for the way the composition of the house appears to have been arrived at by isolating different functional elements and then grouping these around semi enclosed courtyard spaces.

In the third section of his monograph Johnson wrote about the exhibition of model housing, the Weißenhof Siedlung, constructed for the Werkbund exhibition in Stuttgart in 1927, which Mies directed. Johnson placed tremendous historical importance on that exhibition, even going so far as to claim it was the most important group of buildings in the history of Western architecture:

..the various architectural elements of the early post-war

years had merged into a single stream. A new international order had been born. Except for Frank Lloyd Wright, whose influence was felt by every architect represented at Stuttgart, all modern architecture of consequence in the Western world at that time was consonant with this order.[28]

In describing the general tendencies of the new order Johnson made some minor modifications to the characteristics that he had previously formulated in The International Style. The dominant theme and primary difference was the idea of the structural building frame, which did not appear in The International Style he wrote:

The international order was based on a new appreciation of the technical and structural inventions of the previous century. Its esthetic characteristics are: 1) the regularity of skeleton structure as an ordering force in place of axial symmetry; 2) the treatment of exteriors as weightless, non supporting skins rather than heavy solids, obedient to gravity; 3) the use of color and structural detail in place of applied ornament.[29]

Notice how Johnson presented the 'regularity of skeletal structure' as a substitute for 'axial symmetry.' In this section of the monograph Johnson presented Mies as a fully fledged practising architect, no longer contributing to the development of the new architecture through theoretical work alone but through actual, realised buildings. Regarding Johnson's history, it is important to note, many of Mies' executed designs of the period 1925 to the time he moved to America were built of brick, they are hard to read as weightless, skeletal structures. For example, the Monument to Karl Liebknecht and Rosa Luxemburg, Berlin, 1926. The structure does evoke a feeling of volume, the back and forth recession of the brick panels implying a series of volumes stacked on top of one another, but there is no frame and the volumes are opaque, solid figures (figure 9). Or the Wolf House, Guben, 1926, is volumetric in the sense of stacked volumes, some of them punctuated by windows, but there is no regular skeletal structure (figure 10). In order to incorporate these buildings into his history Johnson had to make them seem structural, despite their lack of a frame. To this end he returned to Mies' Berlagian influence and the notion of structural honesty:

Mies, with his Berlagian approach, appreciated the fact that brick was a structural material which need not be concealed. He liked the regular rhythm achieved by the repetition of a module and he enjoyed the craftsmanship involved in the coursing and bonding.[27]

Notice how Johnson reiterated the idea of regularity he had already associated with skeletal structure, only now that regularity has been transferred to the 'honest' use of a material, namely brick. Johnson suggested it was the regular rhythm of the repeated brick module that

FIGURE 9

Mies van der Rohe, Monument to Karl Liebknecht and Rosa Luxemburg, Berlin, 1926

FIGURE 10

Mies van der Rohe, Wolf House, Guben, 1926, external view

appealed to Mies, more than the brick texture and appearance, specifically as the module became manifest in the order of the building. Yet it is hard to equate the regularity of a brick module with that of a skeleton structure, the two belong to different scales of building and to different regions of spatial organisation.

Before leaving the third phase of Mies' development Johnson took time to consider Mies' interior design work, including his exhibitions and furniture designs. He admired their spatial generosity and Mies' skill at being able to *'place things in space.'*[30] Johnson praised Mies' *'impeccable craftsmanship'*[31] and his sensibility to materials and colour. Unlike brick, which as we have seen, Johnson regarded as structural, through an extensive use of adjectives Johnson evoked a rich palette of Miesian materials: white chamois, black cowhide, black, orange and red velvets, gold, silver, black and lemon-yellow silks, clear and grey opal glass, white and black linoleum, tawny gold and white onyx. But he said nothing of how the materials related to the new order.

In the fourth and final part of the monograph Mies has moved to America and is engaged in one of the most important works of his entire career.[32] This was the design of the campus for the Illinois Institute of Technology, 1939-58 (figure 11). Here Johnson presented Mies as confidently working within the tenets of the new order. The new campus was to be set out on a single, repetitious module, 24ft by 24ft by 12 ft high, the regularity of which would, according to Johnson, replace the traditional ordering principle of axial symmetry:

...order is not dependent on axial grouping but on a subtler symmetry deriving from the fact that every building, no matter what its size, is based on the same cubic bay, 24 feet by 24 feet by 12 feet high, and that the spaces between the buildings are regulated by the same 24-foot module.[33]

One campus building that Johnson singled out for special praise was the Library and Administration Building, 1946, (figure 12) which he described as *'possibly Mies' greatest single design',*[34] he wrote:

...when constructed, this section will undoubtedly constitute one of the most impressive enclosed spaces in the history of modern architecture.[35]

It is worth attending to Johnson's account of the library because in writing about it he went some way to clarifying his thinking about regularity in honest structure and regularity in skeletal structure, he wrote:

Structural elements are revealed as are those of a Gothic cathedral; the inside and the outside of the enclosing walls are identical in appearance, since the same steel columns and brick panels of the exterior are

FIGURE 11

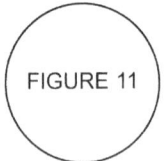

Mies van der Rohe, Illinois Institute of Technology, Chicago, 1939 -'58, montage view of the campus layout

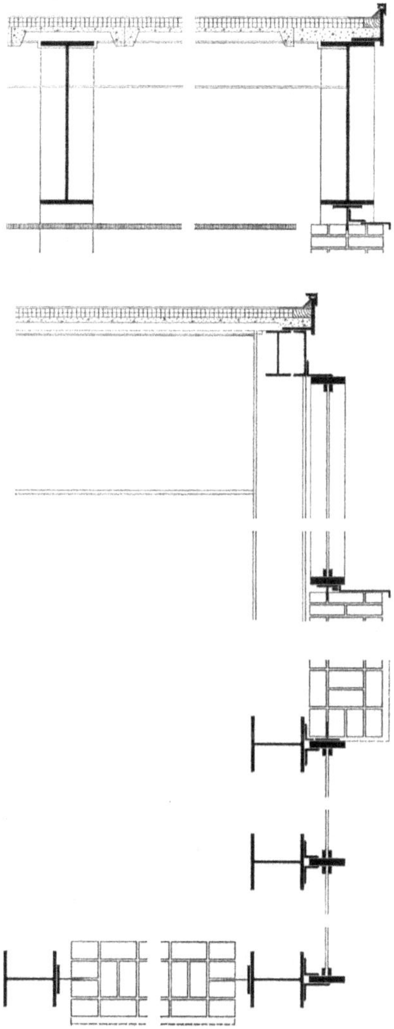

FIGURE 12

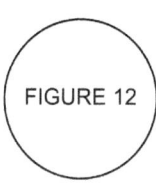

Mies van der Rohe, Campus Library and Administration Building, Illinois Institute of Technology, Chicago, 1946, (unbuilt). Two vertical sections, top and middle, and one horizontal section, relationship of steel members to brickwork.

visible on the interior. In other words, he has conceived the design in terms of steel channels and angles, 'I' and 'H' columns, just as a medieval design is conceived in terms of stone vaults and buttresses. But there is one major difference. He allows no decoration except that formed by the character and juxtaposition of the structural elements. And whereas the medieval architect relied on the collaboration of the sculptor and painter for his ultimate effect, Mies, so to speak, has had to perform the functions of all three professions. He joins steel to steel, or steel to glass or brick, with all the taste and skill that formerly went into the chiselling of a stone capital or the painting of a fresco.[36]

Johnson seems to have understood structure, both honest and skeletal as a species of rational architecture, whereby a systematic logic and process of construction is given expression in finished form. There is some evidence that the same idea was important for Berlage, only Berlage expressed it differently. It is worth looking a little more closely at the difference because when we do we see the similarity dissolve.

Rather than Johnson's interest in order, Berlage was interested in what he termed 'truth.' It is hard to be clear what Berlage meant by truth, he equated it with essence but he was no more clear what he meant by essence than what he meant by truth, for example he wrote:

We want the essence of architecture, which is to say the truth, I repeat, the truth. For in art, too, the lie has become the rule and the truth the exception. We architects, therefore, must try to return to truth, to seize once again the reality of architecture. Now, architecture is and remains the art of construction, the joining together of various elements into a whole to enclose a space. And as even this fundamental principle has become an empty formula, the first priority is to go back to the basics, to construct well. In order to do this quite freely, we must do it in the simplest way. Intrinsically comprehensible objects should be created once again, objects whose bodies are not obscured by cladding.[37]

For Berlage, to construct well meant to construct in a manner that revealed construction as an inherently comprehensible feature of the finished building. Berlage associated his notion of constructing well with truth and reality, however he did not refer to it as structural honesty, that expression was Johnson's.

Berlage set out his understanding of what it is to construct well in the series of lectures he gave for the interior design course at the Kunstgewerbemuseum in Zurich, in 1908. He seems to have found it difficult to explain the notion of constructing well and in the end apologised for his lack of theoretical lucidity and instead used an anecdote to illustrate what he meant:

In all the reflections on architecture over recent years there has been a lot of talk about 'the constructional', and I myself have mentioned it again in these lectures. But this word can very easily lead to misunderstanding. When I maintain to someone who is determined not to understand me that an iron pillar clad with stucco to resemble the form of an antique column is not constructional, he will ask: 'why not? The thing provides support: I can give it any form I like and it will be constructional'. If I enter a hall with a columnar architecture that is enclosed with pilaster vaults above, which is of course an empty space terminated by the floor of the level above, I would say to its builder that the hall is not constructional. This would probably make him very angry and prompt him to ask in reply: 'why not?' - adding that this structure has been formed in this way for centuries and asking if I could do it better than a Sangallo or a Peruzzi. And, finally, if I were to ask the architect of a facade crowned by a tower why in the plan this tower is supported by only a few columns that take the weight of the tower through an iron beam, the architect would probably regard me as mad and even deduce from the plan of a Gothic cathedral that the fourth corner of the tower here rested similarly on a pillar. I must admit that in such cases I am not ready with a conclusive answer. Nevertheless, I know (however pedantic this may sound) that I am right.[38]

Although Berlage failed to give a convincing theoretical explanation of the notion of constructing well, what he meant is conveyed in the examples he gave and also, and more effectively, in the buildings he designed. When Mies acknowledged the influence of Berlage in his own work he did so by referring to Berlage's buildings, as much as to his writing, according to Mies:

Berlage was a man of great seriousness who would not accept anything that was fake and it was he who had said that nothing should be built that is not clearly constructed. And Berlage did exactly that. And he did it to such an extent that his famous building in Amsterdam, The Beurs, has a medieval character without being medieval. He used brick in the way the medieval people did. The idea of a clear construction came to me there, as one of the fundamentals we should accept.[39]

This quote was published in The Architectural Review in March of 1961, it appeared in an article written by Peter Carter, celebrating Mies' 75th birthday. It is important to note, first, Mies did not use 'structural honesty' to refer to what he had learned from Berlage, he used 'clear construction.' Second, Mies indicated he had received the idea of clear construction, not through reading Berlage's published writings,[40] but through the experience of an actual building (figure 13).

In his monograph on Mies Johnson placed great importance on the idea that Mies' architecture can be

FIGURE 13

Hendrik Petrus Berlage, The Amsterdam Stock Exchange, Amsterdam, 1896-1903
above: exterior view, below: interior view

understood through Berlage's influence. Johnson conflated Berlage's attitudes to architecture and building with his own notion of structural honesty. While Johnson's understanding of structural honesty did owe something to Berlage's notion of constructing well nevertheless there was a problem with it. In substituting his own 'structural honesty' for Berlage's 'constructing well' Johnson transposed his own appreciation of the structural building frame (skeletal structure) and its spatial regularity onto Mies' drive for clear construction. While it is impossible to tell from anything Mies wrote what he meant by clear construction there is a good chance he meant something much closer to Berlage's 'constructing well' than to Johnson's 'structural honesty.'

In the biography of Mies by Franz Schulz, published in 1985, there is an interesting story told to Schulz by Johnson. Between 1954 and 1958 Johnson worked with Mies on the now infamous project to design a new office building for the Seagram Corporation on Park Avenue, New York. It was during the construction period and Mies and Johnson were drinking late into the night at Johnson's house. Johnson is said to have told Mies he could hardly see what it was about the Amsterdam Stock Exchange (the Beurs) that Mies admired so much. What is more, Johnson had added, he could hardly see anything of Mies' in it. In response Mies is said to have exploded in anger and left without a word. Johnson told Schulz that to him the incident made no sense. However, the incident does make sense if Mies' aspiration toward clear construction is understood in terms of Berlage's somewhat Romantic yearning after truth, rather than Johnson's yearning for a new order based on regularity. In other words if it is understood as a symptom of the architects interest in beauty and form-giving and not as symptomatic of the kind of architectural rationalism that Johnson's 'structural honesty' would seem to imply.[41]

Ludwig Hilberseimer: Mysterious Relations

Mies' colleague, Ludwig Hilberseimer published a monograph on Mies in 1956. Hilberseimer and Mies had met in Berlin in the 1920s, at that time they collaborated on various projects, both as designers and publicists, dedicated to the promotion of new ideas about architecture. They were also colleagues in the field of architectural education. When Mies took over as director of the Bauhaus in 1930 Hilberseimer had already been running the courses in housing and city planning for several years and when Mies accepted the directorship of the School of Architecture at the Armour Institute, Chicago, in 1938, he immediately appointed Hilberseimer to the staff. At the time Hilberseimer's monograph was published the pair of them were working on the design of a large housing project in Detroit.

What was interesting about Hilberseimer's approach was the attempt to set Mies' work within the framework of a general history and theory of architecture. Because of their shared background and long standing friendship it might be reasonable to suppose Hilberseimer's account of Mies architectural theory and practice was endorsed by Mies himself; but we need to be careful here because there is nothing on record to confirm this was so.

Hilberseimer structured his history and theory of architecture on the basis of a duality of concepts he termed 'structure' and 'form concept.' He argued that architecture arises as a consequence of the correlation between the two. In order to explain what he meant Hilberseimer adduced the Pantheon in Rome and Santa Sophia in Constantinople. These buildings, he claimed, shared the same structure, i.e., the arch and vault, but demonstrated different form concepts. Whereas the form concept of the Pantheon was out of harmony with the structure, because the architects had failed to *'grasp the architectural possibilities of the new structure.,* [42] that of Santa Sophia was in harmony. Hilberseimer thought the dome of the Pantheon, resting as it does on a massive circular wall, was a direct contradiction of the arch and vault principle. At Santa Sophia, on the other hand, the dome was supported on an open structure of piers and ribs, making it seem to hang down from the sky. Thus by a kind of spatial alchemy the arch and vault structure had transcended into architecture.

It is worth noting the role of history in Hilberseimer's general theory was to act as a kind of medium, not unlike the matrix in the Platonic theory of ideas, in which the slow process of transformative becoming takes place:

Centuries passed before an adequate architectural concept was found for the arched and vaulted structure, now best expressed in S, Sophia at Constantinople. As at the Pantheon in Rome, its enormous central space is visible from the entrance. But unlike the Pantheon, whose dome is supported by a heavy circular wall, at S. Sophia the supporting elements are reduced to a minimum, thus creating openness and lightness everywhere. The base of the dome is encircled by a row of windows, which are separated by small piers, the ends of the dome-supporting ribs. The intense light which shines through these windows optically diminishes the size of the piers and makes the dome appear to be unsupported 'to hang,' as Procopius remarked, 'on golden ropes from heaven'.[43]

Hilberseimer used the image of the unsupported dome to signify a transcendent event in the history of architecture. In order to evoke it in his monograph he relied on the literary device of the simile, for the photographic illustration alone could not communicate the magical feeling of suspension as the dome appeared to hang there, as if on golden ropes from heaven.

Hilberseimer believed the times in which he lived had

produced a new structure, like Philip Johnson he used the notion of the skeleton to refer to the new structure. Unlike Johnson however, Hilberseimer understood the essential characteristic of the skeleton structure to be the reduction of the carrying elements of a building to relatively few points.[44] That reduction in turn led to freedom in the use of space, which could now be divided freely, rather then being constrained by the load-bearing function of the wall. Reduction in the load-bearing requirements also led to a dramatic reduction in the weight of the building. Hilberseimer argued that Mies, more than any other architect, was working toward an understanding of the form concept implicit in the new skeleton structure. He wrote:

His architecture, though dependent on structure, is infinitely more than structure. It grows out of and elaborates structure, but attains a transcendence of the material into the realm of the spiritual.[45]

Hilberseimer attributed Mies' ability to achieve such transcendence to his being an artist rather then a designer. For Hilberseimer the distinction depended upon the respective attitudes of designer and artist toward the aims and objectives of their work. He claimed the designer was *'an inventor of everchanging forms.'* [46] The artist, on the other hand, *'strives for beauty.'*[47] Hilberseimer suggested a dual relationship for the architectural attainment of beauty consisting of *'a concept of space'* and *'proportion.'* [48] Just like Mies in his remarks on beauty, Hilberseimer argued it was only possible to perceive space as a relationship between things and that proportions arose in that relationship. He argued that the feeling for proportions was historically variable, determined by the concept of space prevalent in a particular society at a particular moment in time. For Western societies, at least since the Renaissance, the concept of space had tended towards increasing openness. In speculating about the concept of space Hilberseimer was concerned with the human perception of the distances between things, of how far apart things were, or seemed to be and their attendant psychodynamic effects. However, Hilberseimer made no attempt to account for the changes in spatial concepts nor did he try to explain why it was that modern times tended toward skeletal structure and openness. What interested him was the phenomenon of space in architecture per se, which, as he saw it, posed a double problem:

Architecture is placed in space and at the same time encloses space. Therefore a double problem arises - the handling of outer space, as well as inner space. These two kinds of space can be unrelated to each other, or they can, by various means, be united. The outer space can merge with the inner, the inner space with the outer. Or both can flow into one space.[49]

As a consequence of the modern tendency towards openness Hilberseimer believed spatial distinctions between inside and out would ultimately disappear. When that happened a new kind of architecture would arise. One feature of the new architecture would be the dissolution of the bounded, object-like quality of the building. Buildings would no longer appear as bounded forms sitting in an open field of space, such as a piazza or meadow but appear more like a garden, or landscape, in which physical and optical boundaries are more softly defined. Hilberseimer claimed that Mies' architecture already demonstrated *'the flowing together of inner and outer space'* [50] and that this, along with its attendant careful proportions was why it was so beautiful, he wrote:

Whatever he touches gains a kind of splendour which elevates it into the sphere of art, into the realm of beauty. His architecture fulfils Alberti's demands. But we think it is more. Particularly in those of his buildings which are confined to one floor, the two-dimensional plans have an extraordinary and mysterious relation to their three-dimensional appearance in space, the mark of all great architecture. [51]

Notice how irrational was Hilberseimer's description of Miesian architecture, where something two-dimensional, flat and linear, a plan, was mysteriously transformed into a three-dimensional appearance in space. Also notice the similarity here between Hilberseimer's account of what it is like to experience Miesian architecture and the notion of 'going atmospheric' that was evoked by Rosalind Krauss in her account of Agnes Martin's paintings of grids. In the case of the paintings it was the subject stepping back from the painting that triggered the change of spatial texture. Having seemed flat and opaque the painting suddenly appears as a voluminous body, not an impermeable body, but a vaporous, cloudy body, like mist.

Hilberseimer could not explain how Mies' two-dimensional plans were able to transform into the splendour of a three-dimensional appearance in space, in his monograph he wrote that for him it was a mystery. Mies too seems to have been lost for words when it came to theorising the composition of a building, as if he himself had no idea what he was doing when he devised a spatial distribution:

The artistic expresses itself in the proportions of things, often even in the proportions between things. Essentially it is something immaterial, something spiritual. [52]

In their feeling for space and proportions Hilberseimer and Mies suggested more than simply mathematical relationships, they seemed to imply a kind of intelligence of space that could be felt, but not known, it is what they meant by architecture.

Peter Blake: The Miesian Fit

In 1960 a book entitled The Master Builders was published. It consisted of three short biographies, each one comprising a single chapter, the first about Le Corbusier, the second Mies and the third Frank Lloyd Wright. The author of the book, an architect named Peter Blake, thought that this triad exerted an extraordinary influence on contemporary architecture, he wrote:

The fact is that virtually no modern building constructed today would look the way it does if it had not been for the work of one or more of these three men.[53]

The chapter on Mies is interesting because it tells us about Mies' reception at the peak of his fame. Blake wrote of Mies' buildings as evidencing a logical, honest and disciplined approach to questions of structure aligned with a unique approach to questions of function. Blake's discussion of the former reiterated the form/ structure dialectic:

Although Mies was still a classicist in terms of form, it was apparent that structure as an overriding discipline, had begun to interest him more and more. During his year at the Hague he had seen some of the work of H. P. Berlage, the Dutch architect whose unaffected work in brick seemed to Mies to express the honest, structural possibilities of that material to perfection.[54]

Blake made no attempts to theorise the notion of 'honest structure,' he merely assumed it as the driving force behind Mies' interest in the design of skeletal structures:

Once Mies became disenchanted with formalism and began, through Berlage's work to think in terms of structural clarity and honesty, it could only be a matter of time for him to investigate the logical consequences of steel, reinforced concrete and glass, and to arrive at a statement of 'honesty' as he saw it when applied to these new materials. To him the answer was perfectly clear: steel and concrete represented strength; these would be the 'bones' of his buildings. Glass was a shimmering veil that could be draped over the skeleton to form the 'skin'.[55]

In discussing Mies' approach to function Blake pointed out how his buildings were able to combine functional practicality with supreme generality precisely because they were not adopted to any function at all, he wrote:

The only function one could be sure of in any building built to last was the function of flexibility of use throughout its lifetime. So, the only kind of building which would make sense, in terms of functionalism, would be a building not adjusted to any function at all![56]

Notwithstanding their popularity, Blake's views on

and function in Miesian architecture were not quite the same as those expressed by Mies himself. In 1958 the Norwegian architect and theorist Christian Norberg-Schulz conducted an interview with Mies. It was published in Baukunst und Werkform, 11, no 11 and contained some revealing comments by Mies pertaining to the relationship between function and structure. The interview began with Mies claiming his primary interest was clear construction. Norberg-Schulz expressed surprise at this, saying that he had understood Mies' primary interest to be in the variable ground plan. Mies responded by linking the two, claiming that it was impossible to think of clear construction without also thinking of what he termed the 'variable ground plan,' he explained:

The variable ground plan and clear construction cannot be viewed separately. Clear construction is the basis for a free ground plan. If no clear-cut structure results we lose all interest.[57]

There are two things to notice here. First, Mies' use of the terms 'variable' and 'free' clearly referred to the building plan, but there is no reason to suppose he was thinking of the plan in terms of end use, or function. Second, Mies distinguished between 'clear construction' and 'clear-cut structure.' Notice, although clear construction and a variable ground plan are necessary conditions of clear-cut structure, they are not sufficient. Later in the interview Mies gave a further clue about clear-cut structure, paradoxically here it appears as the precondition of the variable ground plan:

...the structure is the backbone of the whole and makes the variable ground plan possible. Without the backbone, the ground plan would not be free, but chaotically blocked.[58]

In the sense that it is what makes the variable ground plan possible Mies was here conceiving structure as an organising format. But the contradiction in his statements on structure should not be overlooked. If structure arises as a consequence of clear construction and a variable floor plan then how can structure be the generator of the variable ground plan? The only way to understand Mies' triad of clear construction, variable ground plan and clear-cut structure is to think of them as interdependent parameters; in other words, to think of them as a relational form. The question then arises, what factors did Mies take into consideration when devising a relational form. In the interview Mies said he always began by asking what has to be built:

We begin by asking ourselves what it is that we have to build: an open hall or a conventional construction type - then we work ourselves through this chosen type down to the smallest detail before we begin to solve the problem of the ground plan. If you solve the ground plan or the room sequence first everything gets blocked and a clear construction becomes impossible.[59]

It seems that Mies approached the design, not from a functional but from a typological perspective, but what did he mean by type? To elaborate on type Mies proceeded to discuss his proposal for a Theatre for the city of Mannheim, 1952 (figure 14). Notice he cites Louis Sullivan's famous formulation, not to refute it but to revise it:

As you see, the entire building is a single large room. We believe that this is the most economical and most practical way of building today. The purposes for which a building is used are constantly changing and we cannot afford to tear down the building each time. This is why we have revised Sullivan's formula 'form follows function' and construct a practical and economical space into which we fit the functions. In the Mannheim building, stage and auditorium are independent of the steel construction.[60]

It seems that Mies conceived functions rather in the way furniture is thought of in a conventional building, as something to be fitted-in latter. With the theatre he listed the primary functions as the stage and the auditorium. Both ideas combine a specific function and a specific form that, Mies explained, were fitted into the space designed to house them. The question then arises as to the nature of the Miesian fit? To answer it we will turn to the design of the Farnsworth House, which Blake dubbed Mies' *'ultimate'* statement of *'universality.'*[61] In studying the Farnsworth House we will learn, not only about the Miesian fit but also about mid twentieth century notions of universal space in architecture.

The Farnsworth House sits in a wood on the banks of the Fox River at Plano, Illinois; it was designed and built between 1946 and 1950, intended to serve as a weekend country house. It consists of three horizontal plates, two of them the same area and vertically aligned, one three meters above the other. Between the two aligned plates span four pairs of columns. The column pairs are fixed to the perimeter edges of the plates on the longer dimension and face one another across the narrower dimension. They are distributed at equal centres and the plates span directly between them, creating a horizontal slice of open space. The term 'clear span' is sometimes used to refer to this kind of spatial arrangement.

The pairs of supporting columns extend down a further one and a half meters to raise the assemblage of plates and open space up and off the ground. The third plate is located to one side of the clear span assemblage, running parallel to the longer dimension but off-set by a dimension equivalent to the centres of the column pairs. The third plate projects out in from of the clear span assemblage,

FIGURE 14

Mies van der Rohe, Project for a NationalTtheatre, Mannheim, Germany, 1953, view of the model just grazing the outer face of two of the column pairs. These serve to support it on one side, on the other side, directly opposite, it is supported by two very short columns. In terms of vertical displacement, the third plate straddles the space between the ground and the underside of the clear span assemblage, which is why the extra columns needed to support it are so short. Between the ground and the third plate and again between the third plate and the clear span assemblage are short flights of steps. The steps are designed to appear as if they are slim horizontal planes floating freely in space.

If a plan and section of the house, as it has been described so far, were to be drawn then that drawing would show very few of the characteristic features associated with a house (figure 15). If not exclusively related to the program of a house, nevertheless, in the description so far given there are two items indicative of purposive intent, most obviously the flight of steps. But the form and location of the horizontal plates too is based upon conventional notions of the purposes of a house. The three meter dimension of the clear span assemblage already begins to imply the spatial idea of the room, albeit a room without walls; and the presence of the third plate has the effect of zoning the clear span assemblage into that area which abuts the third slab and that which does not. The space of the clear span assemblage is further differentiated by the glass screen (figure 16) that wraps around the perimeter on three sides and cuts across the surface of the constitutive plates on the abutting side. The placement of the glass screen has the effect of enclosing approximately two thirds of the open space between the slabs. The glass screen is not necessary to divide the clear span space into two distinct zones that is already effected by the presence of the third plate, what it does is to give a conventional meaning to the covered space that is left, remaindered, outside the glass enclosure: the porch. In some photographs, of the house there are porch/objects lying in the porch/ space (figure 17), a few chairs and some potted plants. Evidence at last that this structure is, indeed, a species of house!

The clear span assemblage has an object inside, almost filling the space from top to bottom, it is three to four meters wide and seven to eight meters long, a simple, prismatic, box form. The box is covered in a veneer of primavera and exudes a deep yellow aura into the space (figure 18). The primevera box is an indented and hollowed out figure, with embedded purposive objects, including rooms, embedded inside. Nested on the outside are kitchen objects, a cooker, a sink, a fridge and there are draws set within a recess that has been formed in the body of the box. On the other side there is a fireplace, set within a recess which, by its placement indicates that when the fire is lit the smoke disappears up inside the primevera box (figure 19). But the most

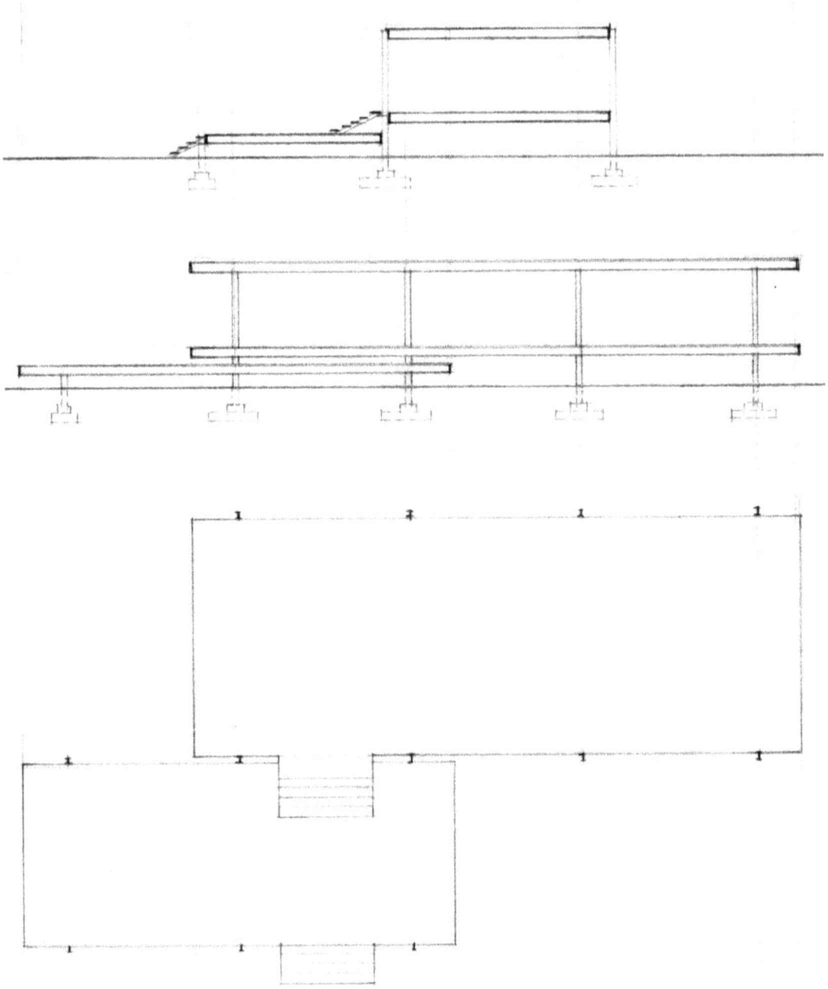

FIGURE 15

Analysis of the Farnsworth House, plan and two sections, stage one

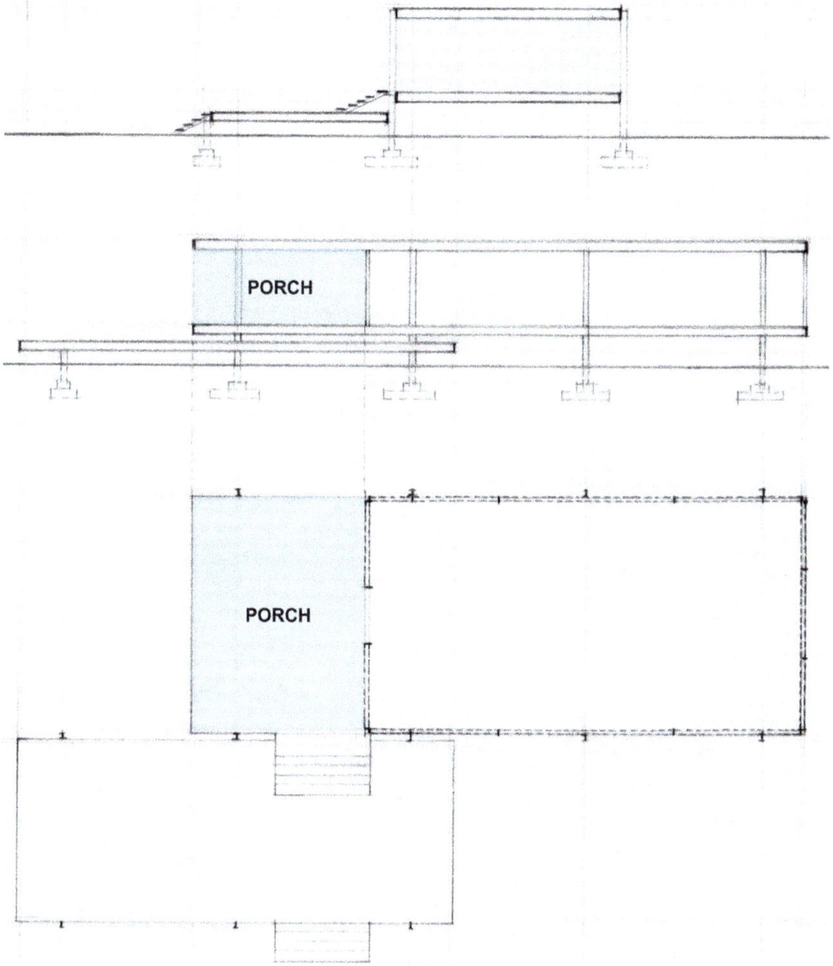

FIGURE 16

Analysis of the Farnsworth House, plan and two sections, stage two

FIGURE 17

The Farnsworth House, two views of the porch, top,1960's, bottom, 1990's

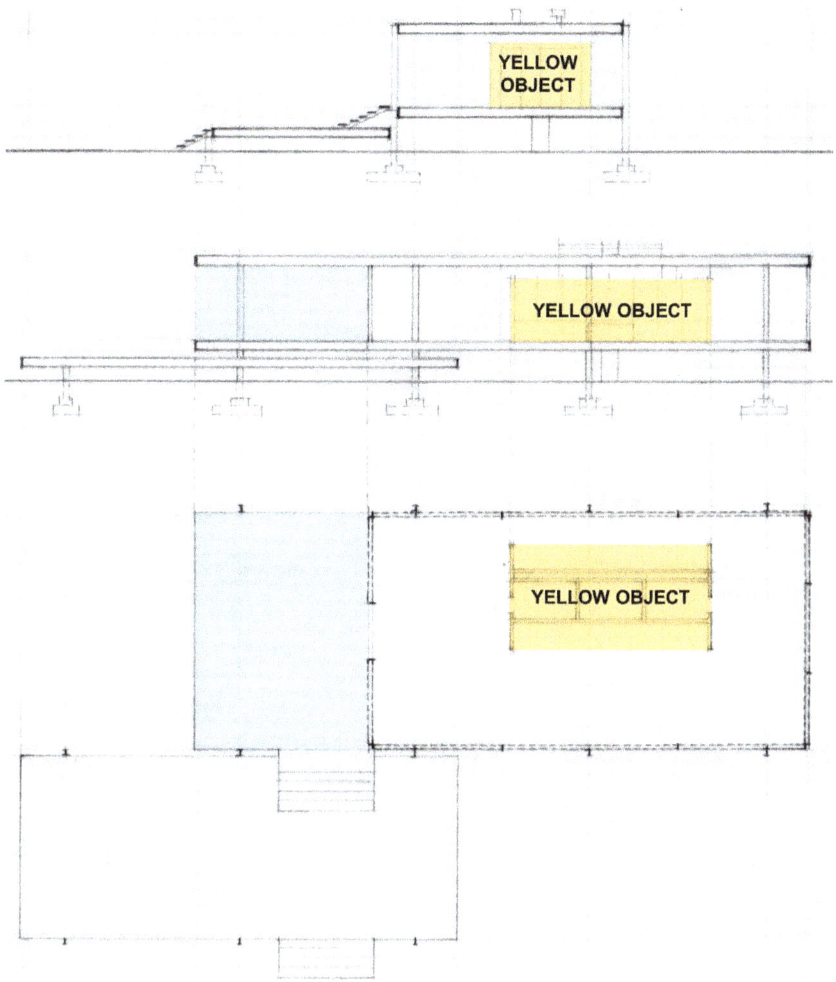

FIGURE 18

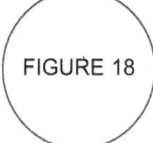

Analysis of the Farnsworth House, plan and two sections, stage three

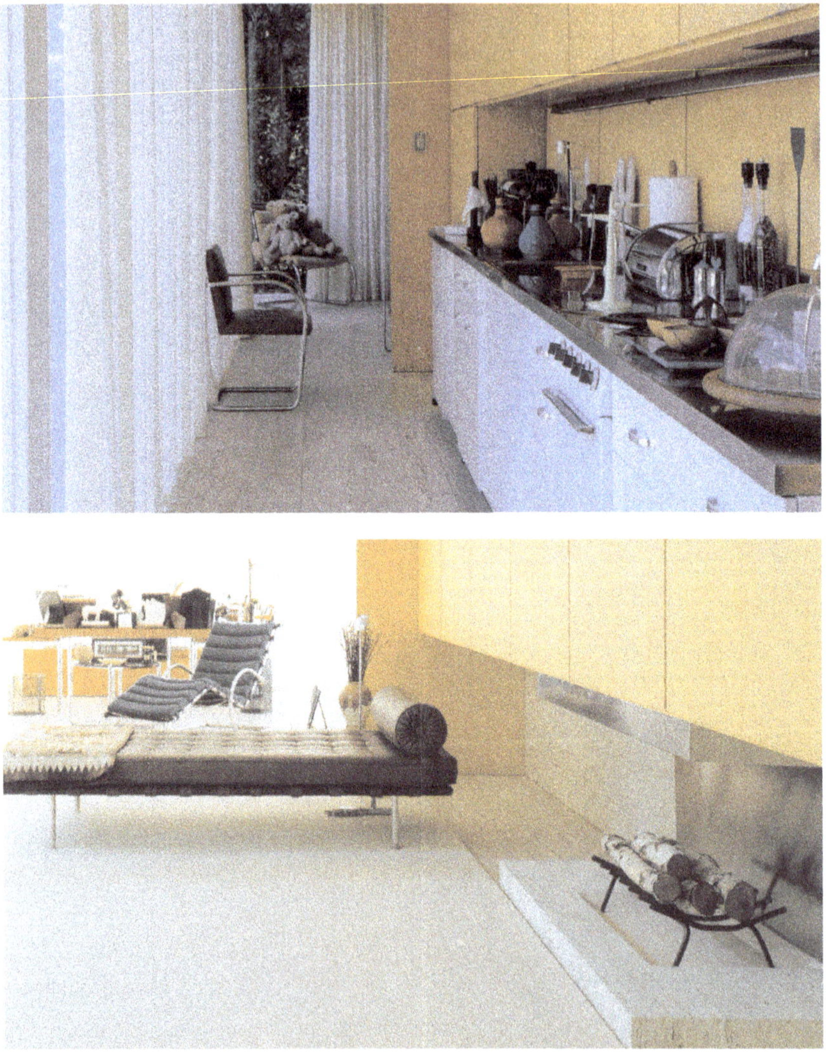

FIGURE 19

The Farnsworth House, two views, top, Kitchen, bottom, Lounge obviously purposive aspect of the primevera box are the doorknobs. The box appears to be made of panels and some of these have door knobs on them (figure 20). The presence of doorknobs turns the panels into doors and signals interior space. Open the doors and there are more purposive objects inside a toilet, washbasin and bath, thus the primavera box contains form/functions: a bathroom, two in fact, one at either end (figure 21).

So what kind of thing is this box fitted within the clear span assemblage which, on the one hand, contains the conventional baths and bathrooms of a house, but on the other hand disrupts house conventions to display cookers and sinks without a kitchen and fire and hearth without chimney breast? The placement of the primavera box (LYO) divides the clear span assemblage into four distinct zones (fig 22): in front of (fLYO) behind (bLYO) to the right (rLYO) and to the left (iLYO). Because the LYO is asymmetrically placed within the space of the clear span assemblage so each of the four zones is a different size and shape. Furthermore, each zone has a different proximity to the porch: zone, iLYO is immediately adjacent to the porch while zone rLYO is furthest away and can only be reached by traversing zones fLYO, or bLYO. All the zones except one contains specific items of furniture (fig 22). Zone iLYO has a dining table and chairs, zone rLYO has a bed and a table-height cupboard. Zone bLYO has no furniture and zone fLYO has a reclining couch, chairs and two coffee tables. It is clear from the nature of their furnishings, their proximity to the point of entry and their interrelationships that zone iLYO corresponds to the conventional type of the dining room, zone rLYO to the conventional type of the bedroom, zone bLYO to the conventional type of the kitchen and zone fLYO to the lounge.

From this analysis of the spatial relationships established between the constitutive elements, the Farnsworth House can be read as a four room house with a porch and a terrace, but with the LYO instead of walls to mark out the sub-divisions of the program. It seems to confirm Mies' succinct if somewhat cryptic statement: *'the schematic is implied by the task and therefore finds its expression in the form-giving.'*[62] And, perhaps of greater importance for the re-writing of architectural history, it would seem to contradict Blake's reading of Miesian architecture as the manifestation of ultimate universality, i.e., an architecture that was not adjusted to any function at all and for that reason was infinitely flexible in use.

Although at first glance the Farnsworth House appeared to be little more than a large empty room it is possible to see that this room was in fact full, full of the program of a house. The house was formed, not by the hard division of walls but by a soft sensibility emanating from the eddies and ripples of inhabited space. Mies had

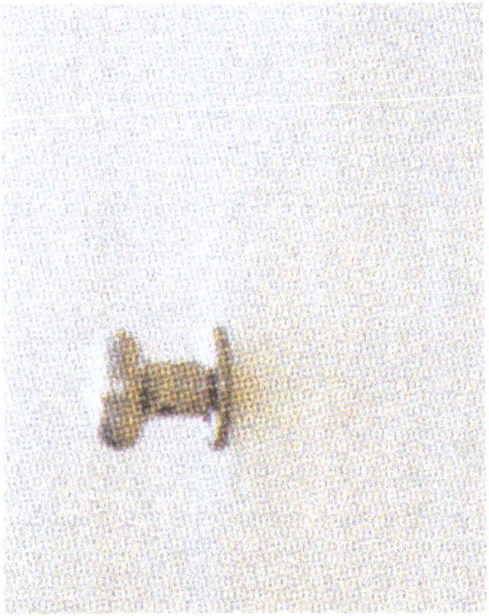

FIGURE 20

The Farnsworth House, bathroom door, doorknob

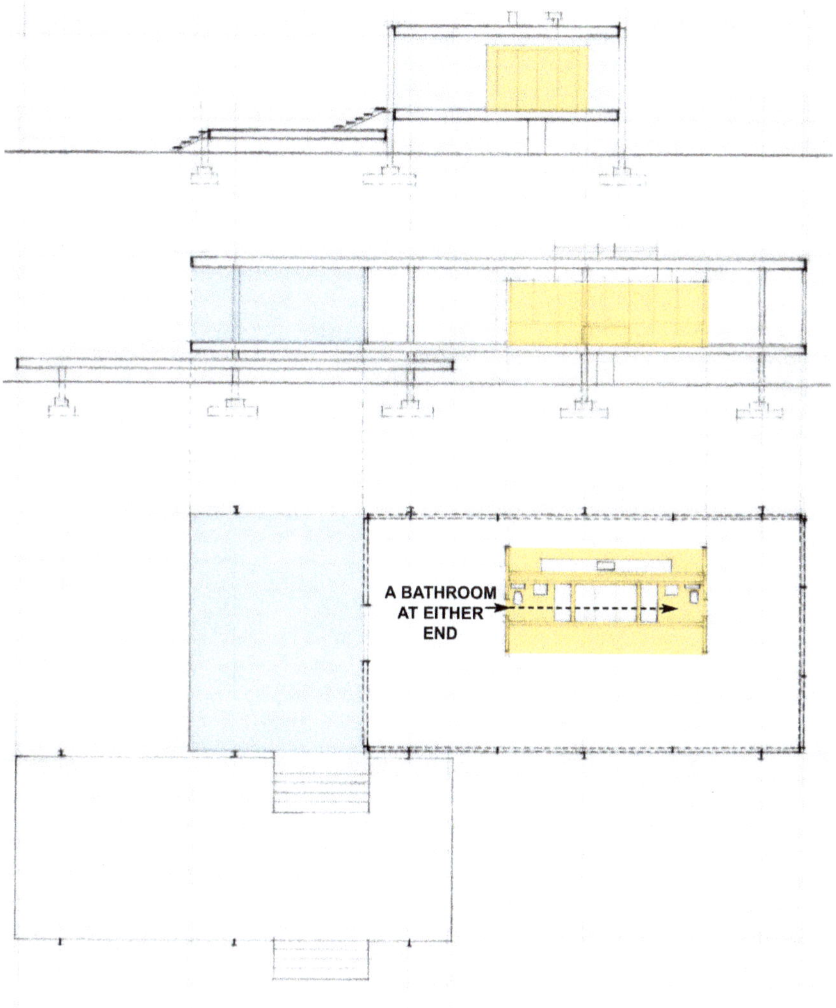

FIGURE 21

Analysis of the Farnsworth House, plan and two sections, stage four

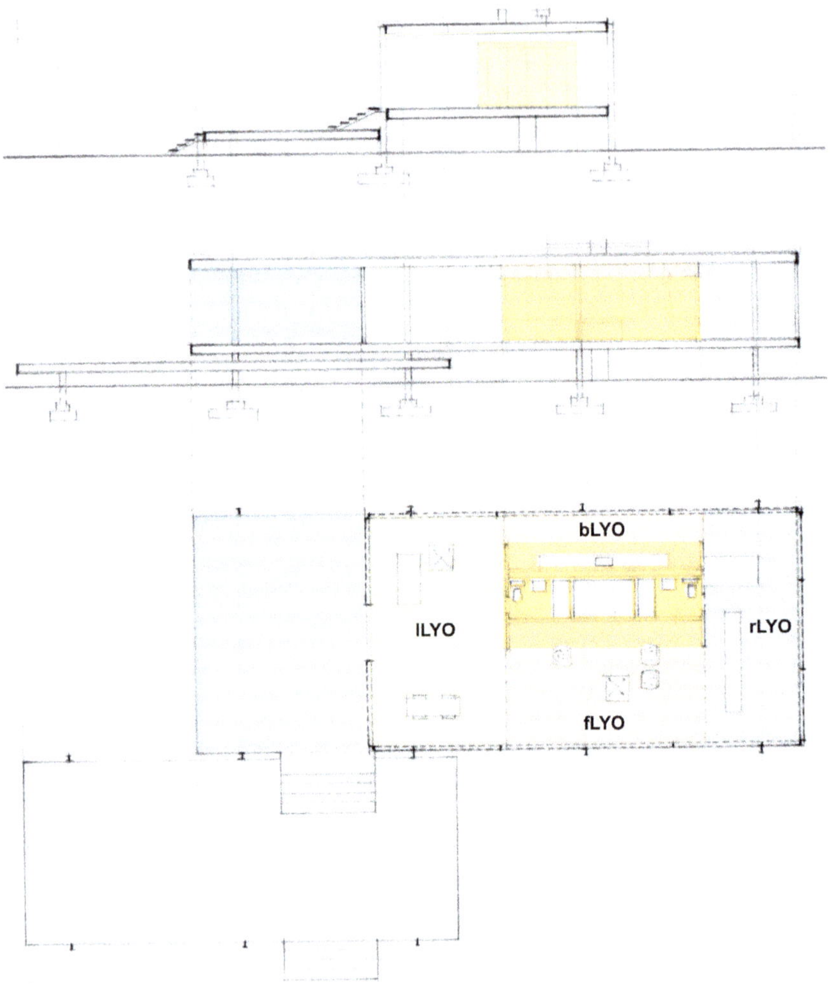

FIGURE 22

Analysis of the Farnsworth House, plan and two sections, stage five conceived the space with a general purpose in mind, namely dwelling. The same soft emanations of general purposive intentions was a characteristic feature of Miesian architecture more generally.

The Role of the Bauhaus (and Mies) in Lefebvre's Conceptualization of Space

In the same year as the Master Builders was published The French Marxist philosopher and sociologist Henri Lefebvre wrote a short essay called 'Notes on a New Town.' It was about Mourenx, a new town under construction near his home town of Navarrenx, in South Western France (figure 23). In his essay Lefebvre wrote about the curious mixture of fascination and dismay he felt as he watched the new town under construction. He was highly aware of and attentive to, the novel practice of planning that underpinned the new town design and he wondered what would arise as a result of the new methods. Levebvre had grave doubts about the validity of planning as a means of producing properly human environments, he wrote:

Here in Mourenx, what do I see? These blocks of flats are also 'technological objects' and machines. Will they be able to provide a new humanism? Are they already providing it? Can they mediate between man and nature, between one man and another? Are they bringing individuals, families and groups together, or are they forcing them apart? Will people be compliant and do what the plan expects them to do, shopping in the shopping centre, asking for advice in the advice bureau, doing everything the civic centre offices demand of them like good, reliable citizens?.....Can spontaneity be revitalized here, can a community be created?[63]

In the light of Lefebvre's doubts it is worth recollecting the statement made in The International Style, the one situated in the discussion of the Siedlung idea as a strategy for extending existing towns and cities, concerned with the relation between function and planning:

The modern Siedlung raises the question of what is meant by function in architecture more pertinently than does any other type of building. The general function is clear both in Europe and in America: to provide a large number of dwellings outside the city but still not too distant from the place of work of the inhabitants. Problems of communications, of retail merchandising and of entertainment are various but they offer no field for architectural controversy. The more of such communal functions that can be incorporated in the same general plan, the more interesting and architectural will be the resultant Siedlung.[24]

Unlike Lefebvre, who offered a critique of the notion of function, the authors of The International Style simply took function as a self-evident principle, advocating the

FIGURE 23

The new town of Mourenx, South West France, view, 1961

introduction of a variety of functions as a strategic necessity for the production of 'interesting' architecture. For them the only questions to be asked of function concerned quantity and variety. In suggesting that people may not actually shop in the shopping centre Lefebvre drew attention to the determinist attitudes underpinning functionalist presuppositions:

Mourenx has taught me many things. Here objects wear their social credentials: their function. Every object has its use, and declares it. Every object has a distinct and specific function. In the best diagnosis, when the new town has been successfully completed, everything in it will be functional, and every object in it will have a specific function: its own. Every object indicates what this function is, signifying it, proclaiming it to the neighbourhood. It repeats itself endlessly. When an object is reduced to nothing but its own function, it is also reduced to signifying itself and nothing else; there is virtually no difference between it and a signal, and to all intents and purposes a group of these objects becomes a signalling system.[64]

Like Mies, Lefebvre saw function as an insufficient basis for the generation of form; but unlike Mies, who tried to articulate what was missing with terms like 'beauty' and 'form-giving,' Lefebvre articulated the limitations of functionalist thinking using terms such as 'surprise' and 'possibility':

Everything is trivial. Everything is closure and materialized system. The text of the town is totally legible, as impoverished as it is clear, despite the architects' efforts to vary the lines. Surprise? Possibilities? From this place, which should have been the home of all that is possible, they have vanished without a trace.[65]

Mies and Lefebvre agreed function was a problem for contemporary architecture, but their values and priorities were different. Mies was interested in the activity of building and in form-giving, Lefebvre was interested in planning and in social relations. These are not mutually exclusive interests, but in a comparison of Mies and Lefebvre they can be forced into opposition, with Mies cast as 'formalist' architect and Lefebvre as 'realist' sociologist. In fact, rather like Mies, Lefebvre did not advocate a total rejection of function, rather he was asking for its organic integration:

Is the functional being integrated into an organic reality - a life - in a way which will give that reality a structure it will be able to modify and adapt?[66]

Lefebvre advocated an 'organic' attitude toward function. For him this meant the integration of function into the formation of the town in such a way as to provide for the social identity of the town as something structural, including the structural need for change.

Lefebvre did not dismiss the phenomenon of the new town as an inhuman and invalid proposition, rather he saw it as the statement of a problem, one to whose solution he felt he should contribute. In formulating an answer Lefebvre asked himself about the difference between this new town and his own village, which must once upon a time have been new:

Wasn't your own village a new town once? It was built on the banks of the Gave, like this one, and because it was alive, it evolved a form. It is precisely because you reject aestheticism that you should take art as your model: art transformed into the art of living. The new town is a challenge to men to create human life! [67]

Lefebvre believed the modern new town was valuable as a kind of on-going experiment, a humanist laboratory for testing everyday life:

Think of it as a place of privileged experiment where at last men are about to conquer and control their everyday lives, through trial and error, successive approximations, abstractions superseded and concrete reality achieved, which is the path knowledge must follow towards predictable and unpredictable totality. [68]

As a contribution to the project of 'predictable and unpredictable totality,' Lefebvre believed that he could usefully develop a new concept. It was this ambition that led him, some ten years into the future, to write The Production of Space.

As suggested by the title, the concept Lefebvre tried to develop in The Production of Space hinged on the notion of space as a medium that needs to be understood dialectically, as both product and producer of social relationships. Lefebvre believed that it is natural and necessary for any society to produce its own space. The process of spatial production is not instantaneous but involves a slow development over time. It is effected through an intrinsic and continual process of self-presentation and self-representation on the part of the subject society. Lefebvre argued, one problem with the growth of modern, capitalist societies was the tendency to suppress the production of space through organic means. In capitalist societies the necessary processes of self-presentation and self-representation were suppressed and instead, he argued, space was produced by the top-down imposition of abstract concepts about space. Lefebvre argued that the modern state was the prime culprit in the imposition of space by means of concepts, rather than allowing for spatial development through organic processes. The state's abstract spatial concepts and their imposition were, in general, strategised and communicated by means of planning and design.

Lefebvre used a number of different terms to refer to the

kind of state-imposed, conceptual space he abhorred, sometimes calling it 'abstract political space,' sometimes calling it 'global space.'

Although Lefebvre blamed the modern state for imposing abstract concepts of space he understood the actual work of formulating those concepts as a task assigned by the state to specialists and experts, such as planners and architects. Lefebvre was deeply suspicious of the motivations of specialists and experts. He thought they were prone to delusions about the social benefits arising fro their work. He liked to point out, no matter how well-intentioned, in the end such specialists and experts had no choice but to defer to the dictates of oppressive and repressive commands coming from the state, he wrote:

Surely it is the supreme illusion to defer to architects, to urbanists, to planners as being experts or ultimate authorities in matters relating to space. What the 'interested parties' here fail to appreciate is that they are bending their demands (from below) to suit commands (from above), and that this unforced renunciation on their part actually runs ahead of the wishes of the manipulators of consciousness.[69]

Lefebvre was suspicious of architects and urbanists for two reasons. First because he was suspicious of all groups claiming to be specialists in what he termed 'the morphology of everyday life.' Second because, as he saw it, contemporary architecture and urbanism was unthinkable outside of the historical phenomenon of the Bauhaus. For Lefebvre the Bauhaus was not only the place where those techniques of planning and design, instrumental in the imposition of space, had been invented but was actually the historic location of the conceptualization of space, he wrote:

It might be asked at this juncture is there is any way of dating what might be called the moment of emergence of an awareness of space and its production: when and where, why and how, did a neglected knowledge and a misconstrued reality begin to be recognized? It so happens that this emergence can indeed be fixed: it is to be found in the 'historic' role of the Bauhaus. Our critical analysis will touch on this movement at several points. For the Bauhaus did more than locate space in its real context or supply a new perspective on it: it developed a new conception, a global concept, of space. At that time, around 1920, just after the First World War, a link was discovered in the advanced countries (France, Germany, Russia, the United States), a link which had already been dealt with on the practical plane but which had not yet been rationally articulated: that between rationalization and urbanization, between workplaces and dwelling places.[70]

Lefebvre credited the Bauhaus with having converted a

vague awareness into a full blown concept of space. The trigger effecting the conversion, he argued, was a perceived link between the efficient organization of industry and the development of cities. Furthermore, in the process of developing a concept of space the Bauhaus people came to see themselves as creators of space:

As Paul Klee put it, artists - painters, sculptors or architects - do not show space, they create it. The Bauhaus people understood that things could not be created independently of each other in space, whether movable (furniture) or fixed (buildings), without taking into account their interrelationships and their relationship to the whole. It was impossible simply to accumulate them as a mass, aggregate or collection of items. In the context of the productive forces, the technological means and the specific problems of the world, things and objects could now be produced in their relationships, along with their relationships.[71]

Lefebvre assumed that when a Bauhaus person, such as Klee, used the term 'space' they were referring to a total environment. He overlooks the fact that Bauhaus people would have used the German expression 'raum,' which doesn't translate into the English 'space' or the French 'espace.' If Lefebvre's assumption was correct and the Bauhaus people did mean space in the way Lefebvre meant space then he was, perhaps, justified in regarding the Bauhaus as the cradle of global space. If, on the other hand, the Bauhaus people used space only in the limited sense of visual and physical perception of boundaries, thresholds and extensions then he was not justified in regarding the Bauhaus to be the cradle of global space.

It is not the aim of this thesis to unravel the semantics of 'space' amongst all those people who were involved in the activities of the Bauhaus. No doubt the term was then, as it is now, used to convey a variety of meanings; and no doubt its use at the Bauhaus involved degrees of ambiguity. Sufficient for the purposes of this discussion is the fact that Lefebvre included Mies amongst those whom he associated with the Bauhaus' totalising attitudes. Lefebvre was, of course, correct to associate Mies with the Bauhaus, he had taught there during the later 1920s and was the institutions director during the last years of its existence, between 1930 and 1933. It is because he associated Mies with the Bauhaus and, rightly or wrongly, he believed the Bauhaus had formulated a global conception of space, that Lefebvre could point his finger accusingly at Mies:

It is certainly arguable that the writings and works of the Bauhaus, of Mies van der Rohe among others, outlined, formulated and helped realize that particular space.[72]

In seeing Mies as a contributor to the formulation and

realization of global space, Lefebvre closed his eyes to Miesian architecture. This was a shame, particularly since Mies was as troubled by the problems of planning and design, as was Lefebvre.

The following section will explore Lefebvre's ideas about architecture, as they emerged in his general theory of the production of space. These ideas will be used as a critical tool with which to investigate Mies' architectural practice. The aim of the investigation is; first, to advance the critical understanding of Miesian architecture which, through a reading of canonical texts, has been developed in this section and, second, to begin to forge a link between Miesian architecture, particularly as framed within Lefebvrian concepts and the project of AIR (nee Cotton) Grid, which is the subject of the second part of this thesis.

1.2: MIESIAN ARCHITECTURE & LEFEBVRIAN SPACE

The aim of this section of the thesis is to identify those elements in Lefebvre's thought that can be utilised to produce an alternative reading of Miesian architecture and to attempt that reading. As well as Lefebvre's thinking the reading The analysis takes as its starting point a question that Lefebvre asked himself in 1960, while he was studying the construction site of the new town of Mourenx:

A few kilometres away from the tower blocks of the new town lies the sleepy old village where I live. Just a few minutes from my timeworn house, and I am surrounded by the derricks of a building estate without a past. ....I know every stone of Navarrenx. In these stones I can read the centuries, rather as botanists can tell the age of a tree by the number of rings in its trunk. But for Navarrenx - as for many other places, villages and towns - a different analogy springs to mind: the image of the seashell. A living creature has slowly secreted a structure; take this living creature in isolation, separate it out from the form it has given itself according to the laws of its species, and you are left with something soft and slimy and shapeless. What can it possibly have in common with this delicate structure, its ridges, its grooves, its symmetries, its every detail revealing smaller, more delicate details as you examine it more closely? But it is precisely this link, between the animal and its shell, that one must try to understand.[1]

In attempting to unlock the link between the creature and its shell Lefebvre produced a kind of architecture without building, a theory of space, in which architectural design features as a mode of spatial production but is by no means conceived as the origins of space. In his architecture of space Lefebvre conceives of space as primary and if architectural structures do arise in space it is because space has produced them and not vice versa.

The Architecture of Living Being

In conceiving space as primary Lefebvre did not have a mathematical notion of space in mind, which presupposes space as a void waiting to be filled. Lefebvre conceived space as fundamental to the actions of living bodies, it is intrinsic to the body, certainly bodies do not create space in the sense of something additional and secondary. In Lefebvre's architecture of space, body and space is thought as an unmediated duality:

Can the body, with its capacity for action, and its various energies, be said to create space? Assuredly, but not in the sense that occupation might be said to 'manufacture' spatiality; rather, there is an immediate relationship between the body and its space, between the bodies's deployment in space and its occupation of space. Before producing effects in the material realm (tools and objects), before producing itself by drawing nourishment from that realm, and before reproducing itself by generating other bodies, each living body is space and has its space: it produces itself in space and also produces that space. This is a truly remarkable relationship: the body with the energies at its disposal, the living body, creates or produces its own space; conversely, the laws of space, which is to say the laws of discrimination in space, also govern the living body and the deployment of its energies.[2]

Lefebvre understood the dual body/space relation as a kind of economy, with its own discernible dynamics. Although some aspects of body/space dynamics can be understood mathematically it is important to remember that they originate in nature and precede mathematical formalisation:

In nature, whether organic or inorganic, symmetries (in a plane or about an axis) exist wherever there is bilaterality or duality, left and right, 'reflection', or rotation (in space); these symmetries are not properties external to bodies however. Though definable in 'purely' mathematical terms - as applications, operations, transformations or functions - they are not imposed upon material bodies as many philosophers suppose, by prior thought. Bodies - deployments of energies - produce space and produce themselves, along with their motions, according to the laws of space.[3]

To illustrate what he meant Lefebvre asked the reader to consider the example of a spider spinning its web, he quizzes the reader on how to think about the space of the spider's activity:

Should we think of this space of the spider's as an abstract space occupied by such separate objects as its body, its secretory glands and legs, the things to which it attaches its web, the strands of silk making up the web, the flies that serve as its prey, and so on?

Lefebvre answers his own question with an emphatic NO:

...for this would be to set the spider in the space of analytic intellection, the space of discourse, the space of this sheet of paper before me.[4]

For Lefebvre it was important to try to think the relation of spider, web and action together, as a basic principle of space. And it was the conundrum of that unity that he wanted his reader to hold in their mind and to attend to. This was because Lefebvre wanted to introduce his reader to the idea that space was a manner of thinking, but one that was quite unlike the kinds of abstract reasoning we tend to associate with the notion of thought. This other kind of thinking, involved in the primeval space of spider, web and action, is a basic factor in the production of habitats and tools, Lefebvre wrote:

As for the web's symmetrical and asymmetrical aspects and the spatial structures (anchorage points, networks, centre/periphery) that it embodies, is the spider's knowledge of these comparable to the human form of knowledge? Clearly not: the spider produces, which manifestly calls for 'thought', but it does not 'think' in the same way as we do. The spider's 'production' and the characteristics thereof have more in common with the seashell or with the flower evoked by the 'Angel of Silesia' than with verbal abstraction. Here the production of space, beginning with the production of the body, extends to the productive secretion of a 'residence' which also serves as a tool, a means.[5]

Through the example of the web spinning spider we are introduced to two ideas of fundamental importance to Lefebvre's architecture of space. First, the idea that there is another, nonintellectual kind of knowledge involved in the production of space and, second that nonintellectual spatial knowledge produces habitats, including tools and residences.

Thus we see at the basis of Lefebvre's architecture of space a kind of anti-intellectual naturalism, evidenced on the fact that animals clearly are capable of reproducing their means of subsistence through their apparently unpremeditated production of habitats and tools.

Although Lefebvre stressed the inseparability of the creature/habitat relationship, it is important to notice that he also differentiates the creature and its habitat. Lefebvre wanted to avoid any suggestion that difference arises only as a consequence of external imposition. Difference is immanent to the architecture of space, produced spontaneously, a feature of its autopoietic functioning.

To communicate this dual sense of spatial architecture Lefebvre referred to a structure that is easy to imagine as simultaneously joined and disjoined: the spider and its web. However, Lefebvre was not suggesting creature/habitat relationships are necessarily manifest in the production of tangible forms, such as shells, nests and webs; rather he was saying the creation of tangible forms is but one instance of a whole range of demarcating and orientating activities that is typical of creature/habitat duality, he wrote:

...that for any living body, just as for spiders, shellfish and so on, the most basic places and spatial indicators are first of all qualified by that body.[6]

Lefebvre understood the entire range of demarcating

and orientating activities and the most rudimentary of spatial indicators as features of his spatial architecture. And, insofar as these referred to specific bodies he called them 'structures.' In so doing Lefebvre was proposing a new way of thinking about structures and living bodies, which, on the whole, tends to be thought in the limited sense of the body's skeletal, gravity resisting armature. With his new way of thinking about body structures Lefebvre was conceiving bodies as distributed within their environment.

Lefebvre described the generation of body structure as a kind of spatial energetics whose key mechanism was that of mirroring. He argued there were two types of mirror: 'imaginary' and 'real.' The first, 'imaginary' mirror, operates within the basic duality of structure and creature that is constitutive of all living bodies. The second, 'real' mirror, contributes a further dimension to Lefebvrian spatial architecture, namely consciousness.

In order to extend the scope of spatial architecture Lefebvre had to explain how it was possible for living bodies to form relationships between themselves. In other words he had to explain how it was possible for his body/space dualities to communicate with one another. This was the role of his second mirroring function. Lefebvre argued that, for all they are inextricable from their environment nevertheless living bodies are irreducible to that environment and this is because they share their environment with other living bodies, necessarily external to them. In order to maintain that externality there is a virtual surface that delimits living bodies and keeps them separate. It is this virtual surface that Lefebvre refers to as the second, 'real' mirroring function of space. He described the mechanism as a kind of radiating energy, emanating out from each living body, coupled to a perceptual system for its reception and interpretation. The energy reflecting between the surfaces of bodies produces a realm of potential messages, it is external to bodies, but they are immersed in it and it affects them:

It is in fact part and parcel of the way in which the existence of space is established. This incessant deciphering activity is objective as much as subjective - in which respect it indeed transcends the old philosophical distinction between objectivity and subjectivity. It becomes more acute as soon as concealed parts of space (the internal portions of things and things outside the field of perception) come to have associated with themselves symbols, or corresponding signs or indices, which are often tabooed, holy/evil, revelatory or occult. It is in this sense that it cannot be properly described as either a subjective or an objective, a conscious or an unconscious, activity; rather, it is an activity which serves to generate consciousness: messages, by virtue of space and of the interplay of reflections and mirages within it, are intrinsic to lived experience itself.[7]

In his descriptions of the endless mirroring operations of space Lefebvre painted the picture of a lively, packed, visceral and kinetic interplay between the realms of the real and the imaginary. And he identified one special event in the play of space, the passage from obscurity into the light:

On the one hand, therefore, space contains opacities, bodies and objects, centres of efferent actions and effervescent energies, hidden - even impenetrable - places, areas of viscosity, and black holes. On the other, it offers sequences, sets of objects, concatenations of bodies - so much so, in fact, that anyone can at any time discover new ones, constantly slipping from the non-visible realm into the visible, from opacity into transparency. Objects touch one another, feel, smell and hear one another. Then they contemplate one another with eye and gaze. One truly gets the impression that every shape in space, every spatial plane, constitutes a mirror and produces a mirage effect; that within each body the rest of the world is reflected and referred back to, in an ever-renewed to-and-fro of reciprocal reflection, an interplay of shifting colours, lights and forms. A mere change of position, or a change in a place's surroundings is enough to precipitate an objects passage into the light: what was covert becomes overt, what was cryptic becomes limpidly clear. A movement of the body may have a similar goal. Here is the point of intersection of the two sensory fields.[8]

Lefebvre located human consciousness at this moment of passing into the light, it is a consciousness that knows itself, he called it 'living being.'

In his theoretical development of the emergence of living being out of the mirroring functions of space Lefebvre put together a fascinating and complex architecture. Plausibly the most interesting aspect of Lefebvrian architecture and the most difficult to picture is the relationship between the two mirroring functions:

1. reflections in an imaginary mirror, which, Lefebvre called 'real'

and

2. reflections in a real mirror, which, Lefebvre called 'imaginary'

The theory posits these differing modes of reflection as giving rise to two different sensory realms: the 'real' and the 'imaginary.' The sensory realm of the real is developed out of the concept of the living body, a duality of energy and structure that is related through reflection in the imaginary mirror of the real. On the other hand the sensory realm of the imaginary is developed out of the concept of communication between bodies. It is a realm of messages produced through the effect of mirroring between the surfaces of bodies. Living being, i.e., being that is aware, arises at the intersection of the two realms.

Lefebvre warned there is an element of danger built into the generation of living being out of the mirroring functions of space. Because, as we shall see, the process involves abstraction and living being is vulnerable to abstraction. Recollect how, in his discussion of the spider spinning its web, Lefebvre used abstraction to imply the analytic space of intellection, the space of discourse. In his discussion of the generation of living being out of the mirroring operations of space he implied that abstraction was something different, something immanent to the mirroring function of space. He argued this other type of abstraction was vital to living being; and yet it opened living being to danger.

In the generation of living being the process of abstraction is one of separation, to know itself living being must be able to create an image of itself. Yet living being can sometimes create images that lead to misrecognition and mistaken identity. When this happens living being becomes confused and overwhelmed, it fails to master its own image. When this happens warned Lefebvre, living being fragments, it looses touch with the vitality of living body, becoming trapped in the void of a space that is merely a figment, an abstract space, he wrote:

The mirror discloses the relationship between me and myself, my body and the consciousness of my body - not because the reflection constitutes my unity qua subject, as many psychoanalysts and psychologists apparently believe, but because it transforms what I am into the sign of what I am. This ice-smooth barrier, itself merely an inert sheen, reproduces and displays what I am - in a word signifies what I am - within an imaginary sphere which is yet quite real. A process of abstraction then - but a fascinating abstraction. In order to know myself, I 'separate myself out from myself'. The effect is dizzying. Should the 'Ego' fail to reassert hegemony over itself by defying its own image, it must become Narcissus - or Alice. It will then be in danger of never discovering itself, space qua figment will have swallowed it up, and the glacial surface of the mirror will hold it forever captive in its emptiness, in an absence devoid of all conceivable presence or bodily warmth.[9]

Although living being cannot exist without abstraction it is essentially a dangerous process and, while it is vital that living being keep on producing images, so it is no less vital that living being does not fixate upon its images but constantly challenges and defies them and produces new ones.

Lefebvre drew an analogy between the process of maturation of an individual living being and the historical development of a society. He suggested the same process that generated living beings was replicated in the spatial architecture of particular societies, this he called 'social being.' In either case Lefebvre believed that abstraction, in the sense of image formation, was a necessary but dangerous process, facilitating the sustenance of living and of social being yet at the same time running the risk of *'the expulsion of the physical body outside of itself.'*[10]

Apollo and Dionysus

One important influence for Lefebvre's spatial architecture was Friedrich Nietzsche's notion of two distinct yet related aesthetic impulses, the Apollonian and the Dionysian, Lefebvre wrote:

The Nietzschean distinction between Apollonian and Dionysian echoes the dual aspect of the living being and its relationship to space - its own space and the other's: violence and stability, excess and equilibrium. Inadequate as this distinction may be, it is certainly meaningful.[11]

Although Lefebvre thought the Nietzschean duality was insufficient, or in some way incomplete; he clearly located his own thinking about space in the Nietzschian tradition. The connection is particularly interesting in the context of this study, aimed at linking Lefebvre and Mies since Mies too came under the influence of Nietzschean thought.[12]

Nietzsche's first book, *The Birth of Tragedy,* published in 1872, attempted to construct a unified theory of nature and culture. Nietzsche was himself influenced by the thought of Arthur Schopenhauer, particularly the ideas expressed in The World as Will and Representation, first published in 1819. What was radical about Schopenhauer's thinking was the way he posited nature, not as the benign creation of a divine being but as a blind field of wilful impulses and energies. For Schopenhauer nature was demonic however, he argued, most human individuals and groups tended to deny the ominous truth of nature and instead to immerse themselves in comforting, illusory worlds. Schopenhauer had little time for such delusions, he believed the only way to confront and come to terms with demon nature was through the total suppression of desire. Although Nietzsche took Schopenhauer's point about nature, his outlook was more optimistic, certainly he did not want to sacrifice desire. Nietzsche proposed instead a working, active relationship between man and nature, one that was structured, not on the basis of individual denial, as was Schopenhauer's nihilism, but on the basis of collective redemption through cultural unity.

Like Lefebvre, Nietzsche conceptualized nature in terms of a duality, but whereas Lefebvre looked to the couple real/imaginary, Nietzsche concentrated on the Apollo/Dionysus couple. Nietzsche thought of the couple in terms of energetics, referring to it as an artistic impulse that arose spontaneously, quite aside from the desires and activities of artists, their patrons and audiences:

Thus far we have considered the Apollonian and its opposite, the Dionysian, as artistic energies which burst forth from nature herself, without the mediation of the human artist - energies in which nature's art impulses are satisfied in the most immediate and direct way - first in the image world of dreams, whose completeness is not dependent upon the intellectual attitude or the artistic culture of any single being; and then as intoxicated reality, which likewise does not heed the single unit, but even seeks to destroy the individual and redeem him by a mystic feeling of oneness. With reference to these art-states of nature, every artist is an 'imitator', that is to say, either an Apollonian artist in dreams, or a Dionysian artist in ecstasies, or finally - as for example in Greek tragedy - at once artist in both dreams and ecstasies.[13]

Notice how Nietzsche's evocation of the eruption and gratification of artistic energies presented the phenomenon as occurring spontaneously, the individual was merely an instrument of nature, a selfless participant in the production of images and dreams, or intoxicated reality. Lefebvre was careful to avoid this aspect of Nietzsche's thinking, he did not conceive living being as merely instrumental. For Lefebvre living being was central to nature, a primary value.

In portraying the difference between the two levels of artistic energy Nietzsche contrasted two psychophysiological states: dreaming and dance. To each of these he gave the name of a classical pagan god and he associated it with a characteristic activity, dreaming with Apollo and dancing with Dionysus. Elaborating on the Apollonian energy level, Lefebvre explained how:

The joyous necessity of the dream experience has been embodied by the Greeks in their Apollo: Apollo, the god of all plastic energies, is at the same time the soothsaying god. He, who (as the etymology of the name indicates) is the 'shining one', the deity of light, is also ruler over the beautiful illusion of the world of fantasy.[14]

As the god of 'plastic energies' Apollo presided over a particular range of art forms, each of which was associated with the dream state. Nietzsche included architecture in the Apollonian category, regarding it as a plastic art and thus associated with beautiful illusions and fantasy. An important difference between Lefebvre and Nietzsche and, indeed, between Mies and Nietzsche, is that neither of them would have accepted Nietzsche's categorization of architecture as an art of illusion and fantasy. However, it is also important to note that Nietzsche's understanding of illusion and fantasy did not carry the negative connotations that those notions might have had for Lefebvre and for Mies.

Nietzsche did not regard images as necessarily

deceptive or fetishistic, but he did point out that it was essential for their proper functioning that they be understood for what they were, i.e., merely appearances, and not be mistaken for reality.[15] In conveying his understanding of the social role of images the analogy of dreaming was very important to Nietzsche, because dreams too had an important function, which he understood as that of soothing and healing.

Elaborating on the other, Dionysian energy level Nietzsche explained how:

Either under the influence of the narcotic draught, of which the songs of all primitive men and peoples speak, or with the potent coming of spring that penetrates all nature with joy, these Dionysian emotions awake, and as they grow in intensity everything subjective vanishes into complete self-forgetfulness.[16]

Nietzsche described with evident enthusiasm the dancing crowds which, ever increasing in number would whirl from place to place under the Dionysian influence. And he warned how corpse-like and ghostly those who, unaffected by the intoxicating substances and atmospheres, must look to the revellers, as they *'roar past.'*[17]

Just like Lefebvre with his mirroring functions, Nietzsche did not regard his two art impulses as opposites, for him the Apollonian dream and the Dionysian dance were inseparable, they existed as a duality. Furthermore, just like Lefebvre, Nietzsche regarded the health of any society to be dependant upon the careful maintenance and well-being of its culture, which was in turn dependant on the dream/dance duality. In order to demonstrate what he meant, Nietzsche turned to the example of Greek tragic drama, which he understood as the most perfect fusion of the Apollonian and the Dionysian into a single art form.

Central to Nietzsche's account of Greek tragic drama was the mechanism of transition between the dream and the dance. Nietzsche understood the transition as a perpetual destruction of appearances, formalised and played out in the ritual of Greek tragic drama. The character of the satyr was important to Nietzsche's account of Greek tragic drama, for him the satyr was 'the true human being,' by which he meant a kind of primordial ancestor of all human beings. Unlike the evolved human being, who shied away from nature, the satyr revered and adored nature, he worshipped nature as a deity. But in order to do so authentically the satyr had to be bold enough to look nature boldly in the eye:

...on the unconcealed and vigorously magnificent characters of nature, his eye rested with sublime satisfaction; here the true human being was disclosed, the bearded satyr jubilating to his god.[18]

Nietzsche understood the process of the Dionysian festival as consisting in two parts. First, a recapturing of the primordial, satyr condition:

The revelling throng, the votaries of Dionysus jubilate under the spell of such moods and insights whose power transforms them before their own eyes till they imagine that they are beholding themselves as restored geniuses of nature, as satyrs.[19]

Seeing themselves as satyrs, the jubilating votaries enact the second stage of the process and project the dream image.

In Greek tragic drama it was the chorus that enacted the satyr transformation. The choral actors chanted the dithyramb, a vehement and wild hymn to Dionysus and in so doing they were transformed, as if their body had entered into that of the satyr. Nietzsche described this relation as one of fusion, as if the actor and the satyr were acting out a dual metamorphosis. In the condition of satyric fusion the actor became oblivious to his real civic and social status:

...the dithyrambic chorus is a chorus of transformed characters whose civic past and social status have become totally forgotten: they have become timeless servants of their god who live outside the spheres of society.[20]

In their fused condition the choral actor lost all sense of individuality, they were staring raw existence, bare unmediated nature, in the face. Caught within their Dionysian ecstasy the actor beheld a vision, that vision was the Apollonian complement of their ecstatic state. By means of the vision the choral actor returned to the non-ecstatic, dream state, of reality, only now it is a new dream, a new reality.

In his account of the Dionysian festival Nietzsche placed great significance on the energetics involved in the process, especially the choral energy. To perform the dithyrambic dance the chorus must have had large amounts of energy to spare. Where did that energy come from? Nietzsche explained the source of the dithyrambic energy as originating in a powerful desire, the desire to experience something never before experienced and to express something new:

In the Dionysian dithyramb man is incited to the greatest exaltation of all his symbolic faculties; something never before experienced struggles for utterance.[21]

The powerful desire that energised the chorus was finally satiated with the projection of the Apollonian vision. As the energy fuelling the revelry reached its peak so a new image, the Apollonian complement of the ecstatic chorus, was disclosed. Life now returned to the low-level energy of the dream state and the Dionysian forces died down. But they did not die out, they were merely waiting, refuelling for the next Dionysian eruption.

Nietzsche's structure of Dionysian and Apollonian art proposed two, interwoven levels of energy, the low-level energy of the dream state and the massive energy level of the dance. The relationship between the two energy levels was cyclical and repetitive. The massive energy of the Dionysian drive was not a once and for all occurrence but constantly returned; the return was born out of the recurrent desire to create something new, the satisfaction of this desire in turn leading to the regeneration of the low-level energy of the Apollonian image. Lefebvre used Nietzsche's interweaving of different energy levels in his dual structure of living being and its relationship to space:

The truth is, however, that in its relationship to itself and its own space the living being uses both minimal and massive types of energy (which in any case are not strictly separable). The organism thus combines apparatuses storing enormous quantities of energy which are discharged explosively (musculature, sexual apparatus, members) with apparatuses designed to respond to very feeble stimuli - i.e. Information - and to consume barely any energy (the sensory apparatus: the brain and sense organs). What we find here is a constitutive dualism. The living being is not merely a data-processing machine, not merely a desiring, killing or producing machine - it is both at once.[22]

Lefebvre was fascinated by the evident capacity of living beings to capture, to accumulate and to release energy. He admitted he could not explain the mechanics of the process, but he was convinced the entire cycle was a necessity of life, something that distinguished it from mere survival:

This surplus or superfluity of energy is what distinguishes life from survival (the bare minimum needed to support life). Captive energy is not generally stored indefinitely or preserved in a stagnant state. When it is, the organism degenerates. It is in the nature of energy that it be expended - and expended productively, even when the 'production' involved is merely that of play or of gratuitous violence. The release of energy always gives rise to an effect, to damage, to a change in reality. It modifies space or generates a new space.[23]

Here Lefebvre was extrapolating from Nietzschian energetics to account for his own energetics of living being. Like Nietzsche, Lefebvre understood the energy of living being to originate in the powerful and recurrent desire to experience something new. For Lefebvre the generation of novelty was a risky but necessary life process, unavoidable if living being were to avoid losing itself in a mere struggle for survival.

Lefebvre and Architecture

Turning now to Lefebvre's understanding of the role of architectural design in his spatial architecture. As we have already seen, Lefebvre credits architecture with the production of living bodies; but he also referred to architecture in a more limited sense of a stage, or setting for events. Architecture conceived as the producer of living bodies seems to imply a more dynamic energetics than architecture in the sense of an artificially constructed environment that can serve as a fixed stage or setting, for events that unfold inside and around it. If there is life in such artificial constructions then surely that life is played out in the activities of the people who make and use them, no doubt people are affected by the built environment, but the idea that their bodies are produced exclusively by that environment seems somehow incredible. On the other hand, to think of architectural design as merely provisional is to take away any sense of urgency, which is presumably why Lefebvre insisted that architecture did more for the environment than just provide a backdrop for events and that it was actually responsible for the animation of bodies, as if architecture was what brought a body to life in the first place:

Architecture produces living bodies, each with its own distinctive traits. The animating principle of such a body, its presence, is neither visible nor legible as such, nor is it the object of any discourse, for it reproduces itself within those who use the space in question, within their lived experience. Of that experience the tourist, the passive spectator, can grasp but a pale shadow.[24]

It is important to note, Lefebvre does not mention architectural design here, it is architecture that produces living bodies. The implication would be, if design is involved, then design is subservient to architecture. But neither does he attribute the animating principle of architecture to the function of the building in use, he attributes it to the corporeal nature of the architecture. The animating principle is reproduced in the users, it does not originate with them. The relationship Lefebvre proposed, between a living body that was produced by architecture and the animating principle of that body is remarkably similar to the set of relationships we were introduced to through the example of the web spinning spider. Recollect how Lefebvre used the example of the spider to communicate the idea of the living body as a bundle of energies that is both the product and producer of space. The mutual relationship between living body and space was governed by laws, 'the laws of space':

Bodies - deployments of energies - produce space and produce themselves, along with their motions, according to the laws of space.[3]

For Lefebvre, architecture, as the producer of living bodies was dialectically linked to the production of space, its prime function being to reproduce the laws of space.

In *The Production of Space* Lefebvre gave an extraordinary account of a particular work of architecture. The work in question was the Church of the Sagrada Familia, Barcelona, built from 1903 onwards and designed by the architect Antonio Gaudí (figure 24). In fact, the Sagrada Familia could hardly be said to have been designed in the conventional sense, for Gaudí's intention throughout the project was the building of a cathedral 'without planning.'[25] This is not to say that Gaudí worked on the Sagrada Familia without deploying techniques of mediation, such as drawing and model-making. What was unusual in Gaudí's approach was the way he structured the relationship between conceiving and making the building. Gaudí did not produce a complete design of the building before work started on site, he produced a model of a physical structure that was sufficient for the purposes of forming a physical and mental framework to serve as a template for building. The subsequent process of design development involved Gaudí in constant activity on site, an activity which included model-making and drawing, but which also included carving and the management of the work of others. The building was not finished in Gaudi's lifetime, it is still not quite finished to this day.

Lefebvre did not mention the unusual circumstances of the Sagrada Familia's production, but it is likely he was aware of them and perhaps saw the slow yet purposeful process of crafting the building as an important aspect of the architecture. But even beyond its unique process of production, the Sagrada Familia was, for Lefebvre, rich with provocation, he described it as the:

...locus of a risible consecration, one which makes a mockery of the sacred, the Sagrada Familia causes modern space and the archaic space of nature to corrupt one another. The flouting of established spatial codes and the eruption of a natural and cosmic fertility generate an extraordinary and dizzying 'infinitization' of meaning. Somewhere short of accepted symbolisms, but beyond everyday meanings, a sanctifying power comes into play which is neither that of the state, nor of the Church, nor of the artist, nor that of theological divinity, but rather that of a naturalness boldly identified with divine transcendence. The Sagrada Familia embodies a modernised heresy which disorders representations of space and transforms them into a representational space where palms and fronds are expressions of the divine. The outcome is a virtual eroticization, one based on the enshrinement of a cruel, sexual-mystical pleasure which is the opposite, but also the reverse, of joy. What is obscene is modern 'reality', and here it is so designated by the staging - and by Gaudi as stage-manager.[26]

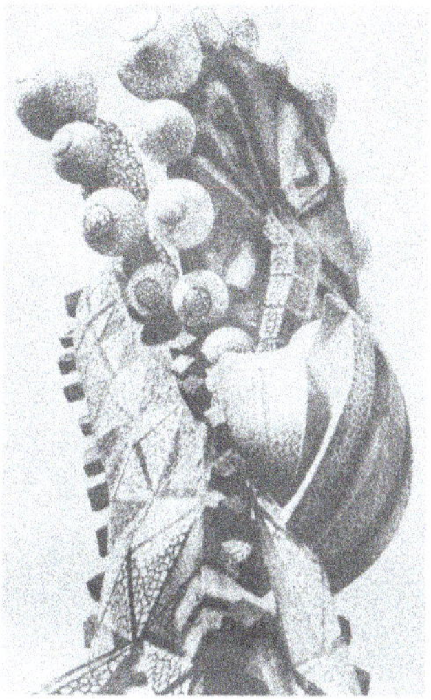

FIGURE 24

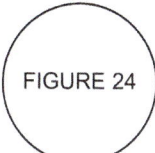

Antonio Gaudi, Church of the Sagrada Familia, Barcelona, from 1903
top left: view towards the spires
top right: view of ornamentation cluster at the tip of a spire

In Lefebvre's description, the Sagrada Familia is made to seem as if it acted as a kind of catalyst, causing an energetic disturbance, a kind of flying of sparks, between two very different types of space: 'modern space' and the 'archaic space of nature' are incited to intermingle and to corrupt one another. In the process we can see an intermingling of both kinds of Lefebvrian mirroring, real and imaginary, and it is fair to assume the church congregation and visitors are commingled and involved in the corruption.

In his account of the catalytic moment Lefebvre refers to two signifying registers, the institution of the church and that of everyday life. Each register generates messages, but thanks to the mirroring function of space the messages are confused. On the one hand they came close to yet fall short of the kinds of authoritative representations expected of the church and on the other they come close to yet fall short of the norms of everyday life. For living being the outcome of the struggle for sense at the Sagrada Familia is a feeling of dizziness and a sense of infinity.

For Lefebvre dizziness and infinity go hand in hand with the kind of abstraction he associated with the continuous process of separation, necessary for the sustained production of self-consciousness. Dizziness and infinity arise at the intersection of the two sensory realms of the real and the imaginary, the same location where self-consciousness appears:

This ice-smooth barrier, itself merely an inert sheen, reproduces and displays what I am - in a word signifies what I am - within an imaginary sphere which is yet quite real. A process of abstraction then - but a fascinating abstraction. In order to know myself, I 'separate myself out from myself'. The effect is dizzying.[9]

Lefebvre was suggesting that the space of the Sagrada Familia produced just such an ice-smooth barrier, or sheen, an environment in which the dizzying abstraction necessary for authentic self-consciousness could occur. The process was socially produced, i.e., not at the level of the individual but at the level of an entire community, including a social strategy for the effective production of architecture. For Lefebvre, the Sagrada Familia was exemplary architecture because it served both as a haven and as a site of provocation, where the painful, but at the same time pleasurable and necessary, sacrifice of self-separation was prompted and protected.

But what about the role of the architect in a work as seemingly affective as this? Did Lefebvre attribute the affectivity of the work to Gaudí's potency as a designer or did he attribute it to the happy circumstances of the city of Barcelona's approach to the church project, or to both? Two factors must be taken into account in answering these questions. First, the circumstances of the Sagrada Familia's production can hardly be described as 'architectural design' in the conventional sense. As already described, Gaudí's involvement in the project was more like that of a medieval master mason than a modern architect. It was surely as much because he knew about the Sagrada Familia's unconventional procurement processes that Lefebvre singled it out as the site of architectural vitality. Second, Lefebvre never referred to Gaudí as the building's architect but as the stage-manager. In crediting Gaudi in this way, Lefebvre placed him in a very particular working relationship with the project. The implication of the term manager pointed towards a practical outlook, concerned with issues of planning and co-ordination, rather than an idealistic outlook, associated with notions of creativity and genius.

In Lefebvre's theory of space the work of architecture lived twice. It lived first as a body, in which the laws of space were reproduced. As a haven for the laws of space Lefebvre's architectural body was invested with both types of reflection necessary for the production of living being: reflection in an imaginary mirror and reflection in a real mirror. The first type of reflection belonged to the relation of energy and structure that was constitutive of the architectural body itself, the building. The second belonged to the relation of the building to the community who inhabited and used it. Through the buildings interactions with the life of the community the work of architecture lived a second time. In order to engage the community the work of architecture had to appear to reflect their world. The work of architecture could only reflect the world of its inhabitants and users insofar as it appeared for them as a meaningful space of representation.

Miesian Architecture: Space and Form

Equipped with this outline sketch of Lefebvre's spatial architecture, the study now returns to Mies, asking what happens if Lefebvre's theory of space is used as a lens through which to read Mies. To begin the study looks for evidence in the things Mies said or wrote, about architecture, paying special attention to the way he used the word space. In his short, aphoristic statements Mies rarely used the word space, on the few occasions when he did, it referred to the physical and visual experiences of expansion that the design would afford the potential user of the building. For example, in 1943 Mies was contacted by the magazine The Architectural Forum and asked to participate in a special issue to be entitled 'New Buildings of 194X'. Initially Mies was invited to put forward a proposal for a church, but he suggested a museum instead. Mies' project of the Museum For a Small City was published in Architectural Forum, no 5, 1943. The proposal was represented by a number of drawings and a text. In the published version there were four drawings:

an exterior view, a plan and two interior views (figures 25, 26, 27 & 28). The first interior view was a perspective construction with overlaid images of a number of artworks and the second was a montage, in which visual depth was inferred by the layering of surfaces. Although the title of Mies' project would appear to place the museum in an urban setting, that of a small city, the drawings conveyed no sense of an urban environment, the Museum For a Small City appeared to be set in a landscaped valley. This would imply that Mies was imagining the small city as a garden city, one where the theme of development was the integration of an urban structure within a landscape environment.

The exterior view showed the undulating profile of a hilly landscape set in front of a clear sky. Laid out at the foot of the hills and filling the foreground was a flat, expansive, concourse (figure 25). In the middle-ground, between the concourse and the hilly backdrop, was a long, low-lying structure. It looked as if the concourse extended below a very flat horizontal slab that was levitating in front of the hillside. Under the slab, and extending out from the slab, were a number of walls and partitions. That the concourse extended beneath the slab was confirmed in the first of the interior views, where the perspectival recession of the concourse surface was drawn into the picture (figure 27). In the foreground three artworks, a painting, and two sculptures establish and stabilise the space.

In the mid-ground a framed transparent screen was drawn, it reached up to the horizontal datum of the slab, which in turn seemed to terminate at the point of juncture with the screen. Beyond the screen was a wall that appeared to slide into the composition from the right; the gridded perspective of the floor surface extended from the foreground, back into the pictorial depth to terminate somewhere beyond the wall. The levitation of the horizontal slab was reinforced by the slim, almost transparent, column which, in the foreground and just obscured by the painting, extended upward and in terminating confirmed the horizontal datum of the slab.

In the second interior view panels of a leafy and of a liquid visual texture were pasted into the background, behind the images of a painting and of two sculptures (figure 28). The textured panels conveyed the sense that nature lay beyond. But the panels were framed within the cadence of a vertical rhythm, meaning they could be read, not as views out but as projections onto a screen. The plan depicted a grid of spots, representing columns, placed upon the surface of the sheet as if it were the floor (figure 26). The merging of the concourse into the ground of the drawing was achieved with subtle fading lines. The grid of columns was encapsulated in two transparent rectangles, one representing the levitating slab, the other the enclosing glass screen. A U-shaped element looked as if it had been pulled out from under the levitating slab, like a draw. Embedded in the

FIGURE 25

Mies van der Rohe, Project for a Museum for a Small City, 1943, external view

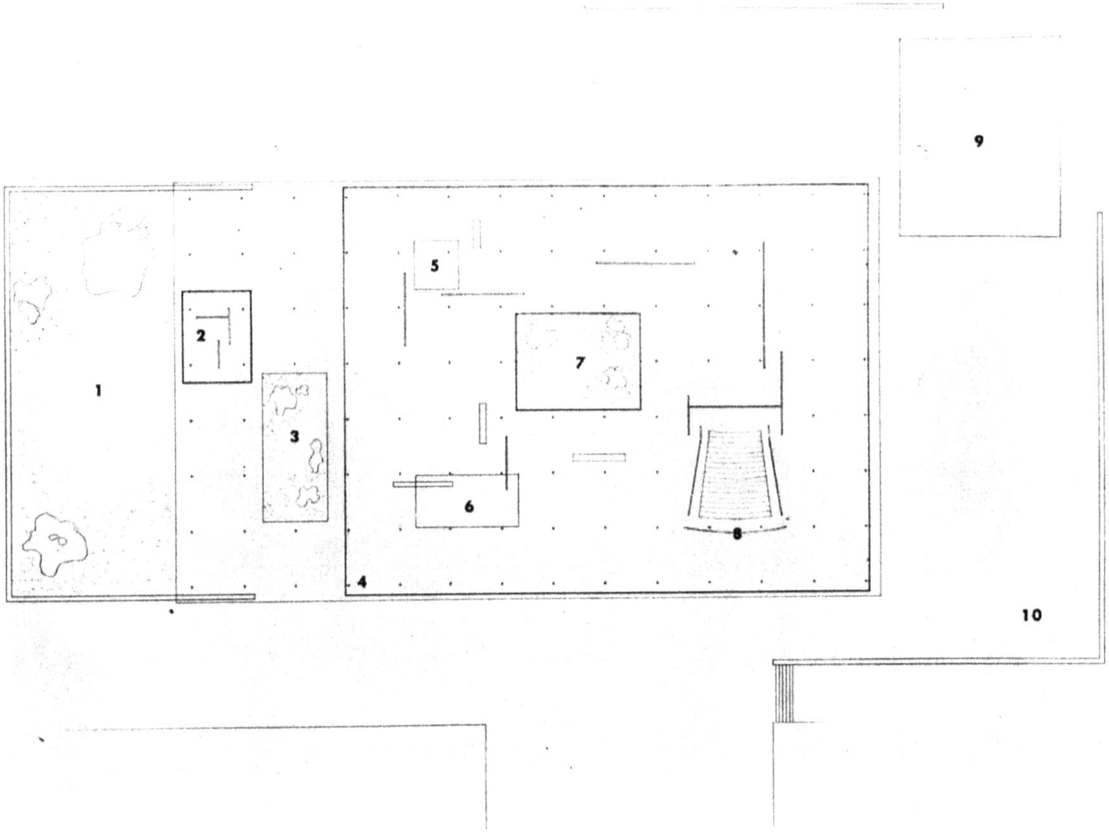

FIGURE 26

Mies van der Rohe, Project for a Museum for a Small City, 1943, plan

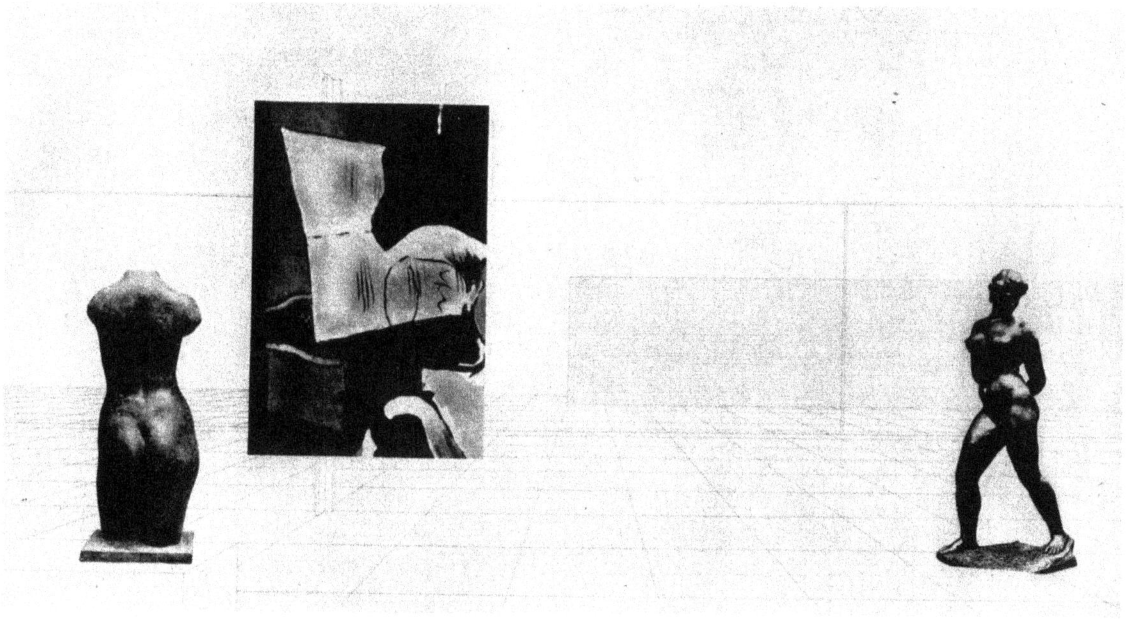

FIGURE 27

Mies van der Rohe, Project for a Museum for a Small City, 1943, interior view

FIGURE 28

Mies van der Rohe, Project for a Museum for a Small City, 1943, interior view gridded field of columns were rectangular and linear elements, representing screens and volumetric subdivisions of the area beneath the slab. The arrangement of these elements upon the drawing surface had something of the 'look' of a Suprematist painting, as if they were floating, loosely bound into a formation in the air.

In his text of the Museum for a Small City Mies emphasised the idea that the museum was a place where artworks are there to be enjoyed, not locked away. Clearly, Mies associated the openness and transparency of his museum design with the enjoyment of art; yet in the drawings there were no visible signs of human occupation, so by whom was the art to be enjoyed? One plausible answer to this question could be found in Mies' text and in the way he used the word space. In the Museum For a Small City the term 'space' appears in a number of different contexts. First paired with the term 'freedom,' where Mies wrote of the sculpture as enjoying 'spatial freedom':

The first problem is to establish the museum as a centre for the enjoyment, not the interment of art. In this project the barrier between the art work and the living community is erased by a garden approach for the display of sculpture. Interior sculptures enjoy an equal spatial freedom, because the open plan permits them to be seen against the surrounding hills.[27]

Mies evoked a sense of spatial freedom through the equivalence of garden and interior; notice how the sculptures inside the museum were to enjoy an equal spatial freedom to those outside in the garden. Mies had arranged the design so as to ensure the sculptures inside would be seen against the hilly backdrop of the surrounding landscape. In this context his use of the word space alluded to the idea of a visual and tactile experience of an open, uncluttered expanse, full of light and air. But it should be noted, Mies equated spatial freedom with the dissolution of a presupposed psychological barrier; that between the works of art and the living community. In his desire to re-unite the living community with art Mies was faintly echoing the Nietzschean idea of culture, i.e., the idea that art was necessary for social well-being. And it might well be that Mies' suggestion of a garden approach was an indirect reference to the Nietzschean concept, a symbolic reminiscence of the Nietzschean idea that art is a form of energy originating in nature.

Having associated space with the notion of freedom Mies proceeded to use the term in a different context, now associating it with the interior of the museum, which he referred to as an 'architectural space':

The architectural space, thus achieved, becomes a defining rather than a confining space. A work such as Picasso's Guernica has been difficult to place in the usual museum gallery. Here it can be shown to greatest advantage and become an element in space against a changing background.[28]

Here Mies used space in the sense of a room or a covered and enclosed area, but notice how he distinguished the kind of room he was proposing from the conventional museum gallery by saying it was 'defining' as opposed to 'confining.' In setting the notion of definition in opposition to the notion of confinement Mies again alluded to freedom, only now in the sense of a liberal distance between perceptual boundaries. The distances in question arising, first, between the elements of the architectural construction and, second, between the artworks on display. Initially it may seem as if the freedom Mies championed here was exclusively for the artworks, rather than the visitors and users of the gallery. However, if, as Mies suggested, the background of the gallery space is to change, then that change could only be registered in the consciousness of perambulating visitors as they wandered about the gallery, enjoying the art and the extended views out to the surrounding landscape. The important point to notice here is that Mies envisioned the users of the museum as mobile and their mobility was integrated into his concept of space.

There was one further use of the term space in Mies' text, where he used it to designate specific functions. The primary designation was that of exhibiting, but Mies included other spatial designations that were separated out from the primary function:

Under the same roof, but separated from the exhibit space, would be the offices of administration. These would have their own toilet and storage facilities in a basement under the office area.[29]

In his text of the Museum for a Small City Mies did not the use the word space in the way Lefebvre used it. However, this did not mean Mies' thinking about space was totally unaligned with Lefebvre's, or that Mies failed to appreciate the importance of architecture in the vital and productive sense that Lefebvre did. Mies used his text to describe the experience of the museum as he imagined it in use. Lefebvre understood the successful relationship between architecture and the community of users depended upon the extent to which the community could recognize itself in the work. In his text Mies referred to the necessity of removing the barrier between the community and the artworks, but he did not explain why. However, it is fairly safe to assume he believed that in so doing the community would, in some way, be able to recognize it self in the artworks.

In his description of the Sagrada Familia Lefebvre wrote evocatively about the vital relationship between the community and the architectural space. In his description of the Museum For a Small City Mies implied a similarly vital relationship, but he did not attempt to evoke it through drawing or writing. Perhaps what held him back was a distrust of representation, which never could present life as such.

Although Mies' seems to have been reluctant to allude to lived experience in his project descriptions there is an earlier text, written in 1928 that did attempt a more spirited account of the relationship between the occupants and the architectural work. It took the form of a letter, addressed to the firm of S. Adam, who had commissioned Mies to design them a new department store.

The letter was divided into four paragraphs. In the first paragraph Mies introduced it as an opportunity to outline the thoughts behind his proposed design, justifying his approach in terms of the professed needs of the client, he wrote:

'The variability you want is best served by an undivided expanse of the individual floor levels; for that reason I have placed the supports in the exterior walls.' [30]

In the case of a department store it may be assumed the variability Mies referred to here is based on the need to constantly change the displays of goods for sale. As a consequence of the need for variability Mies was suggesting the design of the department store, far from expressing difference, should consist in an undivided expanse; rather like the sky or the sea on a clear day, a calm expanse untroubled by incident. However, the calm expanse was not to be left entirely without incident because the efficient functioning of the department store required the introduction of three stairwells, passing through the undivided expanse of each floor-level and facilitating vertical movement through the building. Each stairwell was to have an elevator, but the secondary stairwell, which, for practical reasons was to be placed at the centre of the building, would have two freight elevators. The two other stairwells were to have elevators for the building's visitors. Inside the stairwells were toilets for the employees, while next to the stairwells were toilets for managers and customers.

In the second paragraph of his letter Mies warned the client against placing taste before purpose:

You have indicated in your requirements that in general a building with vertical articulation would conform to your tastes. May I say in all frankness that in my opinion a building has nothing to do with taste but must be the logical result of all requirements that result from its purpose. Only if these are established can one speak of the intrinsic forming of a building. You need layered floor levels with clear, uncluttered spaces. Furthermore you need much light. You need publicity and more publicity.[31]

Mies elaborated upon the importance of intrinsic forming, first on the ground that it protected the building from obsolescence and second on the ground that it ensured the building's instrumentality. Mies then reminded his client of the necessity, not only for the architect, but also for the client to approach the project with a good dose of boldness, thereby paving the way to announcing his intention that the enclosing skin of the building should be made entirely out of steel and glass:

I therefore suggest to you making the skin of your building of glass and stainless steel, with the bottom floor of transparent glass, the others of opaque glass. Walls of opaque glass give the rooms a wonderfully mild but bright and even illumination. In the evening it represents a powerful body of light and you have no difficulties in affixing advertising.[32]

Although Mies grounded his reasoning in practical considerations, his writing was by now beginning to express a mild enthusiasm for qualities. The qualities in question were, first; the daytime effect, in the department store interior, of being immersed in a mild but bright illumination and, second, the night-time effect, of the department store seen from the outside, of an even body of light. Having introduced the idea of the department store as a body of light, Mies then returned to the glass skin as a potential surface for writing on:

You can do as you like, regardless whether you write on it 'For the Summer Vacation', 'For Winter Sports' or 'For Bargain Days'. Such a brightly lit advertising on an evenly illuminated background will have a fairy-tale effect.[33]

With the introduction of the 'fairy-tale effect' the portrait of the department store had become quite magical. At this point, following the introduction of magic into the text and only in the last sentence, Mies made a direct reference to the relationship between the department store and its users. However, Mies did not refer to the potential users of the building as a community but endowed them with some anonymity, they are 'people' in whom 'modern times' are embodied:

Your building should bear the character of your business and should fit in with sailboats and with automobiles, or, expressed differently, with the modern times and with people that embody it.[34]

In Mies' description there was a gradual metamorphosis from consideration of practical purposes through ideas about construction and materiality, most notably steel, glass and light to ideas about commerce and exchange: the body of light was to carry brightly lit advertising, as becomes a site of display. Finally, at the end of the account the mutually embodied building and its users appeared: the character of the building would reflect the character of modern times and the people by whom those times were lived. Mies' description of the Adam Department Store is further proof that, like Lefebvre, he regarded the ambition of architecture to be the mutual recognition between the users and the architectural work. In this respect it is worth noting that Mies, like Lefebvre, saw the role of the building manager, in this case his client, the firm of S Adam, as equally responsible for ensuring the mutual recognition of users and building.

So far this discussion of Mies' work has only looked at the second aspect of Lefebvre's spatial architecture, that being architecture's reproductive role in shaping social processes. But what about the first aspect of his theory, the idea that the work of architecture lives as a body through the fulfilment of the laws of space. Is there evidence to suggest that this idea was paralleled in Mies' thought and practice?

In the documented records of Mies' verbal statements there is no elaboration of a concept of space comparable to Lefebvre's. For this reason it would be futile to search amongst Mies' writings for evidence that he thought in terms of the kinds of spatial dynamics present in Lefebvre's thinking. However, there is another term that Mies used far more frequently than he used space, and that was 'form.' In tracing Mies' references to form it is possible to see a parallel to Lefebvre's notion of the living body and its reciprocal relation with the laws of space. Whereas Lefebvre claimed the aim of architecture was the production of living bodies, Mies claimed the aim of architecture was the production of form.

In order to begin to grasp what Mies meant by form it is important to note that he allocated the task of producing form to architecture, not to architects. In so doing Mies implied there were factors determining particular works of architecture that were self-governing, free from the contingent circumstances that inevitably accompany the production of architectural work. For Lefebvre the self-governing factors of any particular architectural work were the laws of space, for Mies they were manifested through something which he called the 'form-giving.'

Lefebvre was able to communicate his thinking about the laws of space and their relationship to the production of living bodies through the medium of philosophical discourse. For Mies that medium was not particularly communicative; he did, however, occasionally attempt a verbal explanation of what he meant by form-giving. On those occasions he would include references to notions such as 'beauty' and 'artistic expression:'

No matter how much function and economics are preconditions for the new building, the ultimate problems are of an artistic nature. No matter how much function and economics determine our building, they say very little as to its artistic value. They do not prevent it however. The artistic appears in step with the structure of purpose and function, or rather, it realizes itself in that structure. But not in the sense of adding to it; rather in the sense of giving form to it. The artistic expresses itself in the proportions of things, often even in the proportions between things. Essentially it is something immaterial.[35]

Form-giving, then, did not refer to the act of physical assembly, of making buildings out of raw materials, it referred to the endowment of purposeful organisation with harmonious and symmetrical relationships.

It was because he believed the production of form to be the proper responsibility of architecture that Mies constantly advised architects to abandon all preconceptions of form, directing their attention instead to the active study and practice of form-giving:

Is form really an aim? Is it not rather the result of the form-giving process? Is it not the process that is essential?[36]

In advising architects to direct their attention toward the form-giving process Mies characterised the role of the architect as that of a student or apprentice, this is very different to the role the architect is cast in by Lefebvre, i.e., that of manager. As manager, Lefebvre placed his architect in a command position, the architect is a boss. As a student of form-giving, Mies placed his architect in the position of apprentice, of one who is in a constant process of learning.

As a student of form-giving to what did Mies think the architect should attend if they wished to learn? Mies offered two answers to this question. First, the architect should attend to structure. For Mies, any particular historical epoch has a particular structure. The structure of an epoch is established in the relationship of forces, Mies termed these the 'carrying and driving forces.' Mies believed that it was essential for the architect to be aware of the carrying and driving forces of the times in which they lived and practiced:

It seemed to me necessary to trace the course of development, even if in large jumps, for it alone leads to a comprehension of the condition of our time. We have laid bare the structure of our period and have established that our givens are consciousness, economy, technology, and the fact of the masses.[37]

Mies believed architectural form was the concrete expression of the epochal structure out of which it had arisen:

In all these years I have learned more and more that architecture is not just a playing with forms. I have understood the close relationship between architecture and civilization. I have understood that architecture must develop out of the supportive and dynamic forces of civilization and that in its best examples it expresses the innermost structure of an epoch.[38]

It may seem that Mies was offering little more than a causal model of architectural form, because in saying the form of some particular building arises as the expression of a particular time Mies was attributing the determination of form to historical factors, such as social and economic relations and technological development. However, if that was what he was thinking then why did he introduce a massive contradiction into his statements. For Mies believed there was a second thing to which the architect should attend if they wished to learn about form, that second thing he termed 'life.'

In the documented records there are numerous occasions where Mies insisted on life as the primary motive for the production of form:

Only life intensity has form intensity. Every how is supported by a what. The unformed is not worse than the overformed. One is nothing, the other illusion authentic form presupposes authentic life. But not one that has been nor one that has been thought. Therein lies the criterion. We value not the result but the starting point of the form-giving process. This in particular reveals whether form was derived from life or for its own sake.[39]

Mies gave two seemingly contradictory motives for the production of form, on the one hand regarding form as an expression of historical circumstances, yet on the other hand reading form as the expression of authentic life.

Is it possible to unravel the apparent contradiction by allowing Mies to think, as did Lefebvre, in terms of dualities? In Lefebvre's thought the living body was deemed to consist in a duality of structure and energy, which produced itself according to the laws of space. Perhaps a similar duality was present in Mies' thinking about form. The question certainly cannot be decided on the basis of Mies' verbal statements. But if it is permissible to speculatively credit Mies with dualistic thinking then perhaps he thought of form as an energetic duality of structure and life, a dynamics fuelling a process of form-giving. If this was so then Mies' form-giving, though not identical, was closely related to Lefebvre's laws of space?

The question cannot be answered through the study of Mies' statements about architecture, but there is another way to approach it and that is by paying a visit one of his buildings.

The New National Gallery: Form-Giving

In 1962 Mies accepted the offer to design a museum of modern art in Berlin. The offer was made by the City

Commissioners for Planning and Construction. The commissioners were more anxious to have a building by Mies than they were to determine a specific programme for a museum of Modern Art, which meant Mies was given considerable freedom to establish the basis of the design in his own terms. For this reason it seems reasonable to look at the New National Gallery (NNG) as an uncompromising demonstration of Miesian form-giving.

The organizing strategy of the design was unusual. It was not unusual in relation to developments in Mies' design practice, but it was unusual in relation to established conventions for the design of museums. Clearly, the organizing strategy for the NNG was a development of ideas put forward by Mies in his theoretical project of the Museum for a Small City (MfSC); both designs were dominated by the presence of a large room, constituted by three elements, a floor-slab, a roof-plate and a glass-screen; however, there were differences.

First, in the engineering principles demonstrated in the method of supporting the roof-plate. With the MfSC the large room was occupied by a gridded field of slender, cruciform columns, rising up to support the roof-plate. The presence of the columns compromised the emptiness of the room and disrupted the sense of spatial freedom, which, as we have seen, Mies claimed as the ambition of his design. In other words, with the MfSC the columns could be read as a hindrance, they got in the way. On the other hand, with the NNG the large room contained no columns. The roof-plate was supported on its perimeter by eight, large, tapering cruciform columns, two on each of the four sides (figure 29). The supporting columns were set in from the corners of the roof-plate to divide each side in the ratio of five-to-eight-to-five. With the supporting columns pushed to the perimeter the large room was, almost, completely empty.

Second, in the shape and elevation of the roof-plate. With the MfSC the roof-plate was rectangular in shape. The proportions of the rectangle were thirteen to seven. The elevation of the roof-plate, in relation to the extent of its longest side, was one-to-thirty and in relation to the extent of its shorter side was one-to-sixteen. This meant the space under the roof-plate would have felt rather deep and rather low. On the other hand the NNG roof-plate was square and it's elevation, in relation to the extent of any one side, was one-to-eight. This meant the space under the NNG roof-plate felt quite high, quite open and quite wide (figure 30).

Third, in the relation of the glass-screen to the roof-plate. With the MfSC the glass-screen followed the edge of the roof-plate, except on one of the shorter sides, where it was set back from the edge. This meant the roof-plate over-sailed the enclosed space under it

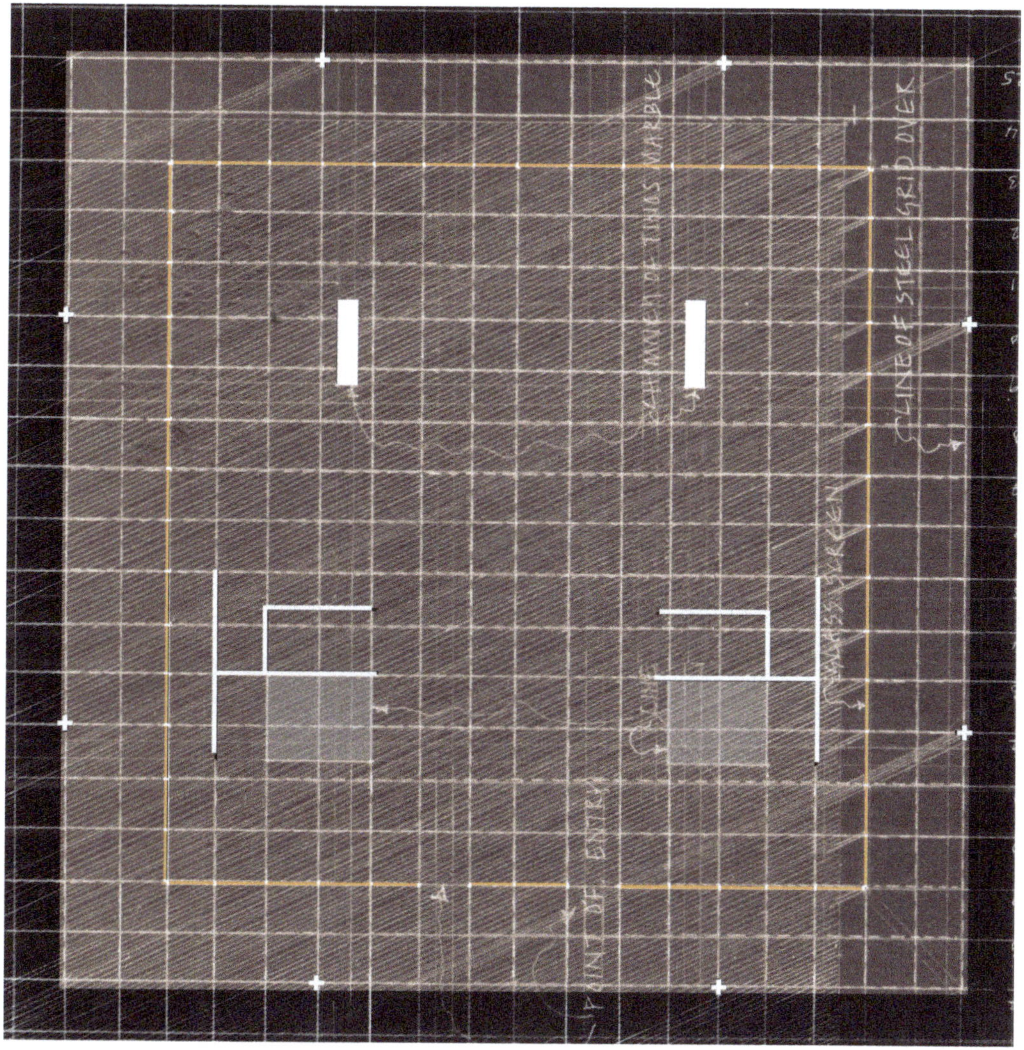

FIGURE 29

Mies van der Rohe, New National Gallery, Berlin, 1962-1968, large room, composite plan Indicating basic spatial relationships

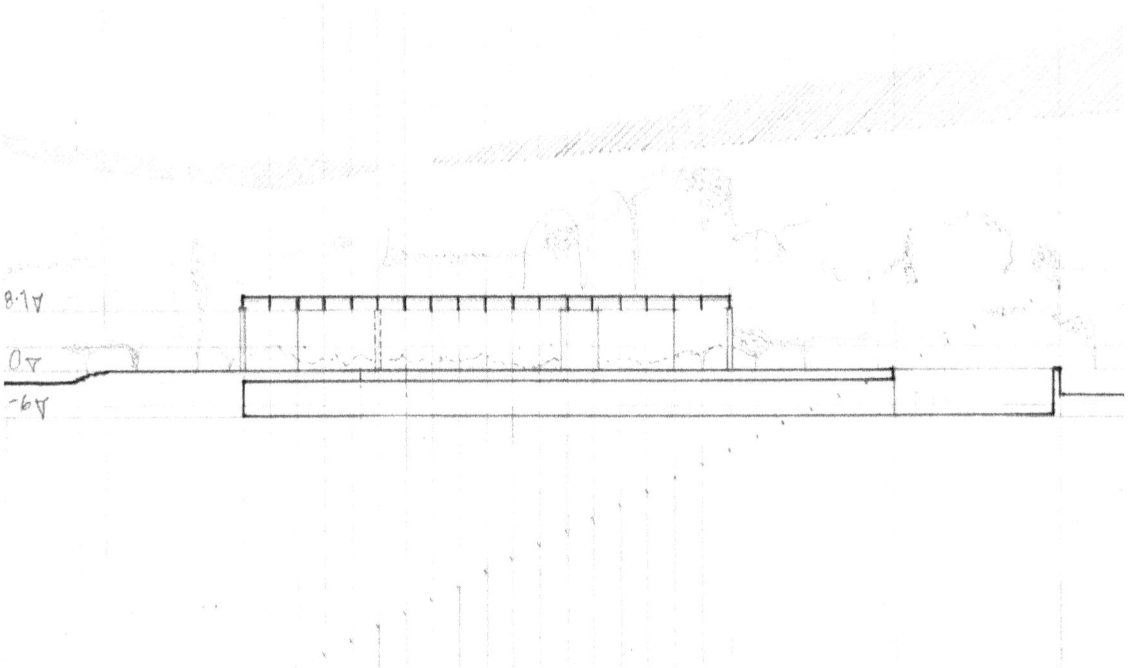

FIGURE 30

Mies van der Rohe, New National Gallery, Berlin, 1962-1968, transverse section on one side only, creating a covered space outside. With the NNG the glass-screen was set back from the edge of the roof-plate by an equal dimension on each of the four sides. The roof-plate over-sailed the room under it, creating an outdoor covered space that circumscribed the room on all four sides (figure 31).

Fourth, in the number, nature and distribution of fixed elements. On the plan of the MfSC there were a number of elements appearing to be fixed in location and determined in shape and size (figure 26). These elements were numbered and in the text of the museum project Mies explained what the numbers meant. Each of the fixed and determined elements was labelled with a particular function. For example, number three, which on the plan drawing appeared as a rectangle and contained coded representations of foliage, was labelled 'open passage,' open because the passage would be constituted by a framed opening in the roof-plate. Or number two, drawn as a rectangle circumscribing one 'I' shaped element and one 'L' shaped element, was labelled 'offices and wardrobes.' While the large room of the MfSC appeared to be quite full of predetermined functions like these, the large room of the NNG had relatively few.

There were only four interruptions in the NNG large room, two mechanical ducts, rising as large shafts of Tinos marble to the underside of the roof-plate and two clusters of low level screens (figure 29). The screens provided for cloakroom storage and were located around the two stair openings leading through the floor-slab and down into the basement. Compared to the MfSC, the large room of the NNG was very empty indeed. At the NNG, thanks to the large basement below, the large room above was free to accommodate emptiness far more readily than that of the MfSC. Whereas the MfSC housed functions inside the large room, sandwiched between the floor-slab and the roof-plate, at the NNG the functions were located under the floor-slab, inside the basement (figure 32). In the NNG basement there were a number of gallery spaces, administrative offices and library, a coffee shop, toilets, rooms for mechanical plant and various storage spaces.

Between the two museums, not only had the functions been relocated in the basement but the field of columns that compromised the emptiness of the MfSC seem to have gravitated there too. But now the plan-profile of the columns was no longer cruciform but square, in fact the NNG columns were sixty centimetres square and their centres were located on a seven point two meter grid, they rose-up from the basement floor to meet the underside of the floor-slab, a horizontal plane marked by the pattern of a rectilinear ceiling grid. The modulation of the grid was identical to that of the columns rising to meet it: sixty-by-sixty centimetres; and they were placed so as to correspond precisely

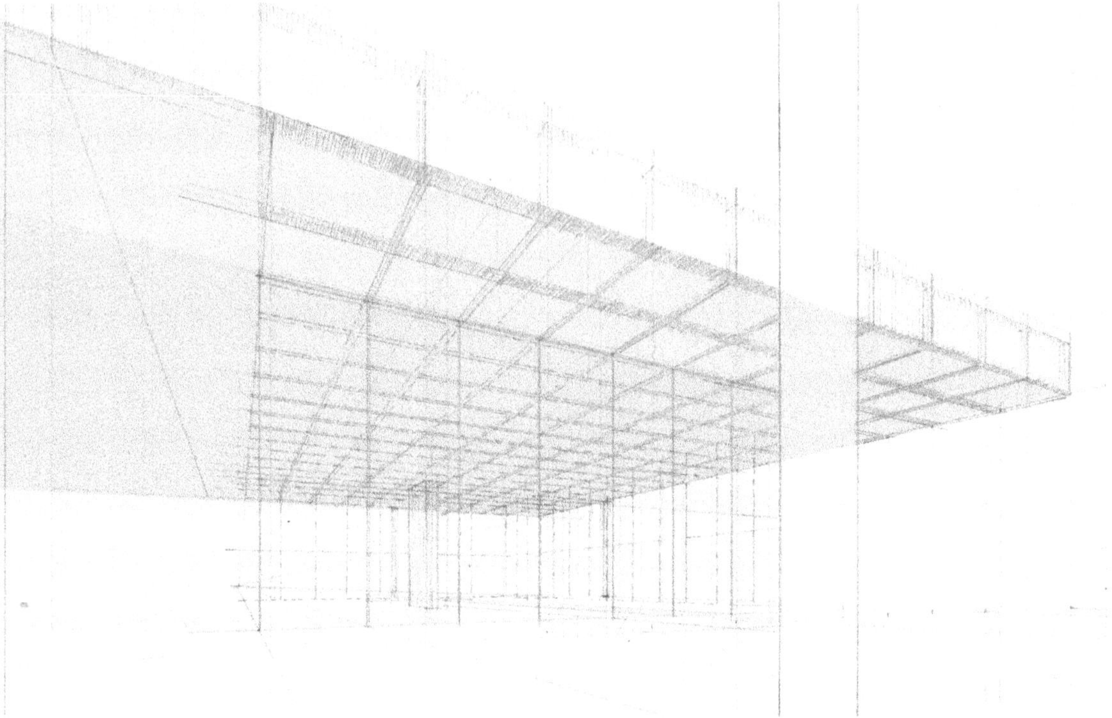

FIGURE 31

Mies van der Rohe, New National Gallery, Berlin, 1962-1968, perspective view

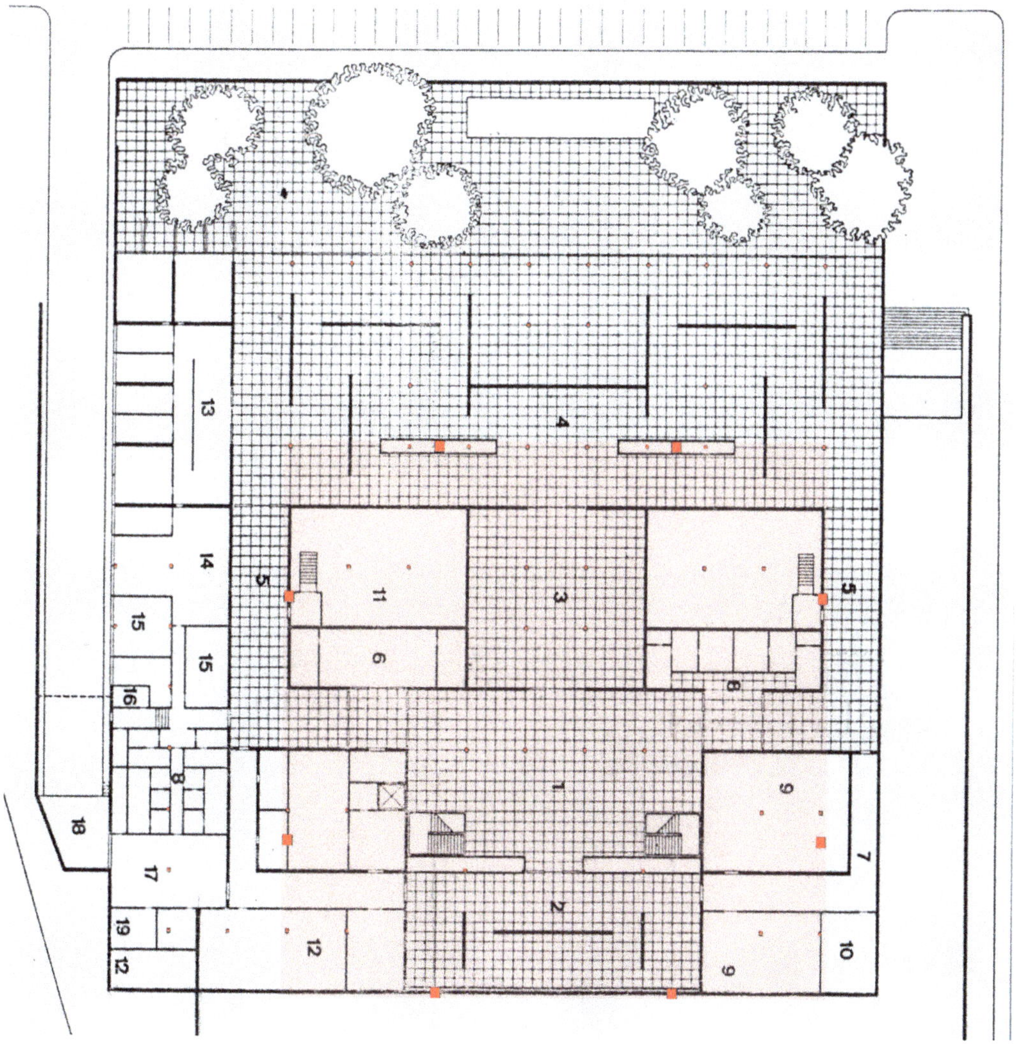

FIGURE 32

Mies van der Rohe, New National Gallery, Berlin, 1962-1968, basement plan (pink tone indicates position of roof-plate over, red indicates position and extent of supporting columns) with the ceiling grid. This meant that, rather than seeming to rise from the basement floor, the columns appeared to have grown down, like stalactites, from the ceiling. Once the drop-down quality of the columns is noticed then it becomes apparent that all the vertical elements sub-dividing the basement were to be read as if they had grown down from the ceiling (figure 33).

If the basement of the NNG could be understood as a transformation of the large room of the MfSC then a further difference has to be noted, this being the difference in the relationship between fixed elements and the column grid. Whereas the fixed elements of the NNG were located on the column grid, sometimes even subsuming columns within their volumetric extent, the fixed elements of the MfSC were off-set in relation to the grid (figure 32). This off-setting could be understood in two different ways. First, the grid could be understood as marking the continuity of an infinite expansion of space, of space in general. If the grid were understood to represent space in general then the fixed elements could be understood as specific moments of space, as space that had congealed in accordance with the requirements of specific purposes. The second way of reading the off-setting of fixed elements in relation to the grid was to avoid their interfering with one another, so the fixed elements did not get in the way of the grid and the grid did not get in the way of the fixed elements!

There is considerable evidence to suggest Mies thought very carefully about the relationship between fixed elements and the grid. One very good place to look for it is in the difference between the way Mies used the grid in his earlier work of the 1920s and 1930s and the way he used it in his later work. For example, between the Barcelona Pavilion, 1928-29 and the Farnsworth House, 1945-50 (work on which began just after the MfSC) there was a demonstrable difference in Mies' attitude to the grid.

The Barcelona Pavilion displayed numerous instances of localised grid patterns, these can be illustrated by looking at the published plan (figure 34). The tile layout covering the surface of the podium was not indicated on this drawing and so there are only three grid presences to be detected: first, the two pools, set into the podium, were hatched in a dense grid pattern; second, the spacing of the cruciform columns implied a grid pattern, third, the mullions sub-dividing the two glass screens appear to be evenly spaced and imply a grid.

Looking closely at the relationship between the mullion spacings of the glass screens and the location of the cruciform columns shows no coherent relationship between the order of screen mullions and the order of the column grid, between the two grids there was dissonance.

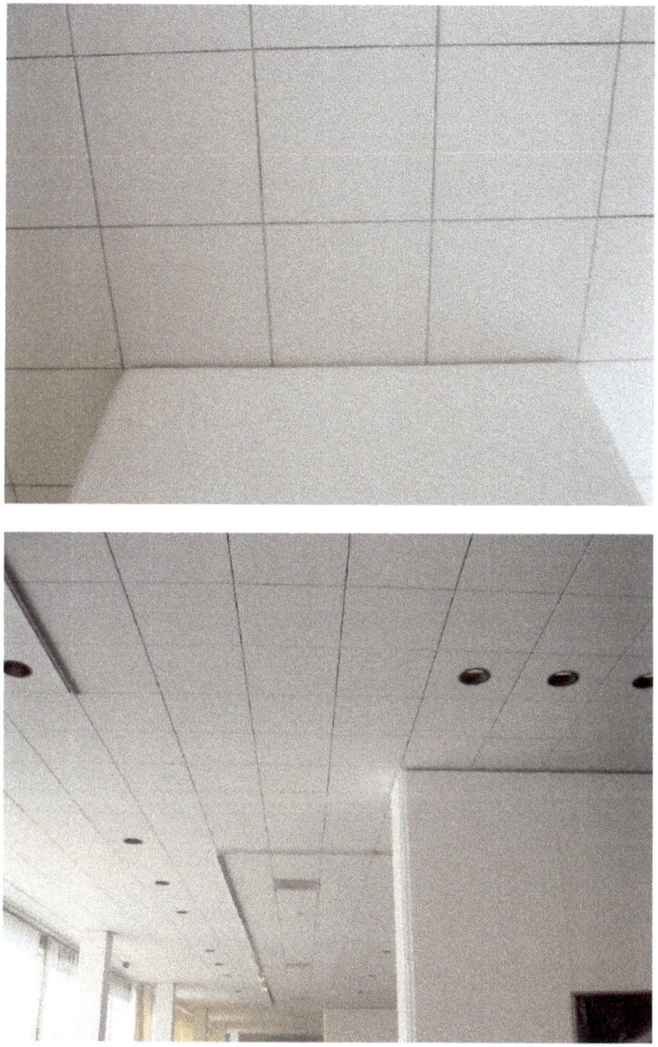

FIGURE 33

The New National Gallery, Berlin, two views of the basement ceiling grid

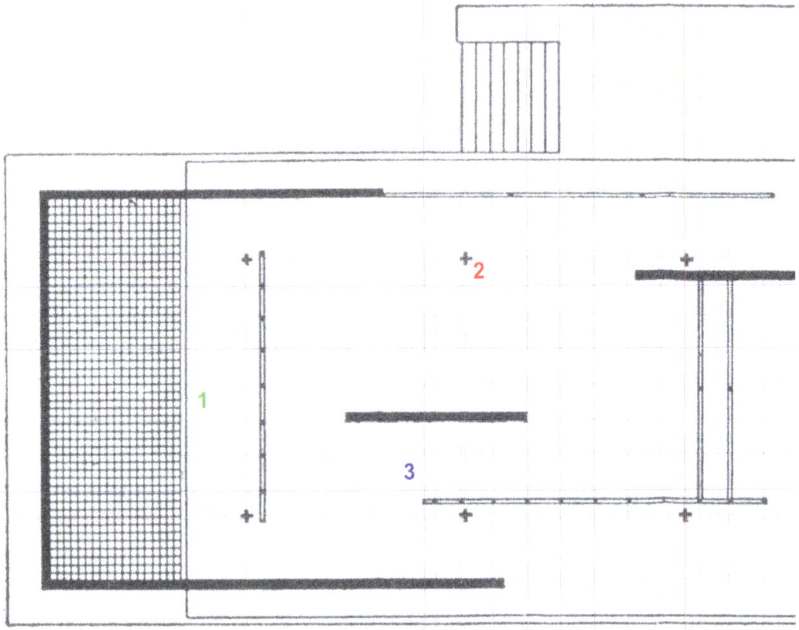

FIGURE 34

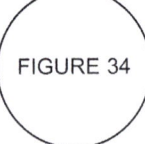

Mies van der Rohe, the Barcelona Pavilion, 1928-1929, detail of the plan

Turning to the published plan of the Farnsworth House, notice the floor surface was marked with the pattern of a grid, but that grid was much more than merely the representation of the paving layout (figure 35). The 'I' shaped columns supporting the roof-plate harmonise with the grid and so do the glazing-bars. Notice the furniture indicated on the plan, every piece has been set out neatly on the grid and the floor tiles are set out on the grid too. In the case of the Farnsworth House and indeed all Mies' later works, the mark of the grid was not literally the pattern of a paving layout, although the pattern of the paving layout did correspond to the grid, the grid had become a structural principle and as such it was perceptible as a faintly tangible network of relationships that permeated and filled the entire space of the architectural body. Once the grid and the fixed elements were harmonised in this structural manner there could no longer be any doubt about it, the grid did not represent a continuous and infinite expansion of space in general. In the case of the Farnsworth House the grid had become fused with the general purposes of dwelling, with the NNG it was fused with the general purpose of installation and enjoyment of artworks.

Recollect the role of structure in Lefebvre's concept of the living body, where he regarded the living body to be a duality of structure and energy, deployed and productive according to the laws of space. As he developed the concept of the living body Lefebvre was careful to emphasize the duality of structure and energy that constituted its unity. The relationship between structure and energy was teleological, neither was the cause of the other but they were bound together through the end purpose of the body. The generative energy of the living body was not caused by the organising effect of the structure and the organising principle of the structure was not caused by the driving force of the energy, the two were mutually productive and their mutual product was the living body.

If we look at the NNG through the terms of Lefebvre's duality of structure and energy then we might think of the structure as manifesting in the grid. But what about the driving force, the energy of the gallery, where, if at all does that appear in the built form? The answer to this question can be seen in the way the grid fluctuates between its manifestation as an invisible and indeed intangible idea, in other words as pure organization, and its physical manifestation as a network of sensuously apprehensible lineaments that are traced across the components of the built form. The components of the building, such as the floor-slab, roof-plate, glass-screen, columns, beams, mullions, sheets of glass, floor tiles and so on, have to be understood as manifestations of energy because in order to make them required a considerable investment in processes of exchange, particularly the transformation of matter into materials through labour.

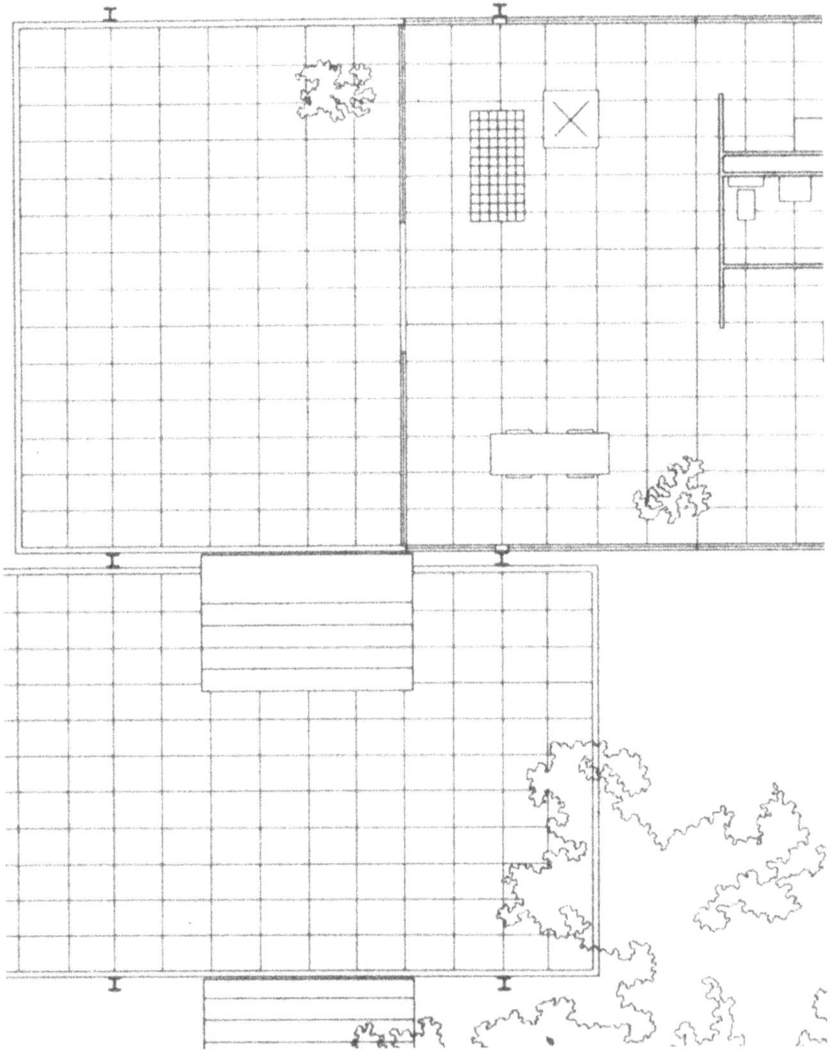

Mies Van der Rohe, the Farnsworth House, detail of the plan

FIGURE 35

A fifth difference, one that is of some significance for the issue of material exchange and labour, is to do with the materiality of the respective roof-plates. In his text of the MfSC Mies gave no indication of the materiality of the roof-plate; in the drawings of the interior views, however, it appeared as a smooth, seamless white surface, propped up on a forest of slender cruciform columns (figure 27). On the other hand, the roof-plate of the NNG appears as a black steel grid, it hovered eight-point-one metres above the floor-slab; and the grid of the basement below was, as already indicated, part of the same structure. Because the materialization of the grid as material form was only partial, so it was only possible to feel its presence in parts. However, as Lefebvre insists, because living being knows the laws of space so it can engage with the structure of the NNG in its totality, as a living body, a unity arising as a consequence of form-giving.

The roof-plate of the NNG is a large steel grid, floating above the top surface of the floor-slab, held in place by eight slender, tapering columns (figure 36). The roof-plate-grid is on a three-point-six metre module, covering an area of eighteen square modules, its depth is one-point-eight metres. The eight columns that support it are eight-point-one metres high, which means the proportional relationship between its depth and the space underneath it is two-to-nine. Between the top surface of the floor-slab and the top surface of the roof-plate-grid there is a modular striation of space, the striating dimension is ninety centimetres.

Between the top surface of the floor-slab and the top surface of the roof-plate-grid space is striated eleven times, nine times between the top surface of the floor-slab and the underside of the roof-plate-grid and twice between the underside and the top of the roof-plate-grid. Between the ninth and tenth of the eleven striations is a thirty centimetre gap, located in the gap is a pinned connection joining the roof-plate-grid to the tops of the columns. The spatial striation is marked on the built form in three ways. First, on the glass-screen that hangs down from the underside of the roof-plate-grid and is set back from the edge by two modules (figure 37). The glass-screen consists of glazed panels set within a black steel frame. There is one horizontal division of the steel frame, this horizontal division marks the third of the nine striations that slice the space between the top of the floor-slab and the underside of the roof-plate-grid; it is located two-point-seven metres above the surface of the floor-slab. Second, in the low-level screens that fix the spaces for cloakroom activities. The cloakroom screens rise to the same height as the intermediary glazing-bar of the enclosing glass-screen, which is a measure of two-point-seven metres above the floor-slab (figure 38). Third, to the back of the space, between the roof-plate-grid and the floor-slab and set within the curtilage of the

FIGURE 36

New National Gallery, Berlin, corner view

FIGURE 37

New National Gallery, Berlin, interior views of the roof-plate and glass-screen

FIGURE 38

New National Gallery, Berlin, views of free-standing oak screens.

glass-screen there are two identical rectangular monoliths, symmetrically placed. They are clad in panels of green Tinos marble and function as service shafts, containing pipes, ducts and mechanical equipment. The shafts appear to reach up to the underside of the roof-plate-grid, although it is not quite clear if they touch it or not. The panels of Tinos marble are cut to correspond to the rhythm of the striations slicing the space between the top of the floor-slab and the underside of the roof-plate-grid. The joints between the Tinos panels are at ninety centimetre centres, there are eight of them, marking the nine equal divisions of space between the top of the floor-slab and the underside of the roof-plate-grid (figure 39).

The space between the top surface of the floor-slab and the top surface of the roof-plate-grid is clearly marked by a modular striation of space, but what about the space below the floor-slab, i.e, the space in the basement (figure 40)? Between the surface of the basement floor and the underside of the basement-ceiling-grid there is no horizontal datum to be seen. Furthermore, the depth of the floor-slab is an unknown quantity. The dimension between the top surface of the floor-slab and the underside of the basement-ceiling-grid would be impossible to determine, impossible that is if it were not for the garden located at the back of the basement (figure 41). The garden appears to be formed as if the amalgam of floor-slab and basement-ceiling-grid had been cut back to reveal the sky. It is possible to do this because the floor slab extends beyond the limits of the roof-plate-grid floating above it (figure 42). The levitating roof-plate-grid covers only a small portion of the expansive area of the floor-slab. The walls that drop down from the floor-slab to enclose the garden are lined with slabs of stone; the stone is coursed in even bands. From the underside of the parapet, which stands up on the edge of the top surface of the floor-slab and the datum of the basement floor there are eight courses and one narrow band of separation. The separation band is between the top surface of the floor-slab and the first of the eight courses dropping down to the datum of the basement floor, these establish a rhythm of spatial striations (figure 43). The band of separation plus two of the eight striations corresponds to the dimension between the top surface of the floor-slab and the underside of the basement-ceiling-grid, the remaining six correspond to the space between the underside of the basement-ceiling-grid and the basement floor. The dimensions of the striations marking the basement space is not the same as that marking the space above; however there is a proportional relationship between them of thirteen-to-eighteen.

But how, if at all, do these vertical striations relate to the horizontal grids marked out on the roofs, ceilings and

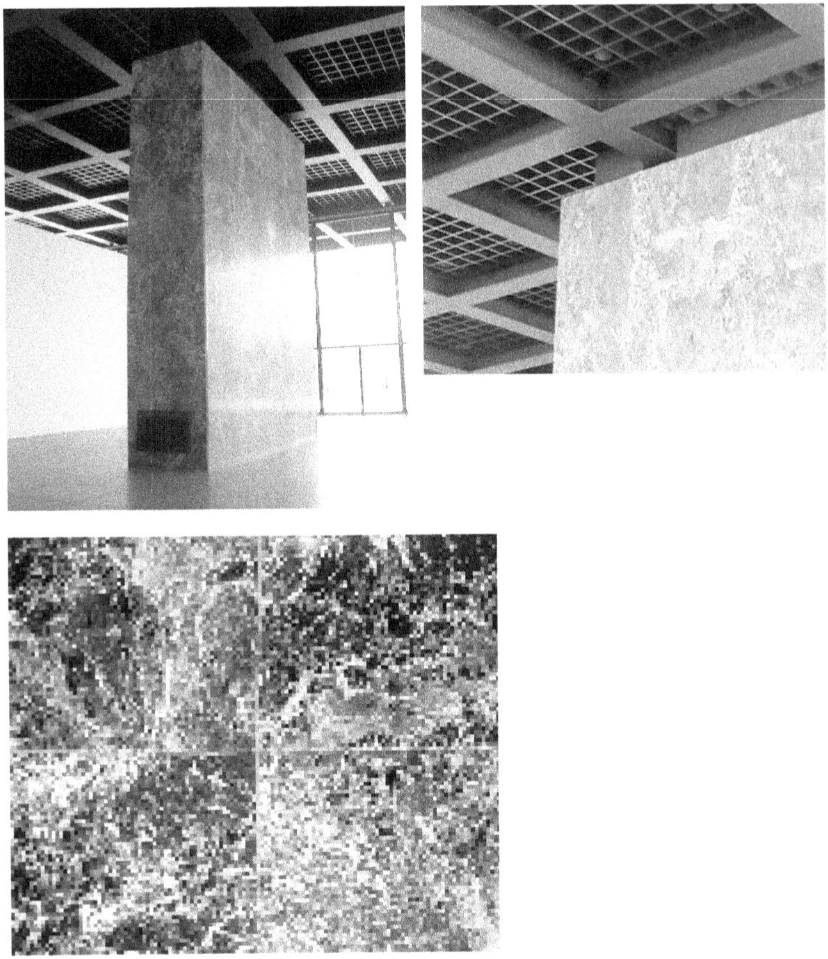

FIGURE 39

New National Gallery, Berlin, views of rectangular shafts

FIGURE 40

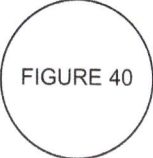

New National Gallery, Berlin, views of the basement

FIGURE 41

New National Gallery, Berlin, views of the garden

FIGURE 42

New National Gallery, Berlin, views from the floor-slab down into the garden

FIGURE 43

New National Gallery, Berlin, views of garden wall

floors of the NNG? The most obvious clue to the relationships between the vertical striations and the horizontal grids of the gallery is found on the surface of the floor-slab (figure 44). The floor-slab is a rectangular figure, very nearly square, its surface marked by the coursing of stone paving tiles. The tiles are square, measuring one-point-two metres, which means there is a one-to-three ratio between the tile grid of the floor-slab and the steel grid of the roof-plate. The correspondence is cleverly played out in the spatial sequence greeting the visitor to the building.

Between the floor-slab and the ground of the surrounding city space there is a change in level. The floor-slab is raised up in relation to the ground datum of the city, which has the effect of presenting it as a clearly defined figure. The change in level drops away across the floor-slab from one side to the other (figure 45), with the main flight of steps located on the side closest to the datum of the city (figure 46). For the subject of experience this means that the journey across the floor-slab is accompanied by an increasing feeling of detachment from the surrounding city space (figure 47), and by an increased awareness of the ambient conditions of the air. As the journey across the floor-slab unfolds so does the awareness of the grid marked out by the paving tiles. Perhaps it is because awareness of the grid is accompanied by an increasing awareness of the ambience of the air that can provoke a feeling of buoyancy, of decreased physical mass, of lightness. As the floor-slab-grid approaches the territory below the roof-plate-grid the enclosing glass-screen, hanging down from the underside, infiltrates the subject's field of perception. In so doing the vertical members of the screen, painted black, like the roof-plate-grid, are seen to continue the lines of the floor-slab-grid, turning upwards, through ninety degrees, to rise in perfect alignment with the grid of the roof-plate floating above. (figure 48). The members of the glass-screen are the material manifestation of the form-giving, fusing the roof-plate-grid and the floor-slab-grid into a unity. In the process of form-giving there is no question that the members of the glass-screen are supporting the roof-plate-grid; they are too fine, too slender, too spindly to support even their own weight in compression, let alone that of the big black grid floating over them (figure 49).

As well as turning upwards, the floor-slab-grid continues on its horizontal trajectory, flowing under the glass screen to the interior. Inside the flow is interrupted on three occasions. First, where it meets the low level cloakroom-screens, here the grid rises to turn through ninety degrees, as if up and over the screens. Second, where it meets the vertical shafts of Tinos marble, again the grid rises to turn through ninety degrees, up and over the shafts (figure 50). Third, where it meets the holes in the floor-slab leading down into the basement, here the grid stops (figure 51).

FIGURE 44

New National Gallery, Berlin, views of the floor-slab

FIGURE 45

New National Gallery, Berlin, Junction to surrounding city space

FIGURE 46

New National Gallery, Berlin, views of main steps

FIGURE 47

New National Gallery, Berlin, views out from the floor-slab

FIGURE 48

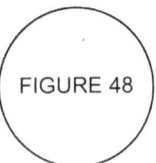

New National Gallery, Berlin, alignment of floor-slab and roof-plate grids

New National Gallery, Berlin, view of glass-screen and roof-plate

FIGURE 49

FIGURE 50

New National Gallery, Berlin, views of screens and shafts

FIGURE 51

New National Gallery, Berlin, hole in the floor-slab

The grid starts again, one-point-five metres below, transformed into the grid of the basement-ceiling. In transforming the grid has shrunk and shifted by half a module. The lines of the basement-ceiling-grid do not correspond to those of the floor-slab-grid above, the lines of the basement-ceiling-grid correspond to the centres of the stone tiles that cover the floor-slab and designate the floor-slab-grid. Furthermore, the module of the basement-ceiling-grid is half that of the floor-slab-grid. From the basement-ceiling-grid columns drop down to the basement floor and here, on the basement floor, the same one-point-two metre measure of the floor-slab-grid reappears. The lines of intersection of the basement-floor-grid correspond to the centre face of the sixty centimetre square columns that seem to drop down from the basement-ceiling-grid (figure 52). The reason for the shift between the floor-slab-grid and the basement-ceiling-grid becomes apparent, it is justified and generated by the desired correspondence between the intersections of the basement-floor-grid and the centre face of the basement columns. In shifting the grid there is the implication of a double force, not only do material columns drop down from above but immaterial columns, phantoms of the form-giving, reach upward from below. The appearance of the form-giving as phantoms arises from the bifurcation of two modes of attention; the source of bifurcation is the subject of perception, in Lefebvre's terms a living being. On the one hand the living being is aware of the grid structure through immediate perception of its partial presence, as manifest in formed elements, such as the roof-plate. On the other hand the living being is aware of the grid structure through mediated perception, having worked out that the grid presence is total. As attention alternates between the modes of immediate and mediated perception so a third condition is produced, this is the condition of imagining. In the condition of imaging phantoms appear, immaterial manifestations of things which are not actually there, such as a field of columns reaching up from basement to support the roof-plate-grid.

A Gravitational Effect

There is a strong parallel to be drawn between the states of attention involved in perceiving the grid of the NNG and the three conditions to which Krauss, quoting Linville, referred to in her account of the painted grids of Agnes Martin. The first condition of viewing the painting, the close up view, where the immediacy of its facture dominates, corresponds to the immediate perception of formed, material elements of the NNG's manufacture. The middle condition of viewing the painting, where the painting 'goes atmospheric' corresponds in the NNG experience to the moment where immaterial, imagining elements start to appear. The third condition of viewing the painting, where the painting closes down, to become a still, opaque, figure set against a white wall, corresponds, in the NNG experience, to the mediated perception in

FIGURE 52

New National Gallery, Berlin, basement, ceiling and floor grid which living being has worked out that the grid is a total presence.

At the Toronto conference Krauss suggested there might be some value in reading the Barcelona Pavilion through the three viewing conditions demonstrated by Agnes Martins' paintings; as Krauss put it, to reading the Barcelona Pavilion in terms of the /cloud/.[40] However, since, as we have seen, the Barcelona Pavilion was not organised on the principle of the grid, the suggestion is problematic. On the other hand, as we have also seen, the trajectory of Miesian architecture did tend toward the grid, which means Krauss' suggested /cloud/ reading was, at least for most of the buildings designed by Mies since 1945, justified. In using the term /cloud/ to refer to the tripartite reading it is the middle term, where the painting 'goes atmospheric' and the building starts to produce phantoms that is privileged. Recollect, what intrigued Krauss about the condition of the /cloud/ was its status as a pure signifier, representing nothing.

In the case of the NNG the psychophysiological condition of the /cloud/ is different to that of the painting, which is primarily triggered through visual stimuli. At the NNG the perception of /cloud/ is as much a gravitational as it is a visual effect. Suspended up in the air, the black roof-plate-grid does not look light and cloudy, it looks massive; yet the perception of mass is not accompanied by any feeling of weightiness. At the points where the grid is supported, i.e., on the eight perimeter columns, there is no sense of compression, as if the grid were pushing down on the supports, to the contrary, there is a sense of tension, as if the grid were tethered to the supports. Recollect and try to imagine the phantom columns emanating up from the underside of the floor-slab toward the mass of the roof-plate-grid. Logically, the force that the phantom columns exert on the roof-plate-grid presses upward, resisting gravity and it is this phantom force that holds the massive black grid up in the air, as if it were weightless.

The defiance of gravity acted out at the NNG requires the participation of the visitors and users of the gallery, in Lefebvrian terms of living being. Just as living being arises at the intersection of two sensory fields: that of 'living body' and that of 'the generation of consciousness,' so the experience of the gallery as /cloud/ can be understood as arising at the intersection of two different sensory fields. Both fields are lodged in the space of living being, they consist, first, of immediate messages about the environment and second, of mediated messages, i.e., knowledge. In its immediacy the NNG is recognised as a material form, in its mediation it is recognised as an organised structure. At the intersection of the two sensory fields a curious interaction occurs, mediated knowledge from the second sensory field appears in the first. In other words knowledge of the organisational structure appears as if it were an immediate message from the environment and living being becomes conscious of the NNG grid as a field of force. Although the field of force is imaginary its appearance is not fanciful and there is nothing arbitrary about it. The field of force is an image that the architecture of the NNG produces: it is an image whose preconditions reside in the form-giving, or beauty, that Mies had locked into the design, it can only be released in the presence of living being. For mere living bodies, or mere generators of consciousness, alone (if such entities exist) it is imperceptible.

The next part of the thesis is a report about an architectural design project. The project was about the development of AIR (nee Cotton) Grid. As the name suggests, AIR Grid was an attempt to create a three-dimensional grid with as little substance as possible. Or, to put this another way, AIR (nee Cotton) Grid explored the possibilities of fusing structure and matter into a single entity.

For the purpose of documenting this thesis the development of the architectural design project is placed after the speculative discourse of this first part of the thesis. But it is important to bear in mind, the documented sequence does not reflect the reiterative process of thinking and making that was the actual mode of working throughout the thesis inquiry. The design research and architectural proposal reported in the second part of this document actually led the inquiry and supported the speculation set out above. Although the thesis documentation separates the two parts there is an inextricable and irreducible link that bound them together in the actual thesis work.

PART TWO
MAKING AND USING AIR GRID

This part of the thesis is a record of the research, development and application of AIR (nee Cotton) Grid. AIR Grid is a three dimensional grid made from embroidery thread, to begin with we referred to it as 'cotton,' but realised that was inaccurate. Like the painterly grids of Agnes Martin, AIR Grid delivers three experiential moments; however, unlike the painterly grids, AIR Grid moments depend less for their effect on viewing distance and more on the angle of vision from which they are seen. In the first AIR Grid moment the subject of experience, 'living being,' is hardly aware of AIR Grid, attending instead to the support armature. In the third AIR Grid moment living being is aware of AIR Grid as a series of parallel, equidistant planes. Depending on the orientation of AIR Grid and the angle of vision the planes align horizontally or vertically or at inclined angels. The third AIR Grid moment is reminiscent of the planes of symmetry used by scientists to understand the formation of crystals. The second AIR Grid moment, between the first and the third, is where AIR Grid 'goes atmospheric.' The experience of AIR Grid /atmosphere/ is misty volumetric and vibrantly colourful.

The first section of this part of the thesis, Making AIR (nee Cotton) Grid, reports upon the material and conceptual research that had led to the development of a technique for making AIR Grid. The second section, Using AIR (nee Cotton) Grid, is a design proposal, it is called The Cotton Caves of Stevenage New Town (CCSNT), it is a response to the question: how might AIR Grid /atmosphere/ be utilised, as a signifier to stand for something unknown but necessary and valuable?

Because this second part of the thesis records a design project the primary mode of representation consists of images. There are three types of image utilised in this thesis, first, photographic recordings of three-dimensional objects, most notably photographs of prototype models of physical AIR Grid structures. Second, CAD and Photoshop drawings of virtual AIR Grid structures and of the architecture of imaginary environments. Third, hybrid images produced by working across the media of physical drawing, physical model making, CAD and Photoshop drawing and model making. Referencing the way artworks are documented in the catalogue of an exhibition, by title, size and medium, the works referred to in this part of the thesis are documented by title and medium, so the catalogue refers to the process by which they have been made. In some cases it includes the size of the original, in dpi or centimetres, or both, as appropriate.

2.1: GENESIS & EVOLUTION

2.1.1 - Drawing the Air

The process of inquiry that lead to the discovery of AIR Grid began with attempts to draw the way Miesian architecture feels. I use the term drawing here to cover a range of techniques, including photography, electronic processing and hand-drawing on paper using pen and pencil, ink and crayon. The drawings were produced in stages, deploying various techniques that were montaged into sequences to produce the images shown in this section. Included in the title of each documented image are the technologies involved in its production.

The images corresponded in some sense to Raymond McGrath's metaphysical reading of Mies, seeming to hint at a looking-glass world beyond. For this reason they were highly problematic, failing to achieve what they set out to do. For how could a contrived image, no matter how ingenious, or delightful to behold, possibly capture what it actually feels like to be in the presence of a Miesian building? At best the images might be understood as caricaturing feelings associated with Miesian architecture, but they could not reproduce the actual feeling of what it is like to be immersed in a Miesian environment.

Mies always insisted on the constructive nature of architectural thinking, even going so far as to lament the covering over of *'constructive thought, the necessary basis of artistic form-giving, with a meaningless and trivial jumble of forms'*[1] and he objected to the decorative smothering of structures in gratuitous shapes, as if, as he put it, buildings were made of *'pastry.'*[2]

In the light of Mies' aversion to applied ornament, increasingly the attempts to evoke the ambience of his architecture through rendered drawing seemed inappropriate. It not only contradicted Mies' attitude to design but also the very idea of practice-based research in architecture. Because, if the images could stand-in as built equivalents, then where did that leave the constructive processes that lead to the production of the built environment?

The realisation that something was missing prompted a confrontation with the basic presupposition behind the production of the drawings, i.e., that an image projected onto a flat surface ever could capture what if feels like to be in a built environment, whether by Mies or any other architect for that matter. The images did prompt feelings, but there was no reason to suppose those feelings were immanent to Miesian architecture.

The cool, matter of fact logic of the way Mies built is inseparable from the way the architecture feels; and yet the architecture is not conceptual, the subject does not think the building, they are affected by it.

RED BALL, ink, tracing paper, photograph & inkjet transparency

SPLASH, ink, tracing paper, inkjet transparency

SKY HOOKS, electronic montage

EYES, ink, crayon, detail paper

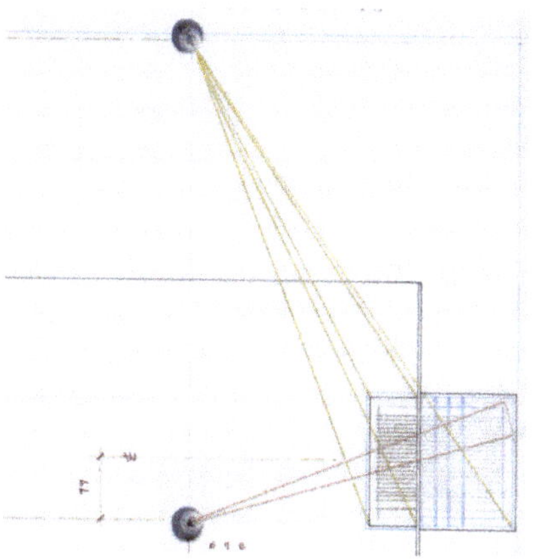

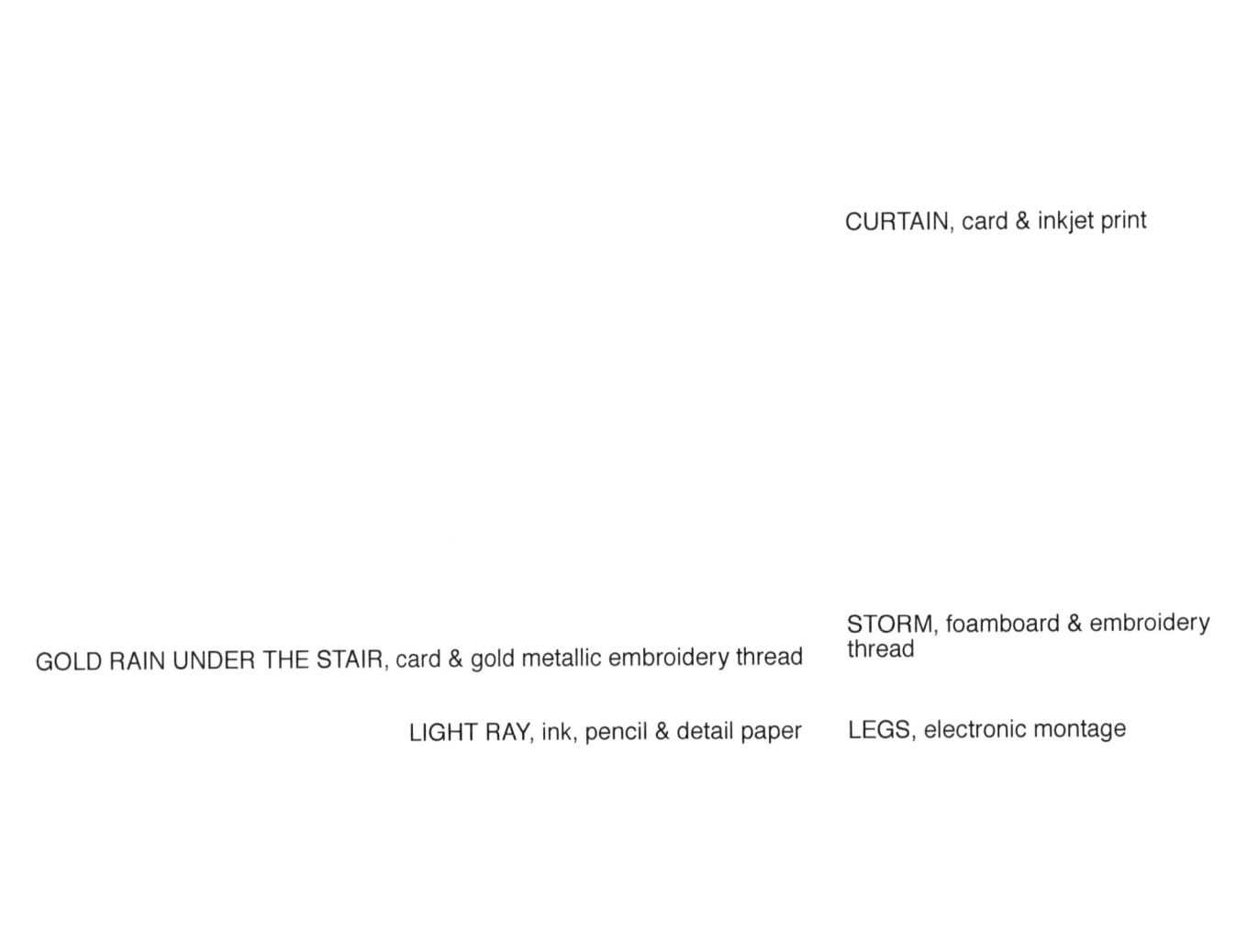

CURTAIN, card & inkjet print

GOLD RAIN UNDER THE STAIR, card & gold metallic embroidery thread

STORM, foamboard & embroidery thread

LIGHT RAY, ink, pencil & detail paper

LEGS, electronic montage

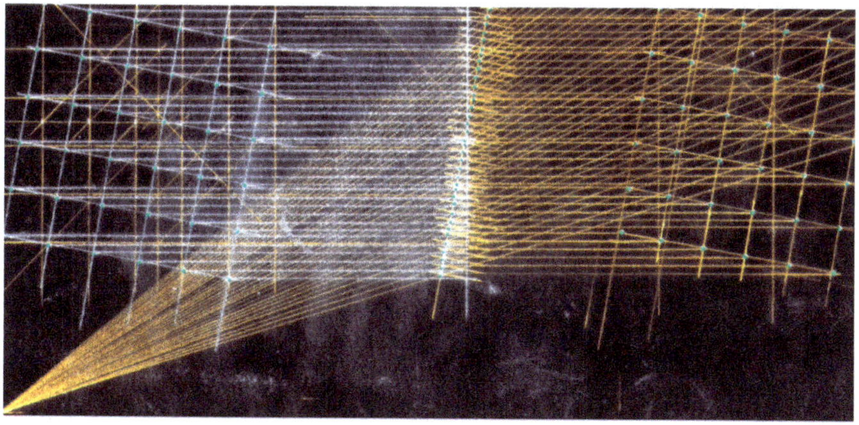

POINTS, ink, pencil & cartridge paper

NEUTRINO, card, embroidery thread

THE WHITE SHADOW, ink, pencil, tracing paper, inkjet transparency

RUBBER COLOURS, ink, tracing paper, inkjet transparency

IVY, ink, card & embroidery thread

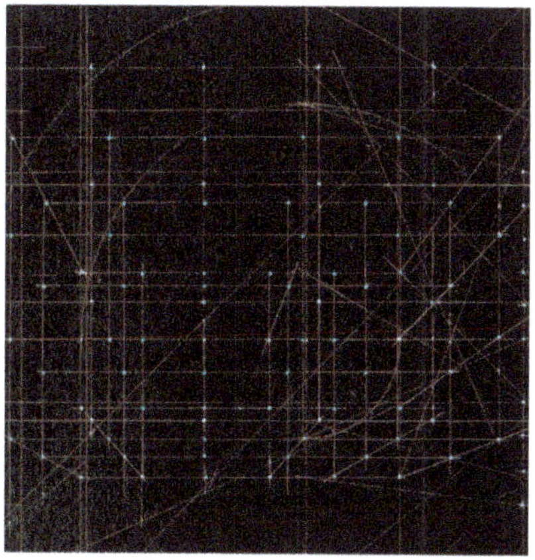
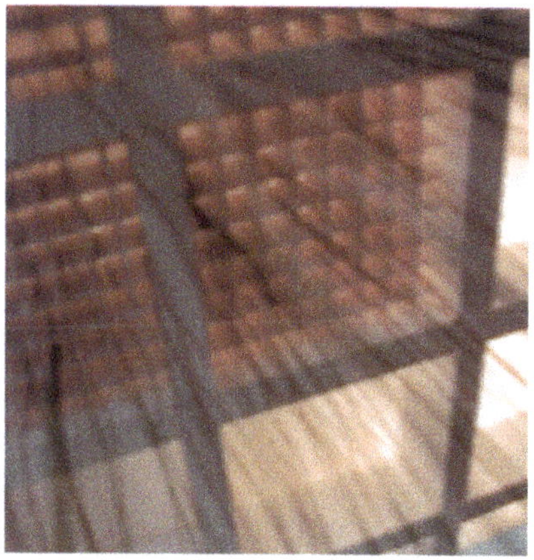
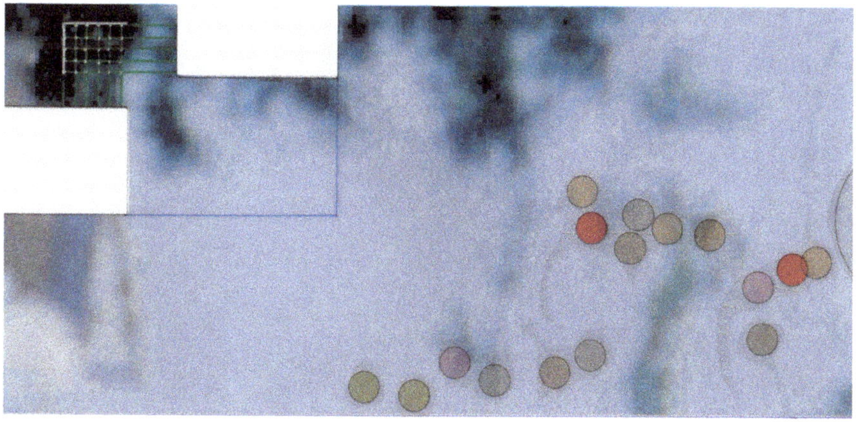

MIES, card & inkjet print

HEP, crayon, card, inkjet transparency

SPIDER, foamboard & embroidery thread

GOLD RAIN, card & gold metallic embroidery thread

DIDDLE, electronic montage

BB, ink, pencil & cartridge paper

BORG, ink, pencil, tracing paper, inkjet transparency

XRAY, ink, pencil, tracing paper, inkjet transparency

METZ, ink, pencil & cartridge paper

DIMIE, ink, pencil & cartridge paper

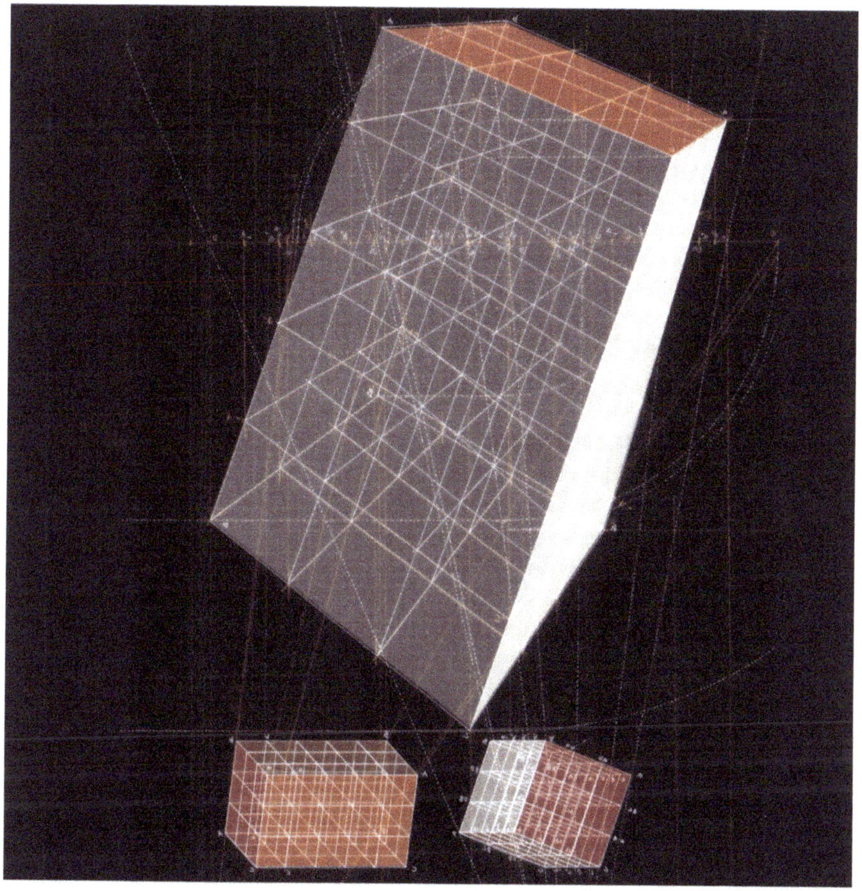

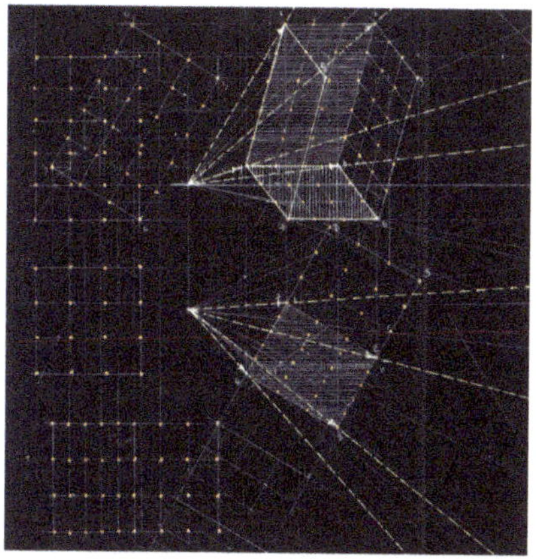

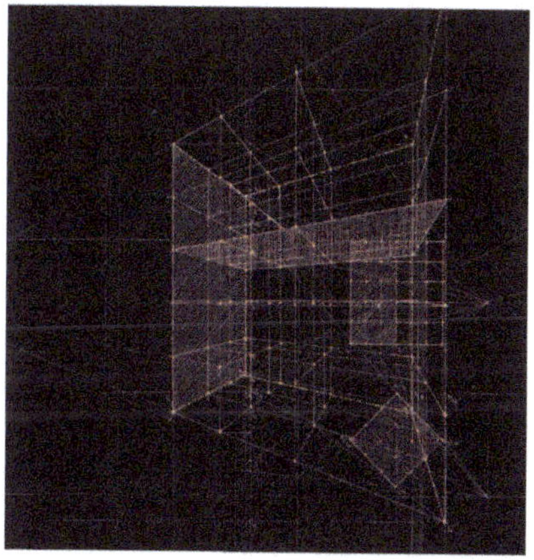

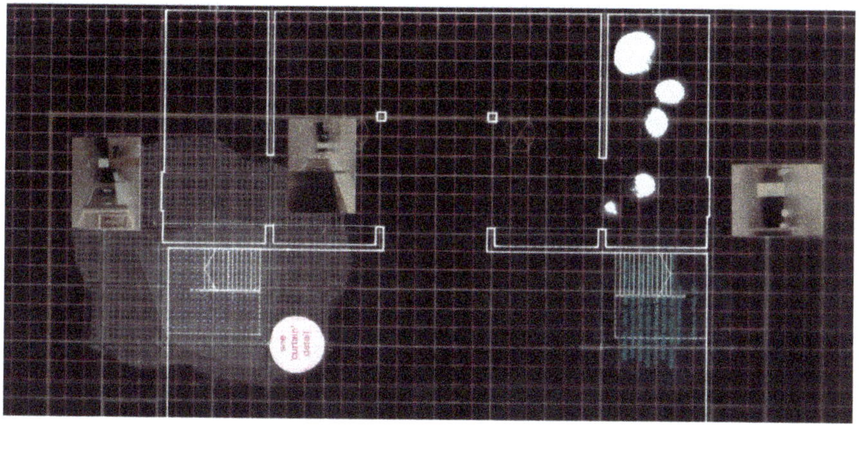

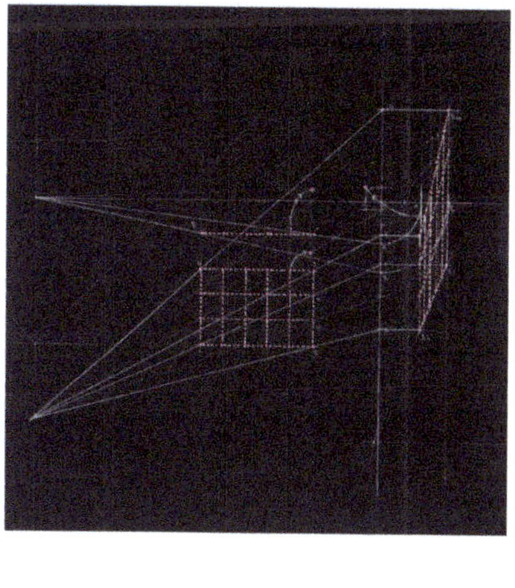

2.1.2 - Mies as Model

The next stage in the inquiry looked at the possibility of using Miesian buildings as models, asking if it was possible to convey the quality of weightlessness that is so often reported of the experience of Miesian architecture?[3] Realising the most immaterial component of Miesian architecture is the grid led to the idea of building just the grid only. The question of how to make a grid, in three-dimensions, out of as little material as possible led to the first experiments with embroidery thread, (at that stage in the inquiry referred to as cotton). Gravity is a problem for the three-dimensional grid made from thread, a support is necessary. The support performs two functions. First it serves as an apparatus for measuring and locating points in space, second it maintains the shape of the grid. Foamboard is a composite material consisting of a polyurethane core, sandwiched between two layers of thin card. The material is light and rigid but not brittle, it is easy to punch small, relatively clean, holes through foamboard (in those days there were no laser cutters to do the cutting and hole-punching work for the researcher). Because of the card surface it was easy to mark setting-out lines on foamboard and it was easy to cut. The grid was made by drawing thread through a network of holes, pierced into panels of foamboard and held taut in the grip of a sharp incision cut into the vertical members of the foamboard armature that gave stability to the holepanels.

The first Miesian work to serve as a model was the 860-880 Lake Shore Drive Apartments, Chicago, 1948-51. The cadence of the grid was extrapolated from a one-to-five-hundred scale plan and section of Mies' design. The design of the foamboard support consisted of two components, the holepanels and a framework of vertical and horizontal brackets, referred to as 'stiffners.' Some but not all stiffners were sliced with a rhythm of fine incisions, corresponding to the rhythm of the holepanels. Because the foamboard yields, the incisions were sufficient to hold the thread taut. Prior to fabrication an electronic model of the Lake Shore grid and support was produced, this served two practical purposes. First it could be used to generate cutting and hole punching templates for the holepanels and stiffners, second it could be used to generate a coloured ground. The coloured ground was pasted to the inner face of the holepanels, the Lake Shore model was given a very dark grey, almost black, lining and was sewn in a pale blue thread. The thread had a light sheen to it, which meant that sometimes it seemed to radiate, not blue, but silver or white.

The second Miesian work to serve as a model was the Seagram Building, New York, 1954-58. The production process for the Seagram grid was identical to that of Lake Shore, but the form and the colours were different. The lining of Seagram was a deep olive green and the embroidery thread was gold.

The third Miesian work to serve as a model was the Office Building, Westmount Square, Montreal, 1965-68, this grid came to be known as Marilyn, her cadence was extrapolated from a one-to-two-hundred scale plan and section of Mies' design. Unlike Lake Shore and Seagram, Marilyn was sewn into an unlined support made from black foamboard. Her colour scheme was not chosen in order to emulate the aura of the original Miesian work, rather it was chosen for the sake of the colour itself. Although she had highlights of white, pink, and honey blonde, Marilyn was primarily red. As with Lake Shore and Seagram, there was both a Marilyn made of thread and an electronic Marilyn, made in the computer.

The fourth and final Miesian work to serve as a model a repeated the Seagram model, only the cadence of this fourth model, like that of Marilyn, was extrapolated from a one-to-two-hundred-scale plan and section of Mies' design. The model came to be known as Chrystophene. Like Marilyn, Chrystophene was sewn into a black, unlined support and her colour scheme, primarily green, was chosen for the sake of the colour. As with all the other models, there were two Chrystophenes, one made from thread the other electronically, in the computer.

Because they were built to a larger scale, Marilyn and Chrystophene were much bigger than the earlier Lake Shore and Seagram grids and as a result the specific AIR Grid effects were clearer, much bolder. With the earlier grids there was a lingering tendency to read them as representational, not only because of the choice of colour scheme but also because the original lift shafts were represented in the grid. One of the saddest moments of the research was the demise of thread-Marilyn and thread-Chrystophene. Unfortunately the support frame for both grids was inadequate to hold the lattice in tension and they lost their shape. All that remains of them today is a number of images taken with a digital camera. In order to sustain three-dimensional grids on the scale of Marilyn and Chrystophene the support structure needed to be reinforced either with more, or with deeper, stiffners.

The electronic grids served two purposes, one practical, the other experimental. First they were invaluable as part of the design and fabrication process for making the thread grids. Second, they could be used to generate perspective views inside the computer, which could be compared to the experience of looking at the thread grid in 'real' space.

Although the electronic grid could not emulate the lustre and the effects of light and shadow of the thread grid, it could reproduce another, perhaps more striking effect, this being the effect of change. With the electronic model the space of the lattice is virtual, there is no gravity in computer space and hence no need of a support to hold the lattice in place. This meant that in the views of the electronic grid the support could be taken away. In removing the support it was possible to emulate views of a purely optical, colour grid. And with the removal of the support one of the three existential moments of the thread grid was removed too, that being the first moment, where living being attends to the support, rather than the grid. With the first moment removed the third and second moments could be studied more carefully. Attending to the existential conditions of the electronic grid revealed an additional moment, somewhere between the second and the third moments of the thread grid. In the additional moment the computer's virtual camera captures the grid as a hybrid of both parallel planes and a misty volume of colour, the relative proportions of each depending upon the direction and angle of the camera. The absolute stillness of the virtual camera views cannot be experienced in 'real' space, where living being is constantly animated by desire, as their living eyes scan back and forth.

By the same token it is not possible for the computer to replicate the animated desire of living being as the creature moves about its environment, This is because virtual animation, whether produced by electronic or photographic means, cannot reproduce the feeling of immediacy that characterises lived space. Virtual animation might be able to simulate movement but it cannot replicate the exact psychodynamics of AIR Grid experience in lived space. When living being watches any animation they are, of course, experiencing movement, but what actually moves are the film stills, the apparent movement of objects in the film is an illusion.

There is in fact no medium in which it is possible to capture what it is actually like to really look at an AIR Grid. All the images documented in this thesis are total failures in that respect. The thesis images serve merely to document and catalogue the process of research and development, to illuminate ideas about the grids, but they cannot substitute for AIR Grid experience in lived space. For this reason it is essential for anyone who is interested in AIR Grid to visit an exhibition of AIR Grid artefacts whilst studying the thesis.

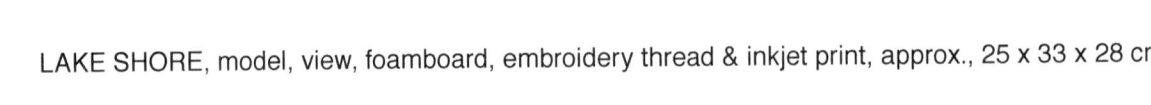

LAKE SHORE, model, view, foamboard, embroidery thread & inkjet print, approx., 25 x 33 x 28 cm

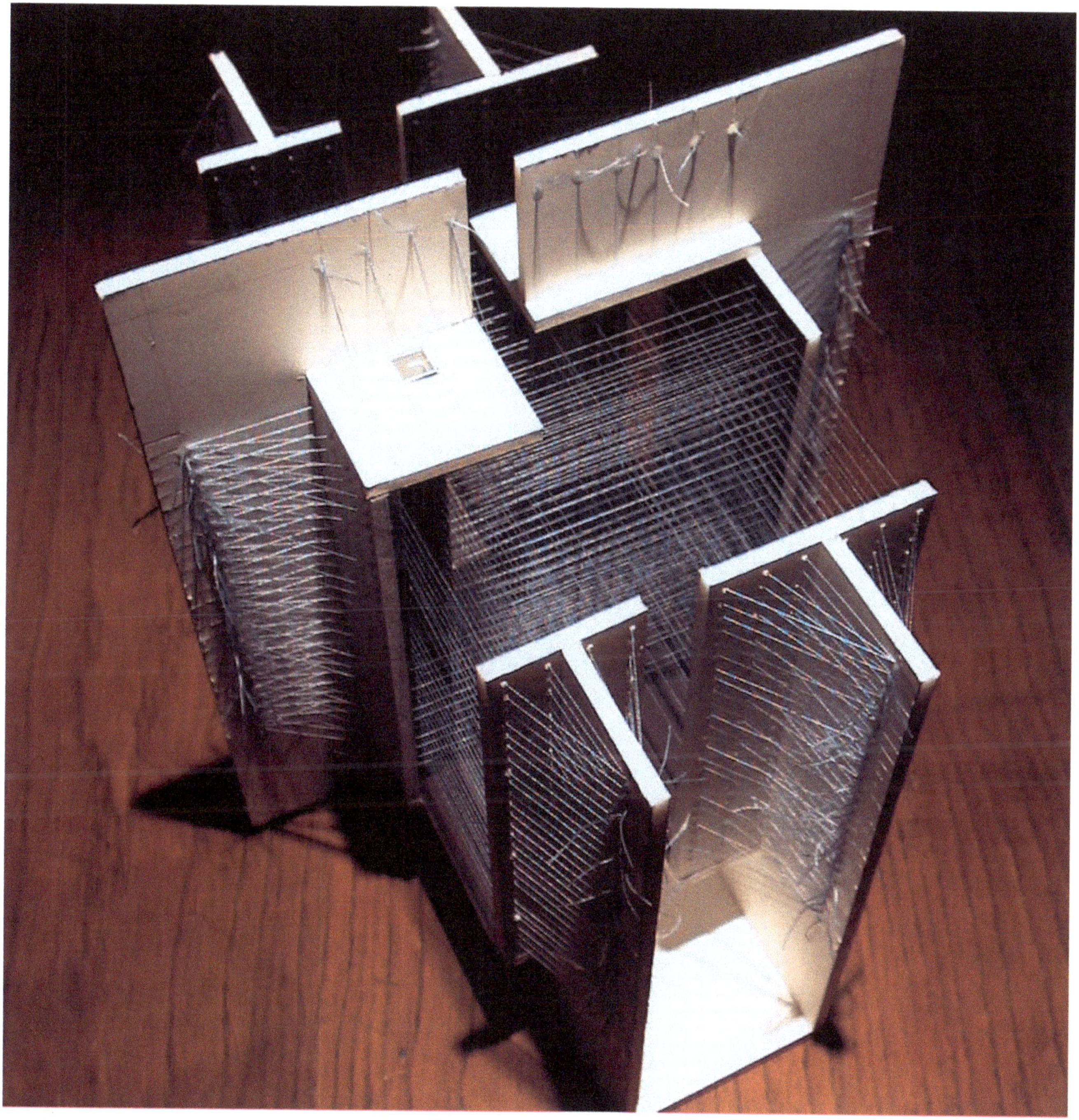

LAKE SHORE, model, interior view, foamboard, embroidery thread & inkjet print, approx., 25 x 33 x 28 cm

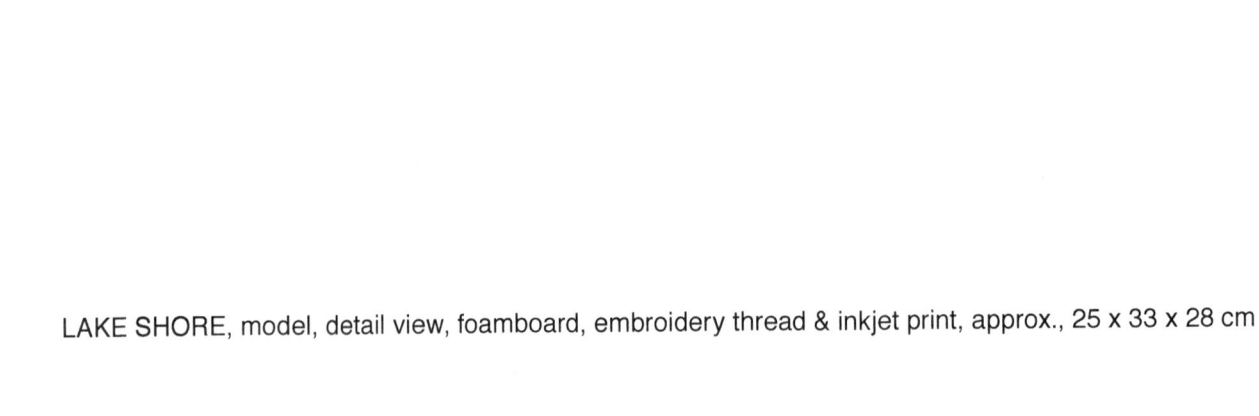

LAKE SHORE, model, detail view, foamboard, embroidery thread & inkjet print, approx., 25 x 33 x 28 cm

LAKE SHORE, electronic model, view

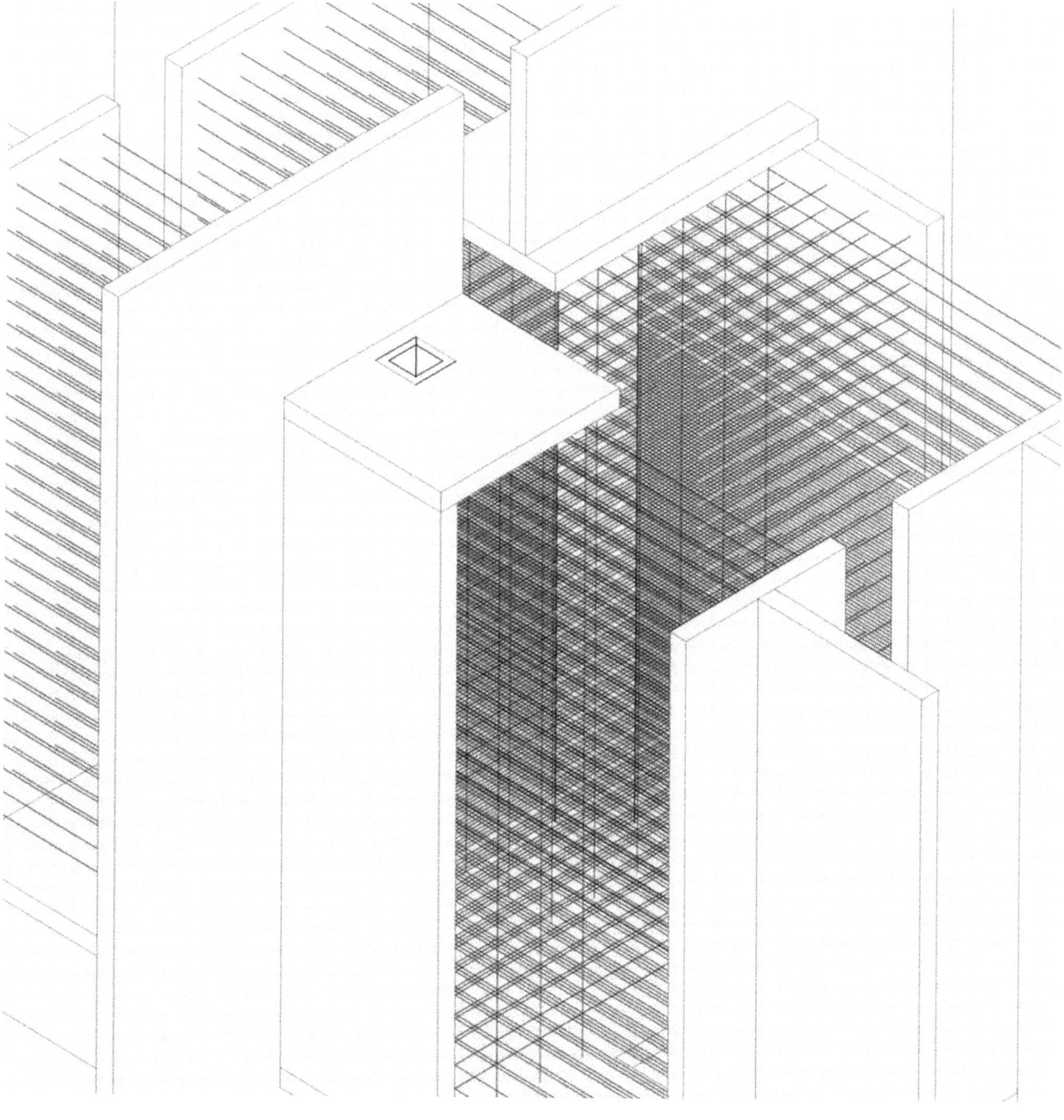

SEAGRAM, model, two views, foamboard, embroidery thread & inkjet print, approx., 25 x 30 x 44 cm

SEAGRAM, model, interior view, foamboard, embroidery thread & inkjet print, approx., 25 x 30 x 44 cm

SEAGRAM, model, detail views, foamboard, embroidery thread & inkjet print, approx., 25 x 30 x 44 cm

SEAGRAM, electronic model, interior view

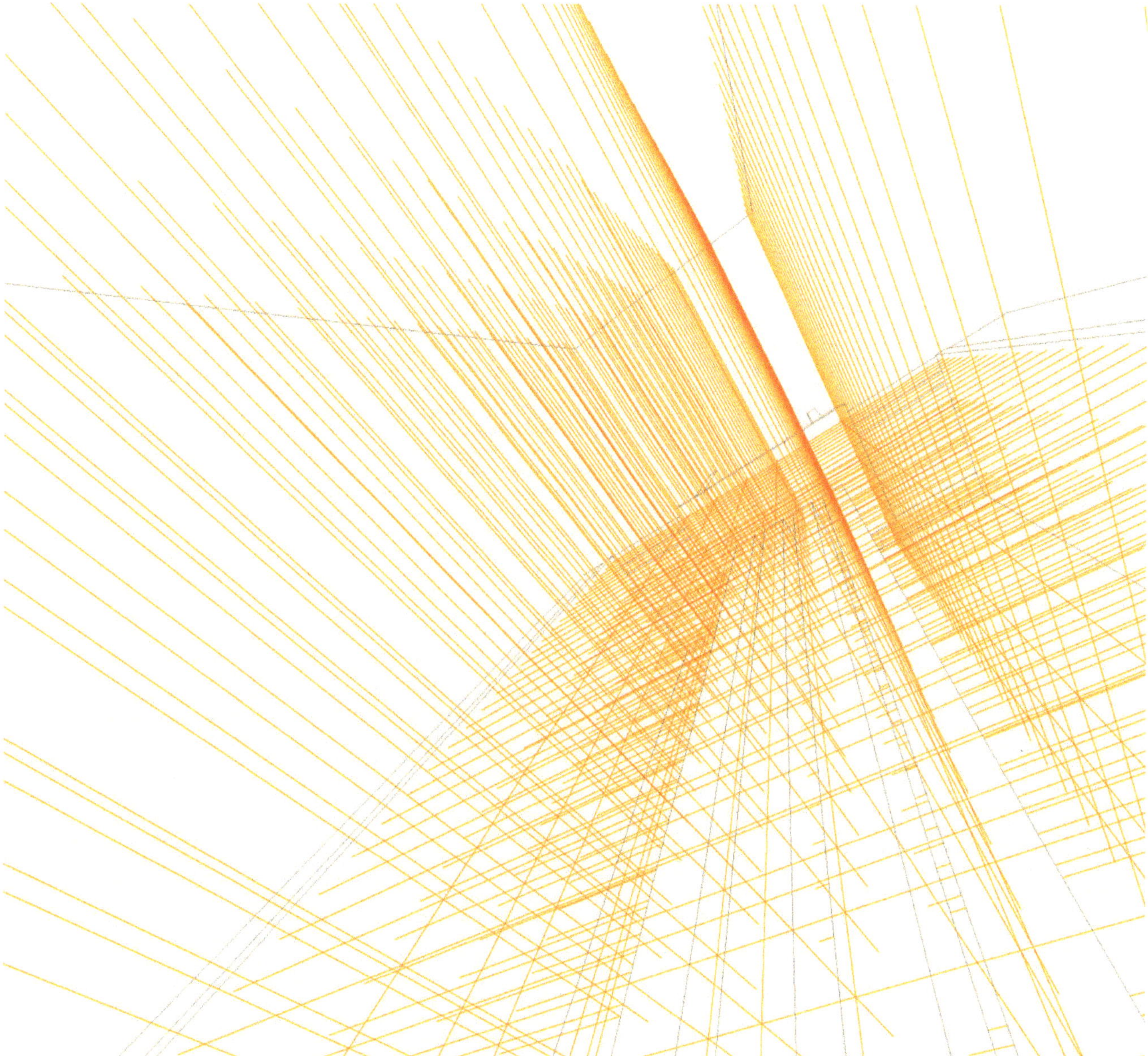

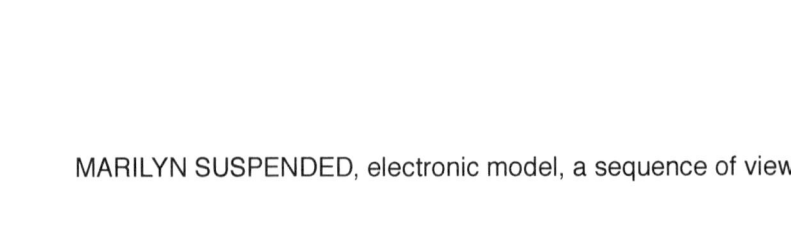

MARILYN SUSPENDED, electronic model, a sequence of views

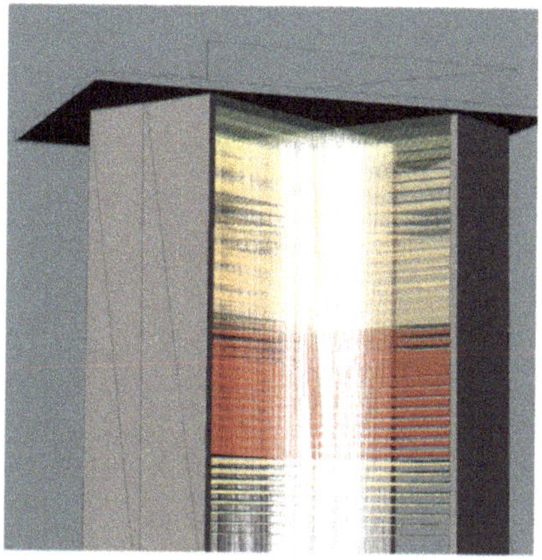

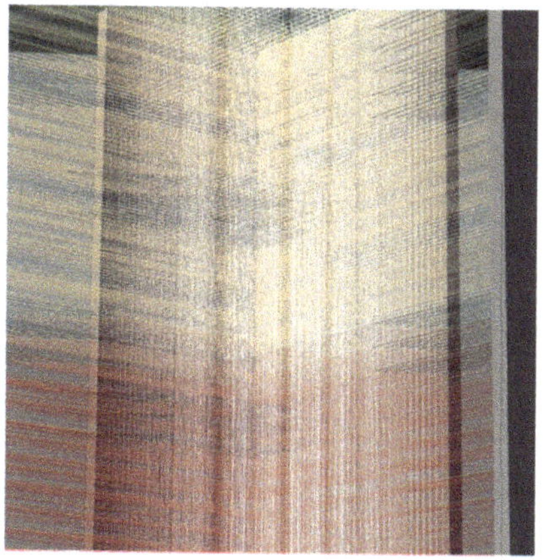

MARILYN UNDER THE TABLE, foamboard, embroidery thread, approx., 60 x 60 x 78 cm

CHRYSTOPHENE, two interior views, foamboard, embroidery thread, approx., 48 x 52 x 78 cm

CHRYSTOPHENE, electronic model, view

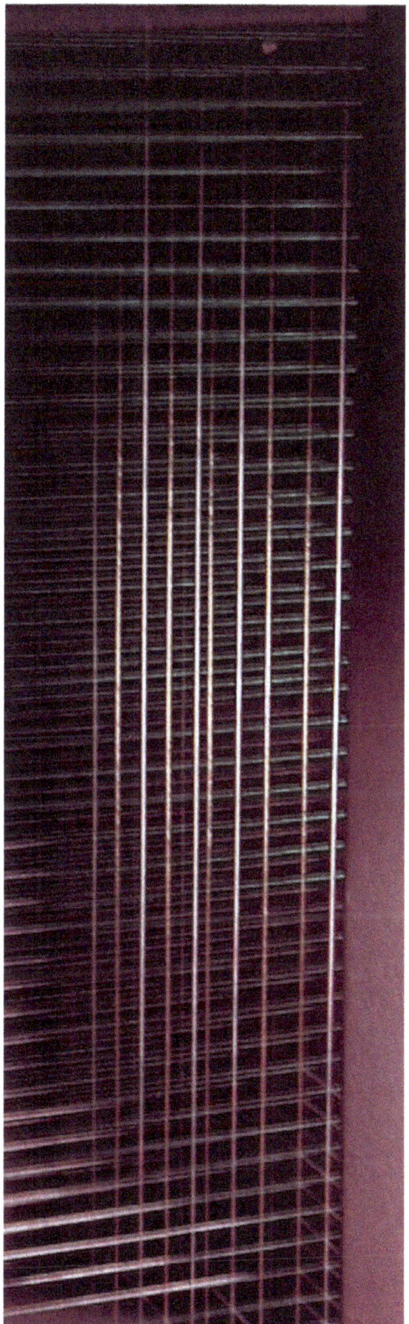
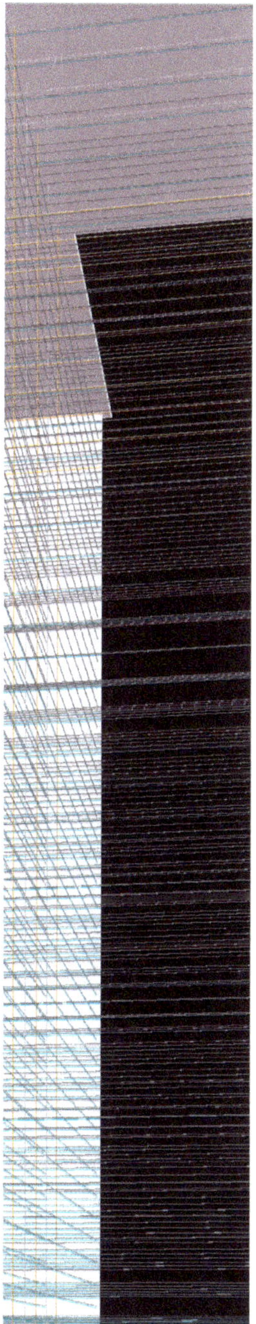

CHRYSTOPHENE, electronic model, two views

CHRYSTOPHENE, interior view,
foamboard, embroidery thread,
approx., 48 x 52 x 78 cm

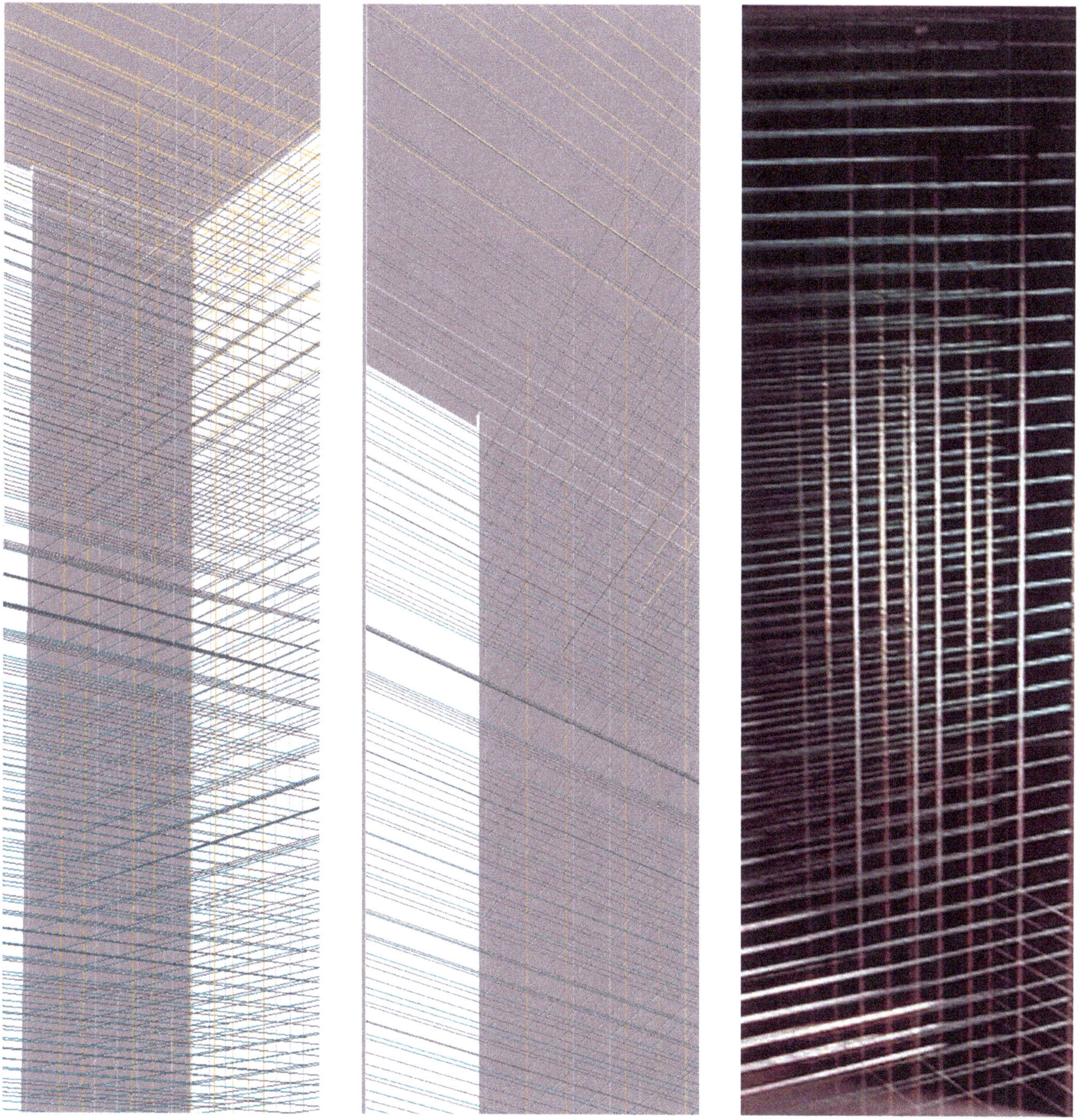

2.1.3 - Test Apparatus

At a certain stage in the inquiry it became necessary to test if the psychodynamics of AIR Grid experience was universal or if it only applied to grids derived from Miesian architecture.

A support apparatus made from black foamboard was constructed. The cadence was based on the simple unit of one centimetre. The holepanels were limited to eighteen centimetres in width and forty-five centimetres in height. The black support was used as a frame for constructing temporary portions of grid in different colours, in each case the portion measured approximately fifteen-by-fifteen-by-twelve centimetres high. A photographic study was made of the temporary grid-portions. The study aimed: first, to ascertain if the block of grid did indeed bifurcate between the third and second moments revealed in the Miesian models. In other words that it did, sometimes, appear as an array of parallel planes and sometimes appear as a volume of mist. Second, the study aimed to record those differing moments. The first temporary grid-portion was sewn with blue threads, the second with red threads and the third with gold threads. The reason for testing three differently coloured portions was to see if colour had a role to play in the bifurcation of the grid.

There was a noticeable difference between the red and the other colours, the red grid-portion looked heavier and when it appeared under the aspect of parallel planes it seemed more like a stack of closed surfaces than an open weave. When it appeared under the aspect of mist it looked heavier than the blue or the gold.

The tests with temporary grid-portions demonstrated that the qualities of the AIR Grid, as observed initially in the Miesian models, did not apply only to grid cadences derived from Miesian architecture. At this point in the inquiry it seemed reasonable to state that the phenomenon under study was irreducible to the Miesian architecture by means of which it had been discovered; but it was not inextricable from that line of inquiry. It was at this point in the inquiry that the phenomenon was given a generic name, at first we called it Cotton Grid, then changed Cotton to AIR. It should not be forgotten that at this stage in the inquiry the successful manufacture of AIR (nee Cotton) Grid had been restricted to portions of a limited size.

TEST APPARATUS BLU01, 1 cm cadence, black foamboard & blue embroidery thread, portion size, approx., 15 x 15 x 12 cm

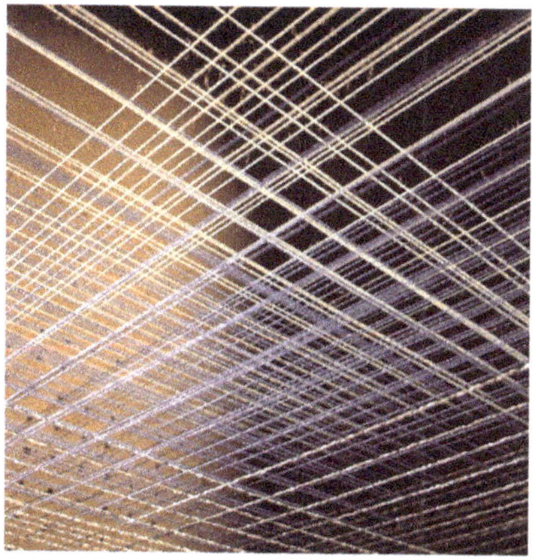
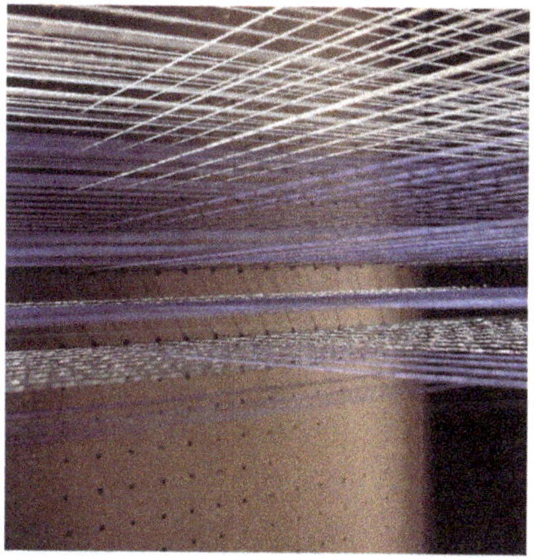

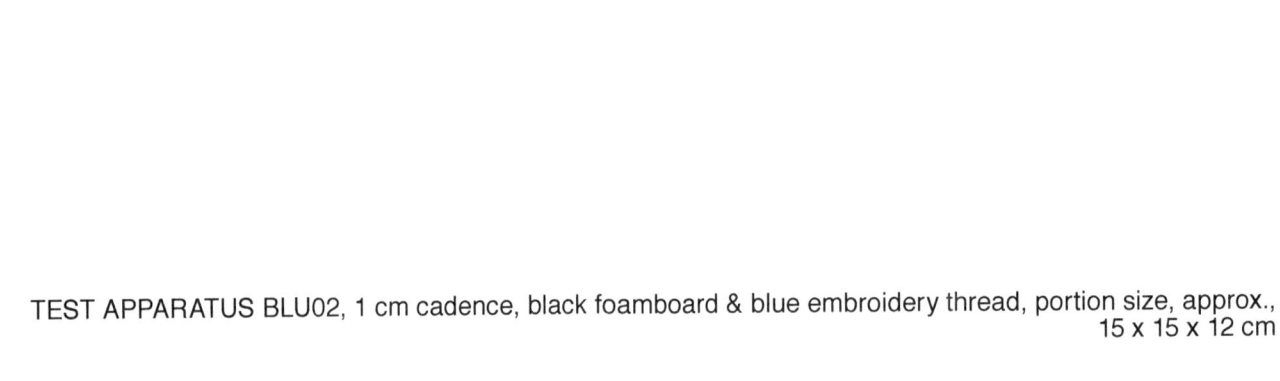

TEST APPARATUS BLU02, 1 cm cadence, black foamboard & blue embroidery thread, portion size, approx., 15 x 15 x 12 cm

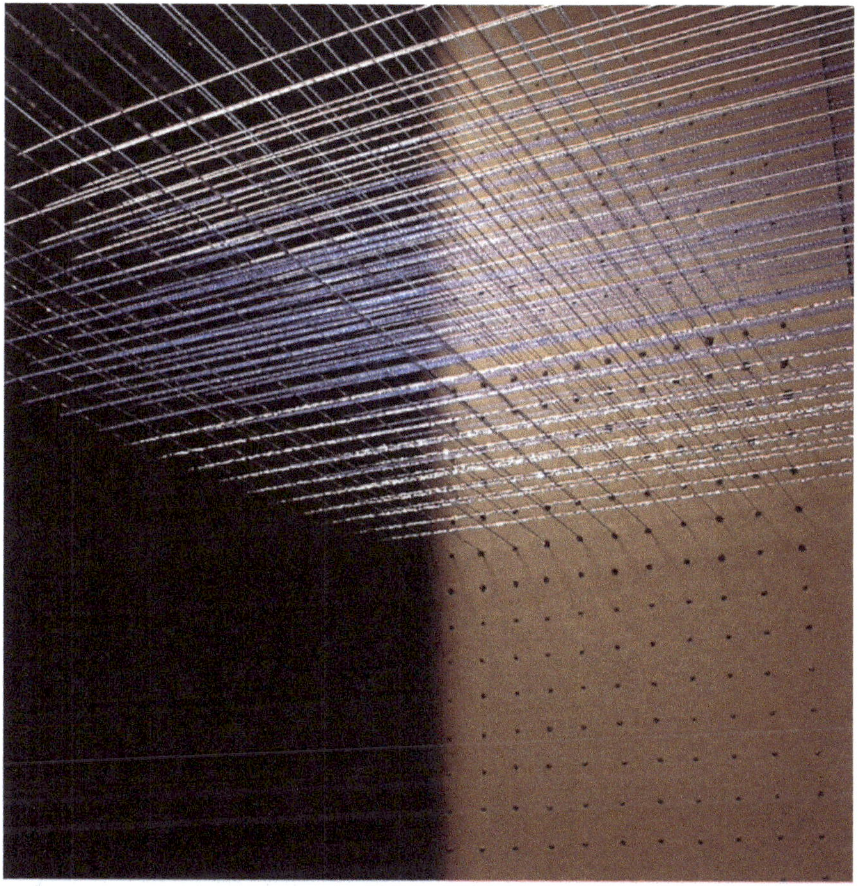
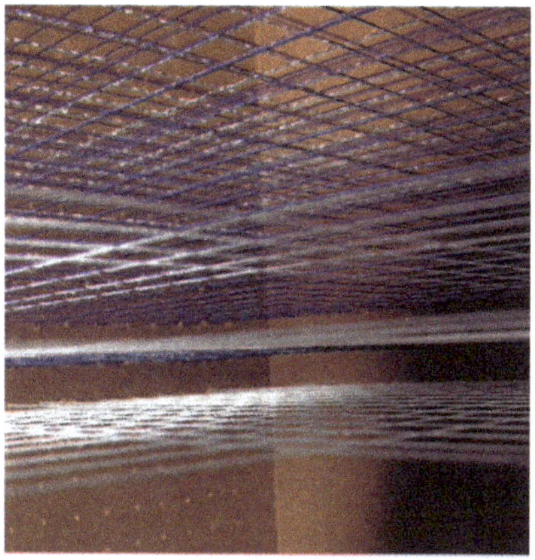

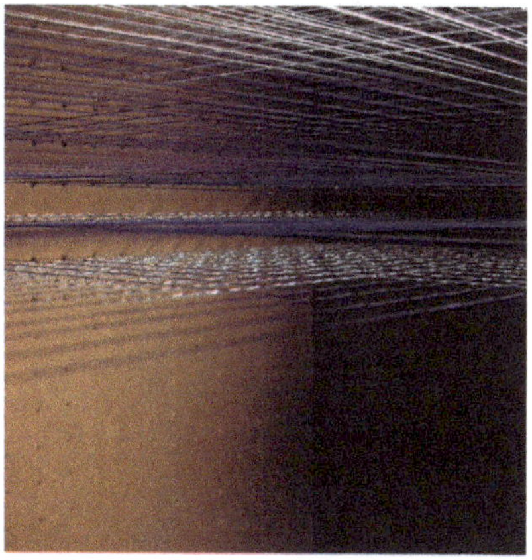

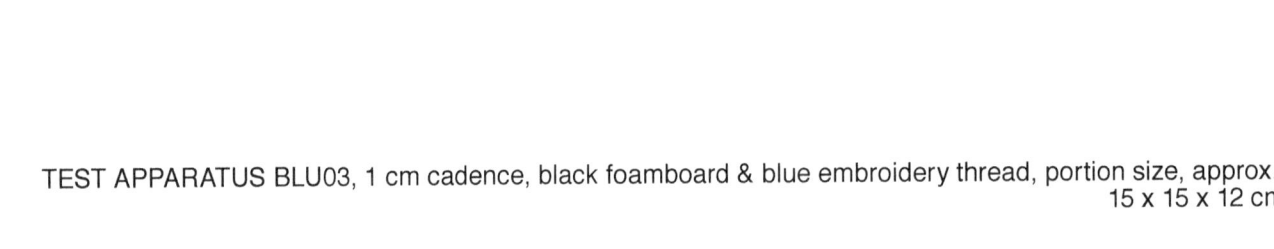

TEST APPARATUS BLU03, 1 cm cadence, black foamboard & blue embroidery thread, portion size, approx., 15 x 15 x 12 cm

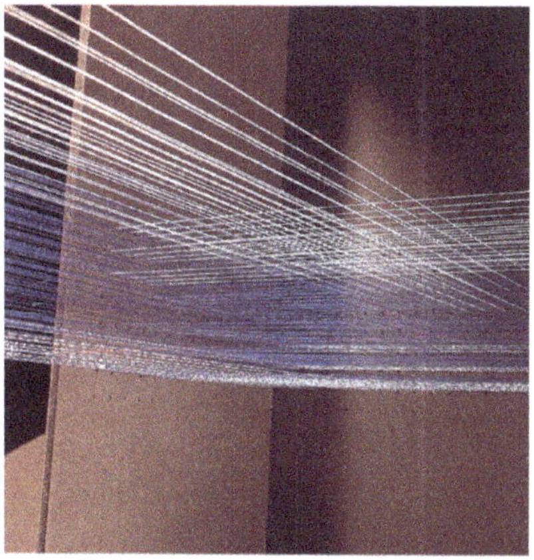
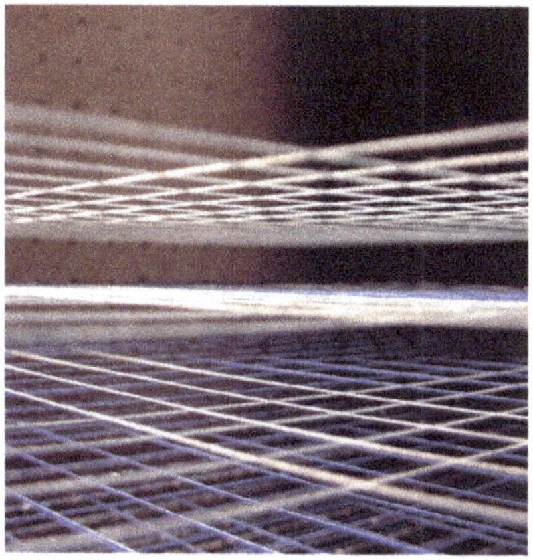
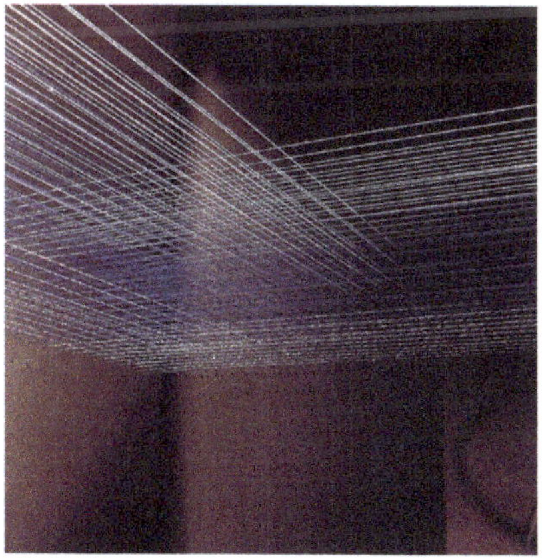

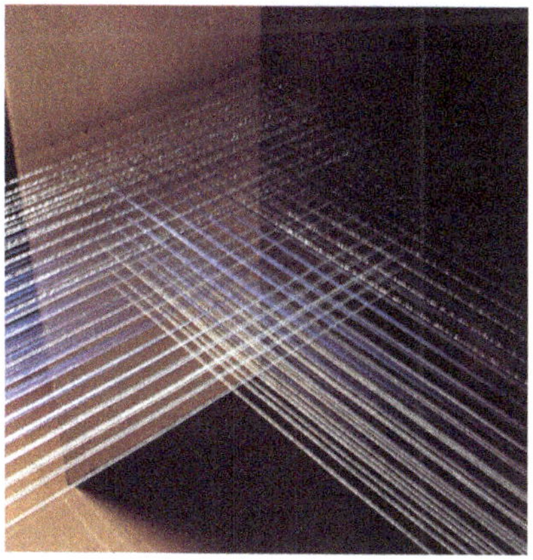

TEST APPARATUS RED, 1 cm cadence, black foamboard & red embroidery thread, portion size, approx., 15 x 15 x 12 cm

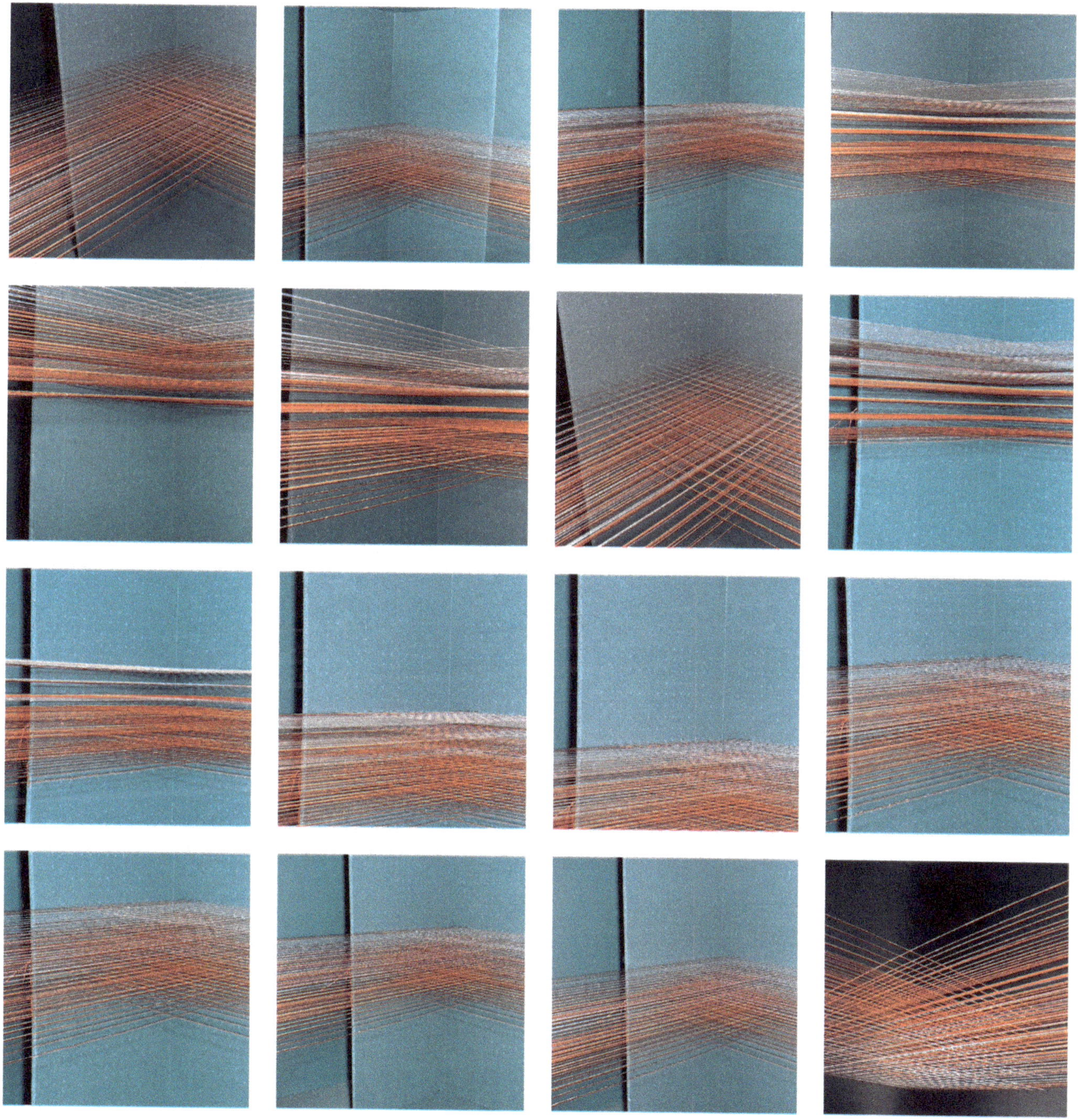

TEST APPARATUS GOLD, 1 cm cadence, black foamboard & gold embroidery thread, portion size, approx., 15 x 15 x 12 cm

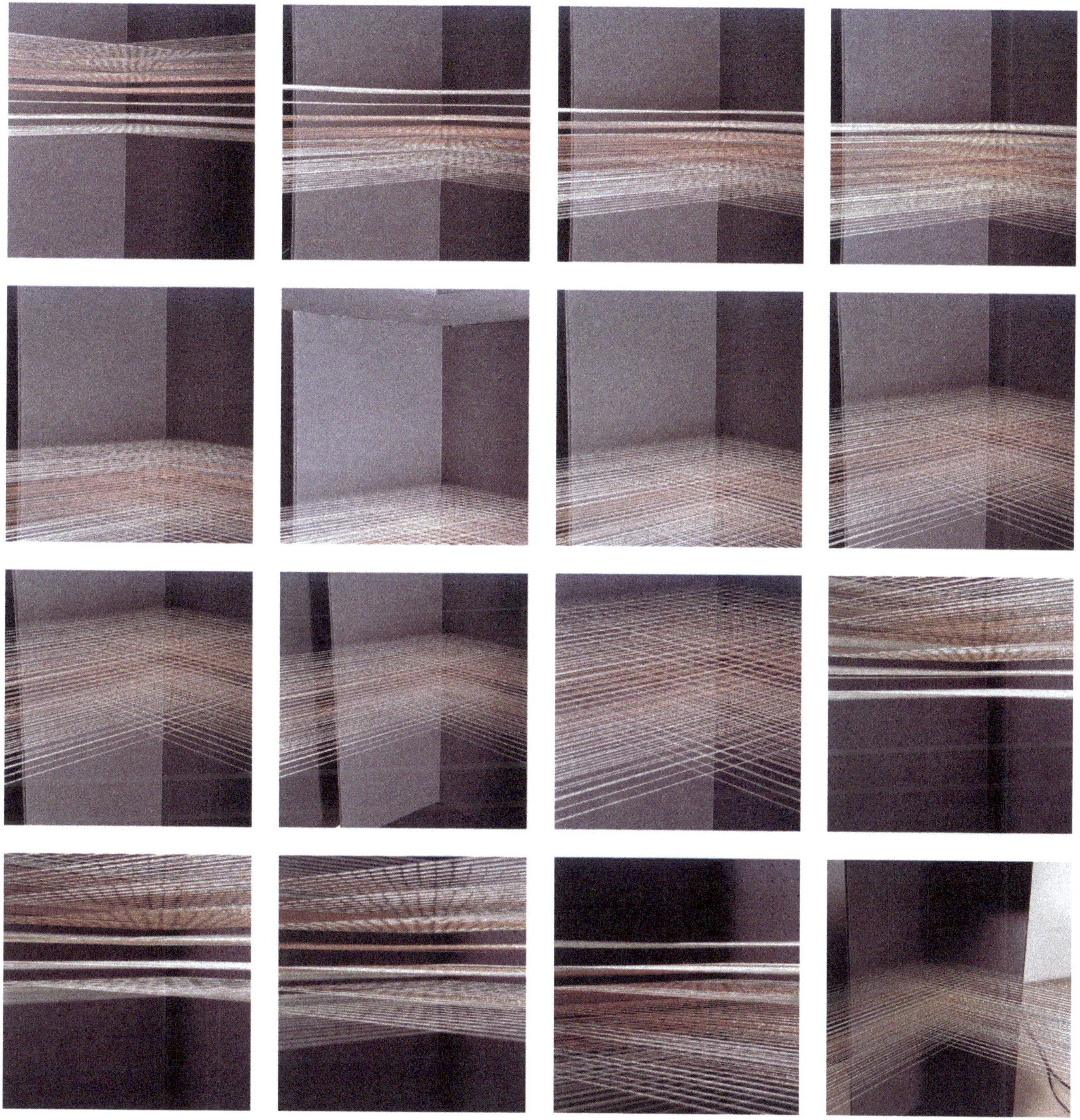

2.1.4 - Domestic and Dark Space

Looking into AIR (nee Cotton) Grid evokes a spatial feeling. It is possible to explore that feeling, but not by going into AIR Grid space in person. The body of a human-sized living being cannot enter into AIR Grid space because that space is already occupied by the AIR Grid lattice; and yet the desire to get inside AIR Grid space can be very powerful.

The question arises, is there a place for AIR Grid space in the everyday world? Attempts to address this question began with the idea of burrowing into the corner of a room, of hollowing out a small alcove in which an AIR Grid structure could sit, radiating out but at the same time drawing away from the world around it. Two grids were produced, a white, gold and orange grid (named Polia) and a blue grid (named Vectorah). Each grid was given a hypothetical location, both in domestic space: Polia in the corner of a room, in a void space between the plaster lining and the masonry outer walls; Vectorah in the bulkhead under a stair. As the design developed, so the placement of the grids in the selected locations seemed more and more contrived. To carry on working with AIR Grid it was necessary to face up to the non-everydayness of the AIR Grid phenomenon.

At the same time a series of experiments were conducted in the blind space of the computer. They were entitled 'Lancelot,' and 'Silk Maiden,' respectively. The experiments were valuable as a means of learning about the possibilities of operating with AIR Grid inside computer space. They also gave some indicators as to the possibility of contextualising AIR Grid, if not in the everyday, at least in a lived world scenario.

POLIA IMMURED, electronic model, a sequence of views

POLIA ATTEMPTING TO FLY, electronic model, view

POLIA, detail views, foamboard & embroidery thread, approx., 60 x 60 x 51 cm

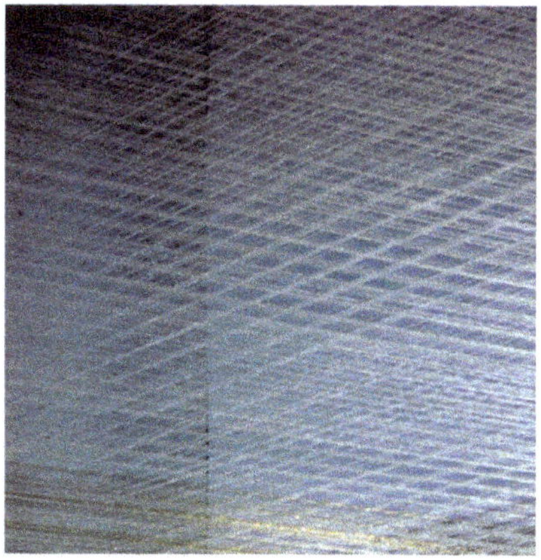

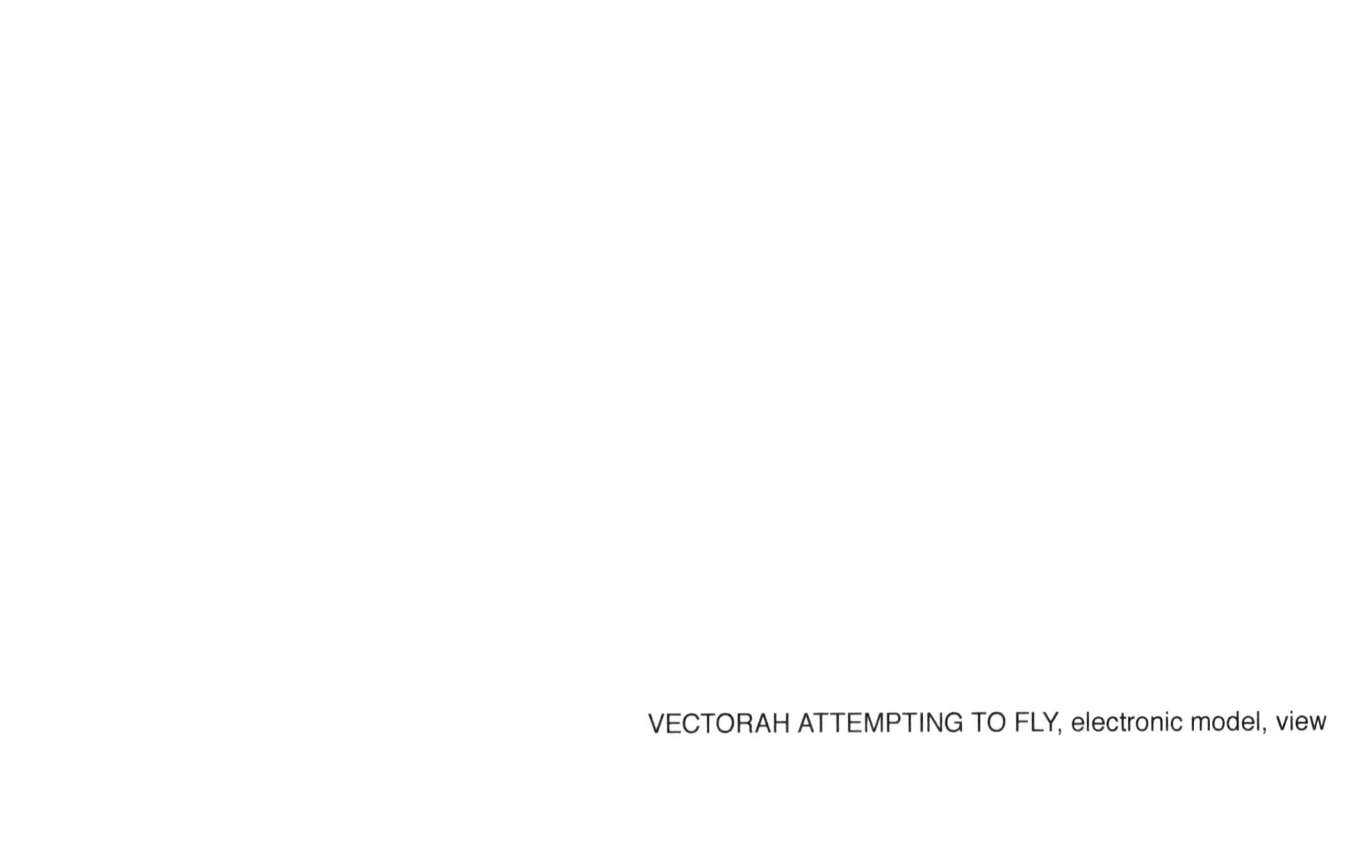

VECTORAH ATTEMPTING TO FLY, electronic model, view

VECTORAH, being made 01, foamboard, embroidery thread, approx., 60 x 60 x 60 cm

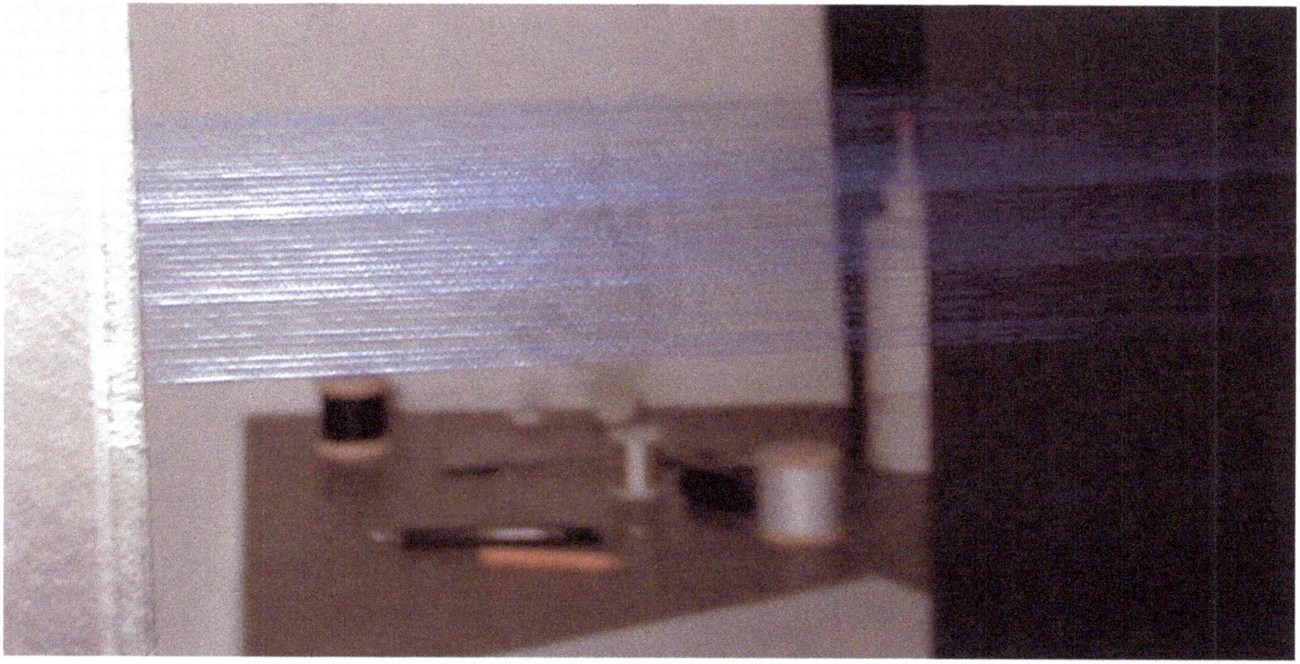

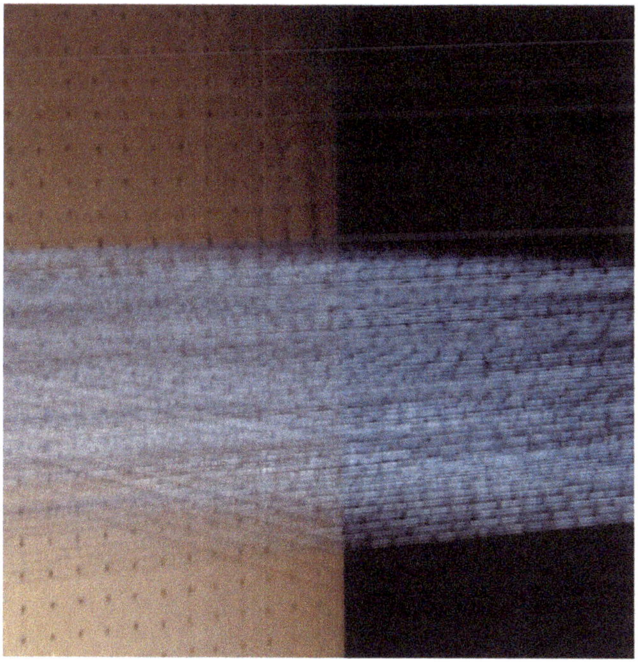

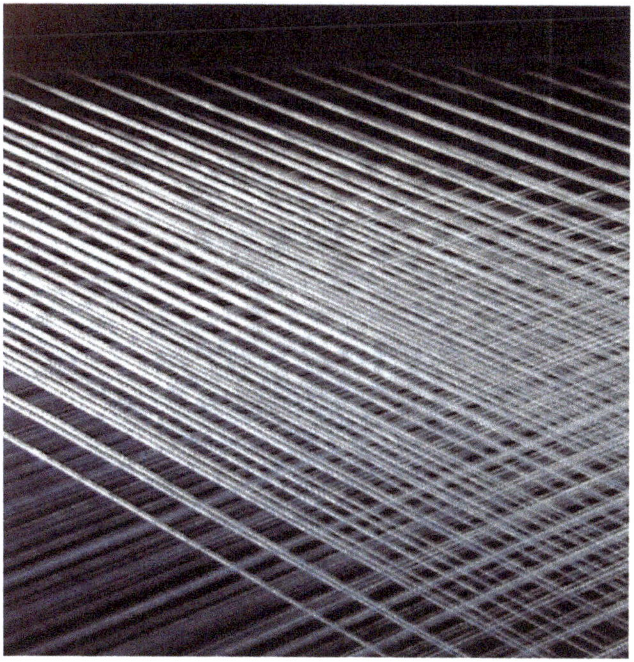

VECTORAH, being made 02, foamboard, embroidery thread, approx., 60 x 60 x 60 cm

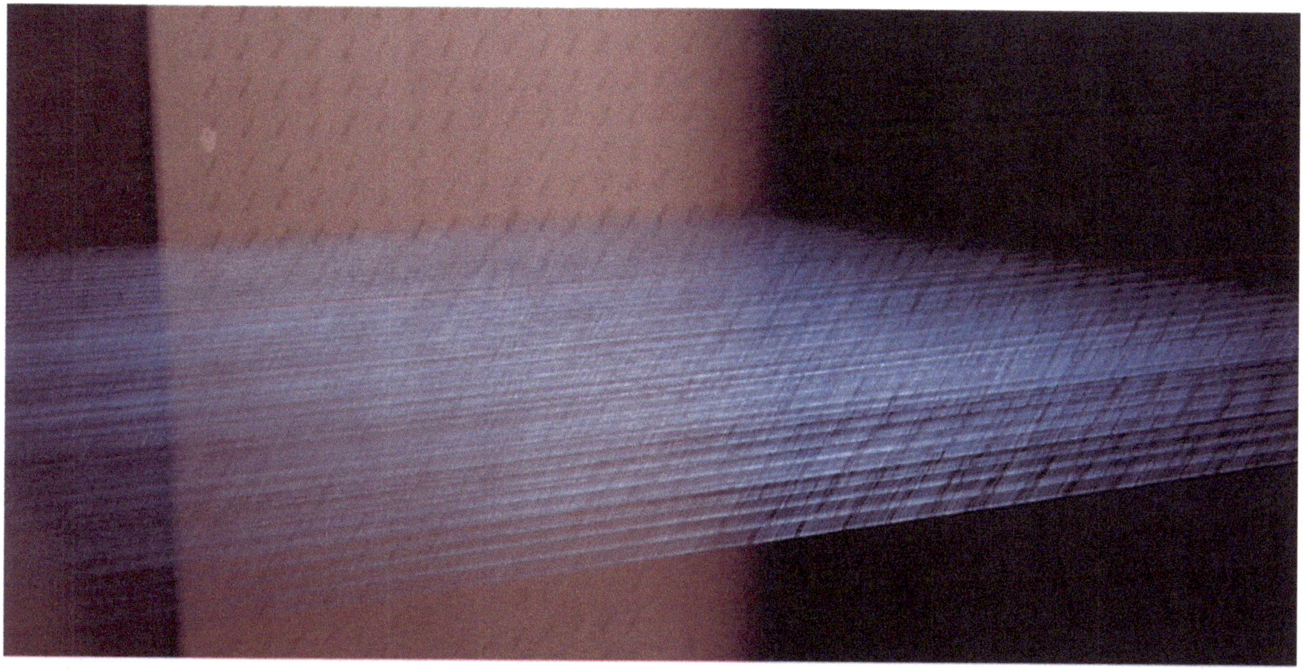

LANCELOT, electronic model, studies in dark space, views 1-16

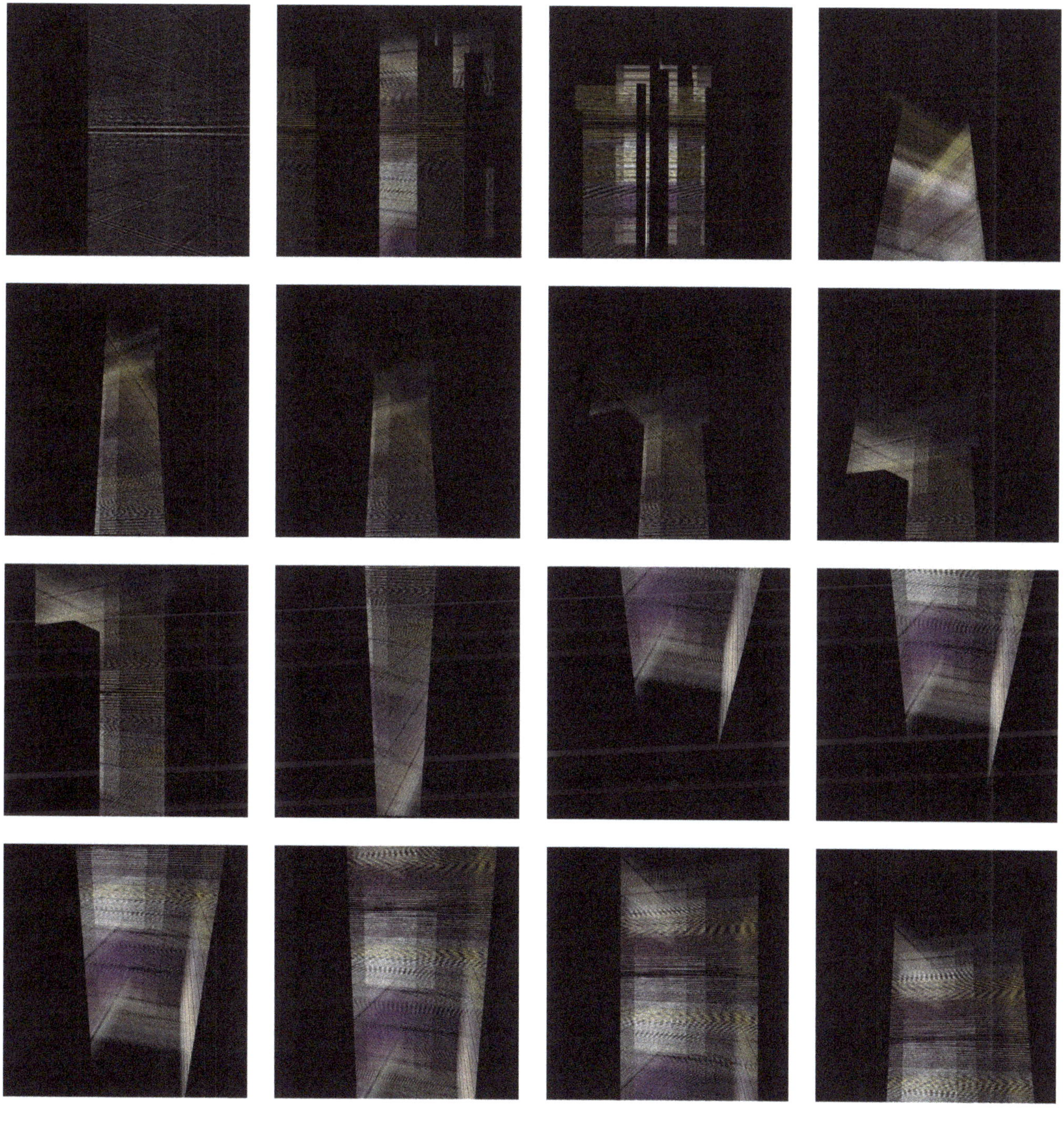

LANCELOT, electronic model, studies in dark space, views 17-32

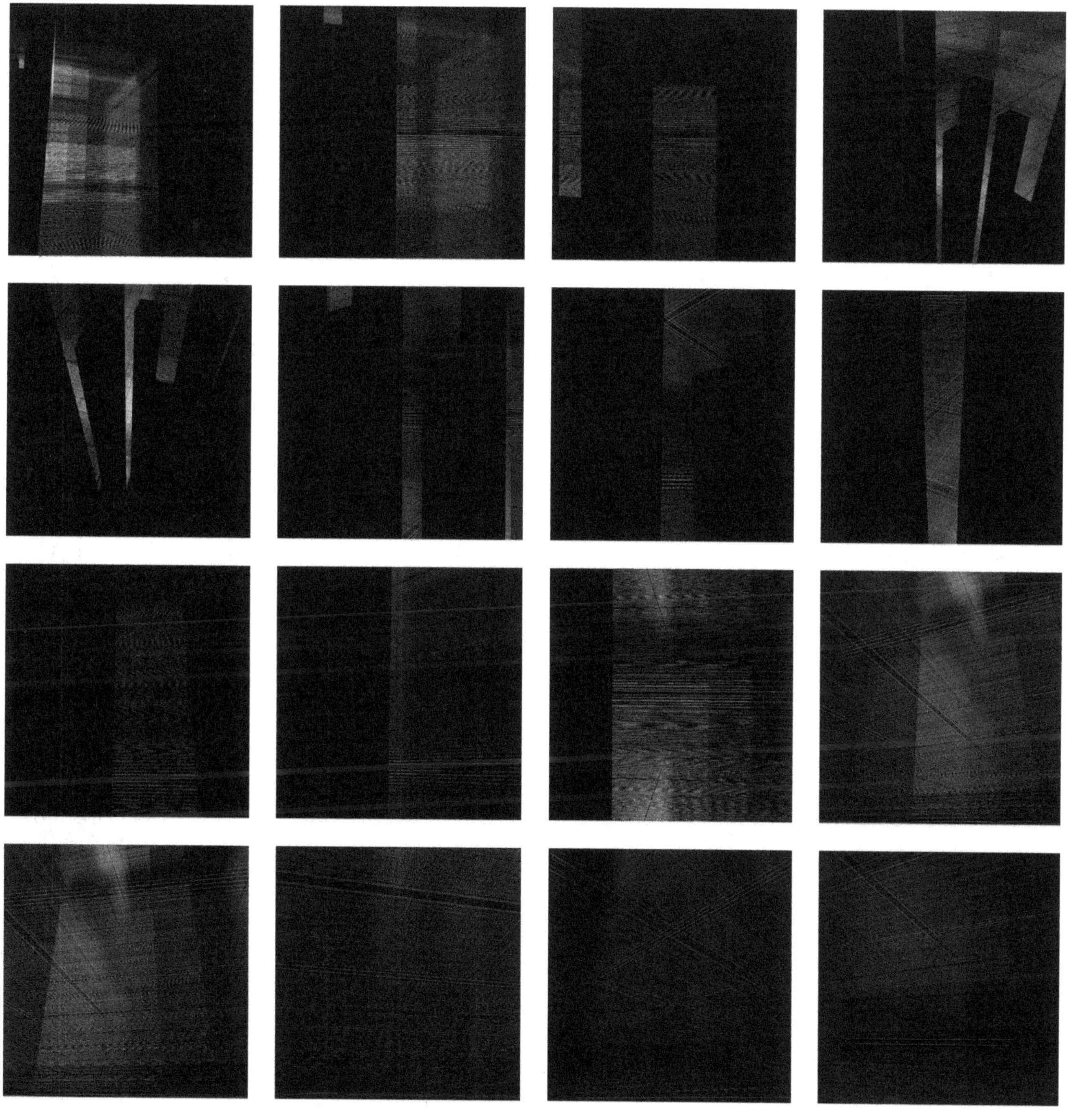

SILK MAIDEN, electronic model, studies in dark space, views 1-16

SILK MAIDEN, electronic model, studies in dark space, views 17-32

2.1.5 - Support Studies

We have already mentioned certain failures of the support, leading to the demise of a number of Miesian Air Grid structures (thread-Marilyn and thread-Chrystophene). In order to solve this problem a considerable amount of research time and energy was invested in the development of the support structure. There were several difficulties inherent in the idea of the support: first, while on the one hand the support is necessary for holding the shape of the AIR Grid lattice, on the other hand it obscures the view. Second, as well as maintaining the AIR Grid lattice the support has to maintain its own shape (if it fails to maintain its own shape then the support cannot maintain that of the AIR Grid). In designing the support it was necessary to balance the desire for a maximum view of the lattice with the requirements of easy sewing and support stability.

After much testing of prototypes the researcher began to work confidently and with some ease, between AIR Grid lattice and support structure. The other thing worth drawing attention to at this stage is the amount of labour involved in the sewing of an AIR Grid. The sewing of AIR Grid is by no means an exciting time for the living being upon whom the task falls. However, there are moments of intense pleasure, for example when the first layer is finished and hovers like a sharp incision in the air, or when the first moment of mist appears. And, as AIR Grid builds up, so hybrid moments begin to occur with increasing frequency, they can catch the researcher off-guard, as it were when they are not looking: an intense cloud of colour, a shimmering uncertainty, the glimpsed view, poised between mist and parallel array.

SUPPORT STUDIES, foamboard & embroidery thread, approx., 16 x 16 x 20 cm

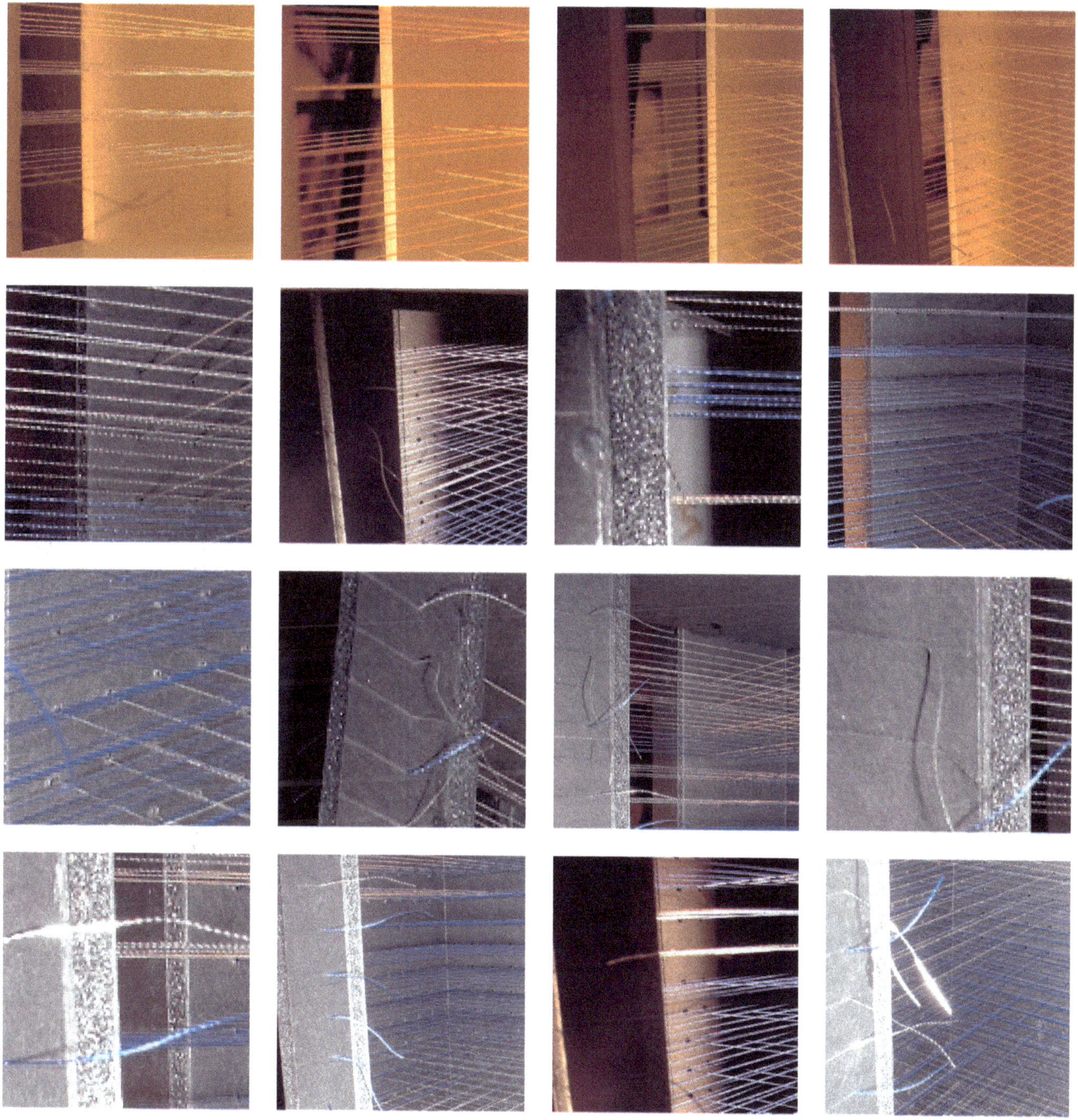

ACQUA SUPPORT STUDY, foamboard & embroidery thread, approx., 45 x 45 x 33 cm

ALCONA SUPPORT STUDY, foamboard & embroidery thread, approx., 61 x 48 x 41 cm

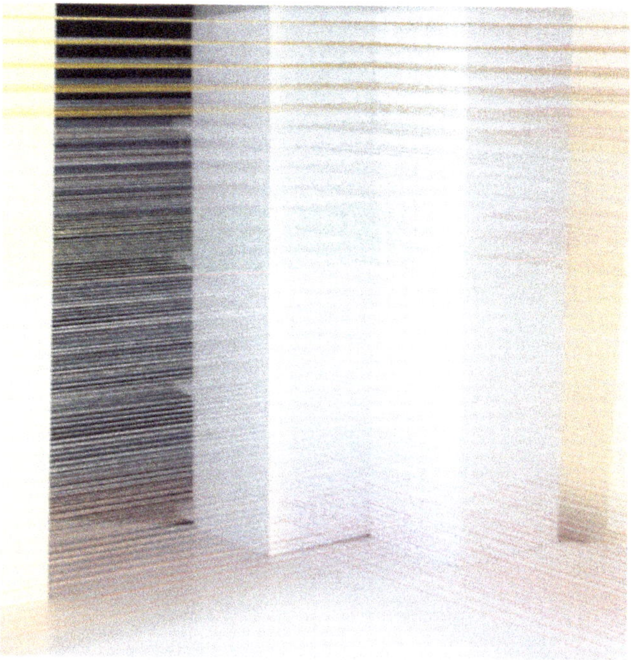

CHROME SUPPORT STUDY, foamboard & embroidery thread, approx., 26 x 26 x 38 cm

ACQUA SUPPORT STUDY, foamboard & embroidery thread, approx., 45 x 45 x 33 cm

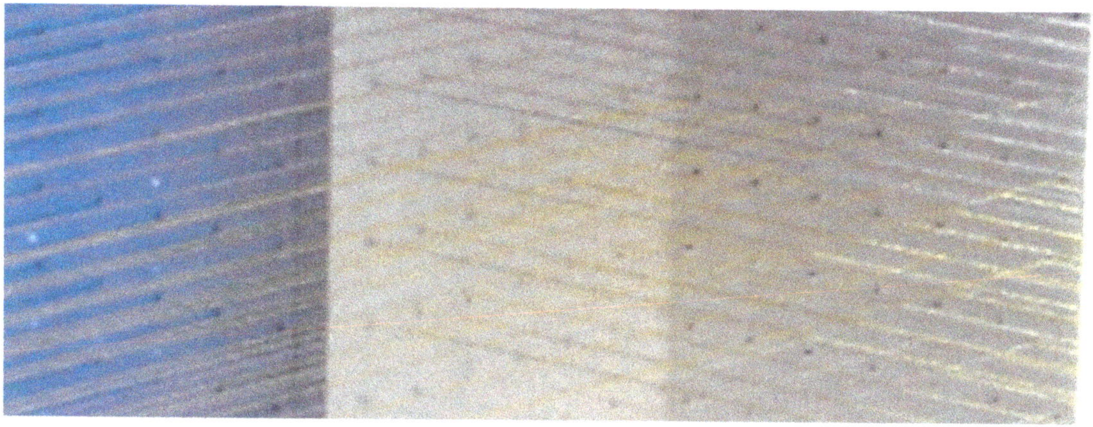

2.1.6 - Form-Giving

AIR Grid was found to be irreducible to the Miesian architecture out of which it arose; but that did not mean there was nothing more to learn about AIR Grid from Mies. In the early AIR Grid work Miesian architecture served as a model and in those first structures the Miesian subject was considered to be an urban artifact, a building set within the space of a city. With the move away from the Miesian model towards generic AIR Grid the implied urban scale of the Miesian model disappeared. If AIR Grid did not represent anything, but simply was what it was then the scale of operation had shifted to one-to-one. The AIR Grid structure dealt in groups of centimetres ranging from fifteen to one-hundred-and-twenty. Returning these dimensions to Miesian architecture we are in the realm of paving slabs, of ceiling tiles, of wall panels.

In the analysis of the New National Gallery, set out in the second section of the first part of this thesis, Miesian Architecture & Lefebvrian Space, the smallest increment of form-giving was identified as thirty centimetres. This increment is the off-set dimension relating the grid lines of the top surface of the floor-slab to the grid lines of the suspended ceiling below. However, what was not mentioned in that analysis is the lighting grid that sits below the roof-plate-grid. It divides the three-point-six metre module of the roof-plate-grid into ten equal increments, each of which is thirty-six centimetres. The common denominator of thirty and thirty-six is six. Six-by-six is the smallest increment necessary for the horizontal divisibility of the NNG form-giving. Now, as we have seen, in the vertical dimension there is a difference between the rhythm of spatial striations above the surface of the floor-slab and the rhythm below. Between the underside of the roof-plate-grid and the top surface of the floor-slab there are nine striations of space, while between the underside of the basement-ceiling-grid and the datum of the basement floor there are six striations of space. The common denominator of nine and six is three. The sum of nine and six is fifteen. Extrusion of six-by-six through fifteen generates a volume measuring six-by-six-by-fifteen. This measure is taken to be the basic unit of an AIR Grid family of proportioned structures.

FORM-GIVING: SUSPENDED GRID, pencil & paper

FORM-GIVING: LIGHTING GRID, card & cotton

FORM-GIVING: MAINTENANCE, digital photography

FORM-GIVING: MATERIAL MODULE, digital photography

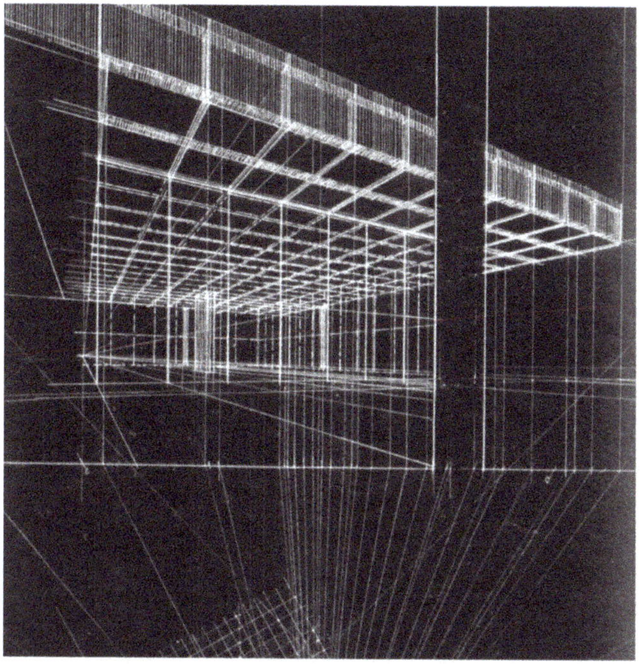
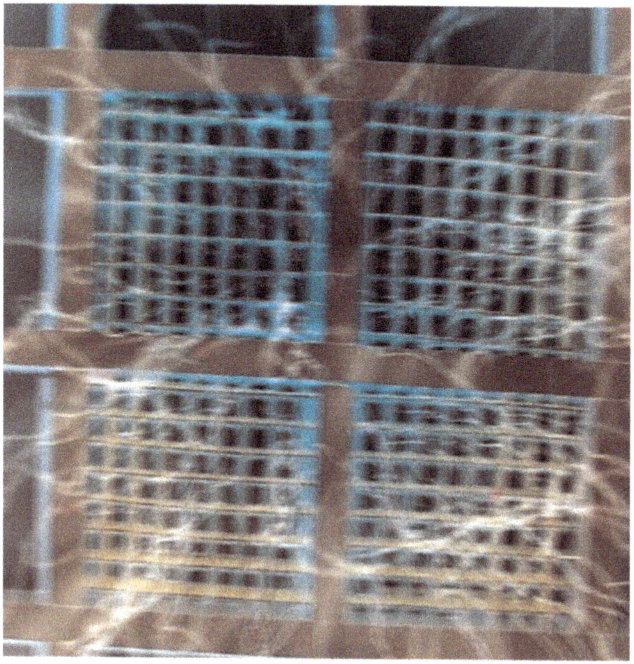

FORM-GIVING, electronic model, view 01

FORM-GIVING, electronic model, view 02

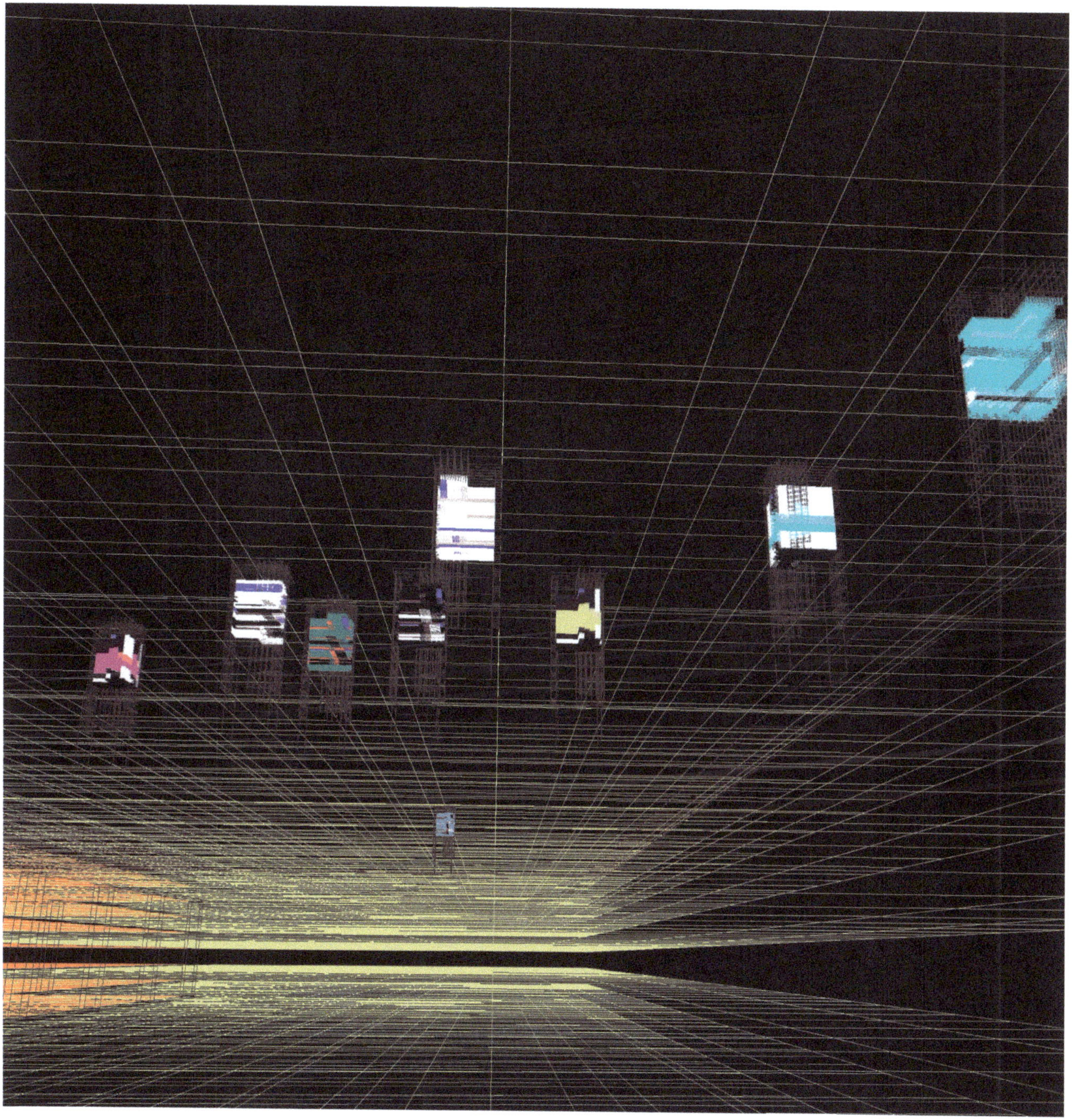

FORM-GIVING, electronic model, view 03

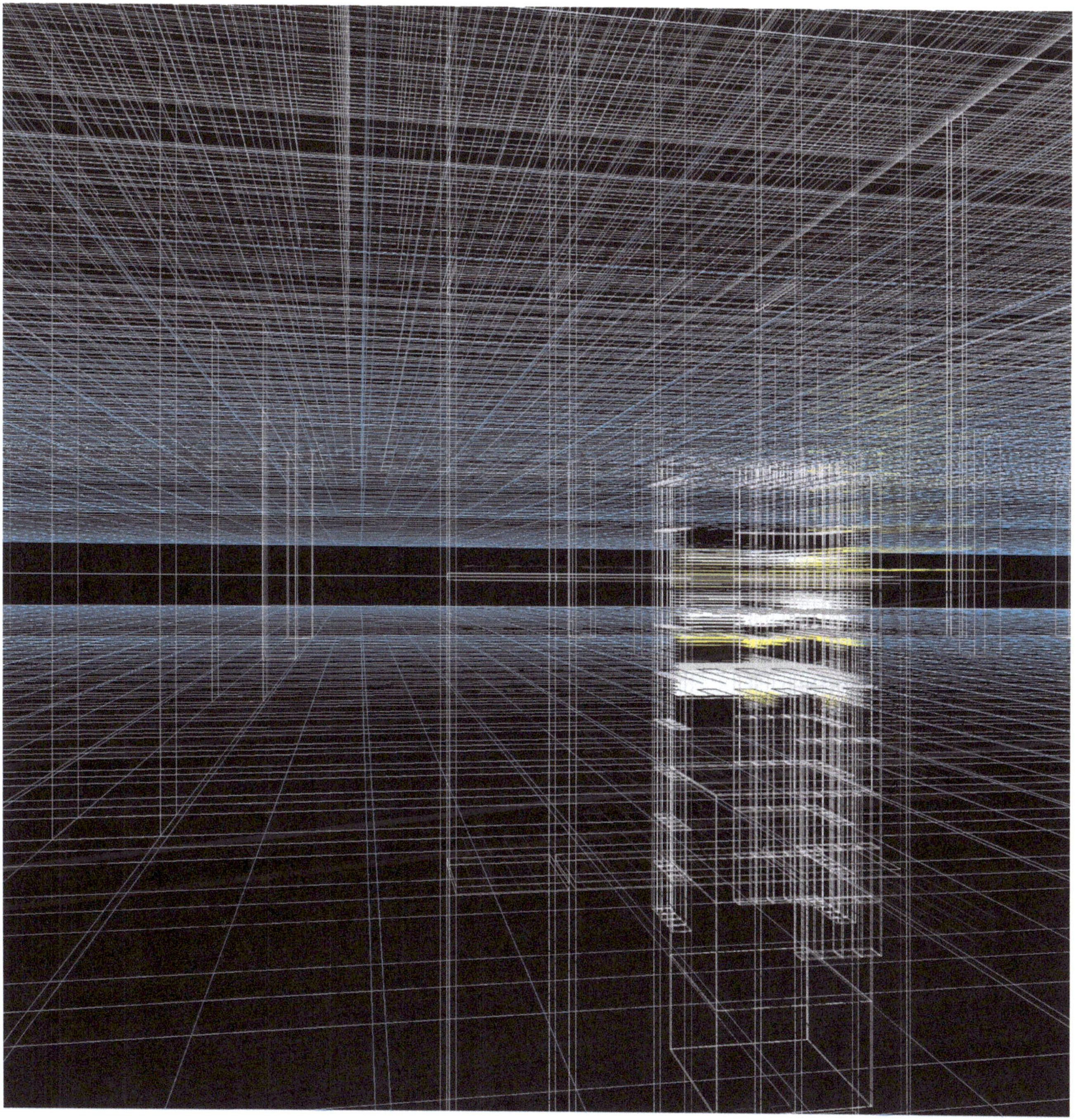

FORM-GIVING, electronic model, view 04

FORM-GIVING, electronic model, view 05 - 08

FORM-GIVING, electronic model, view 09 - 12

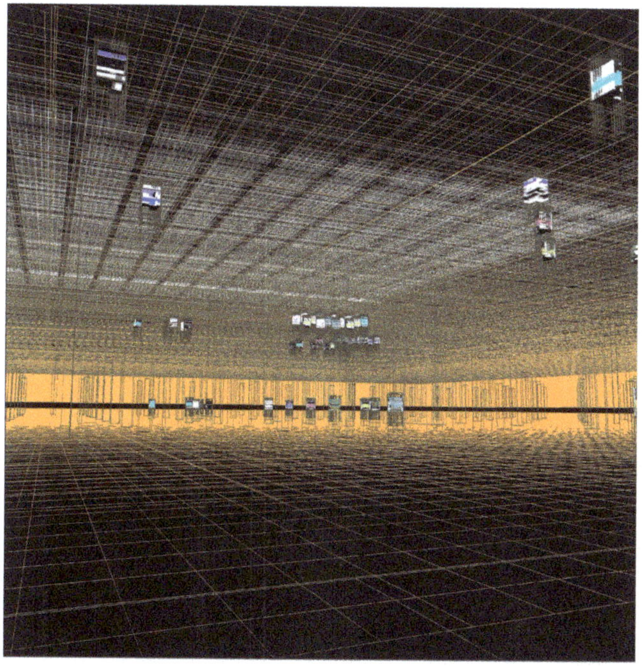
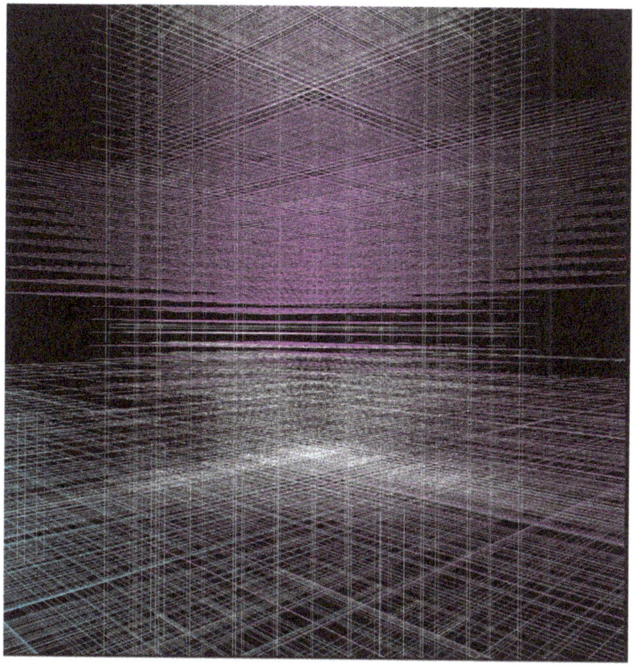

FORM-GIVING, electronic model, order@ A'

FORM-GIVING, electronic model, order@ A''

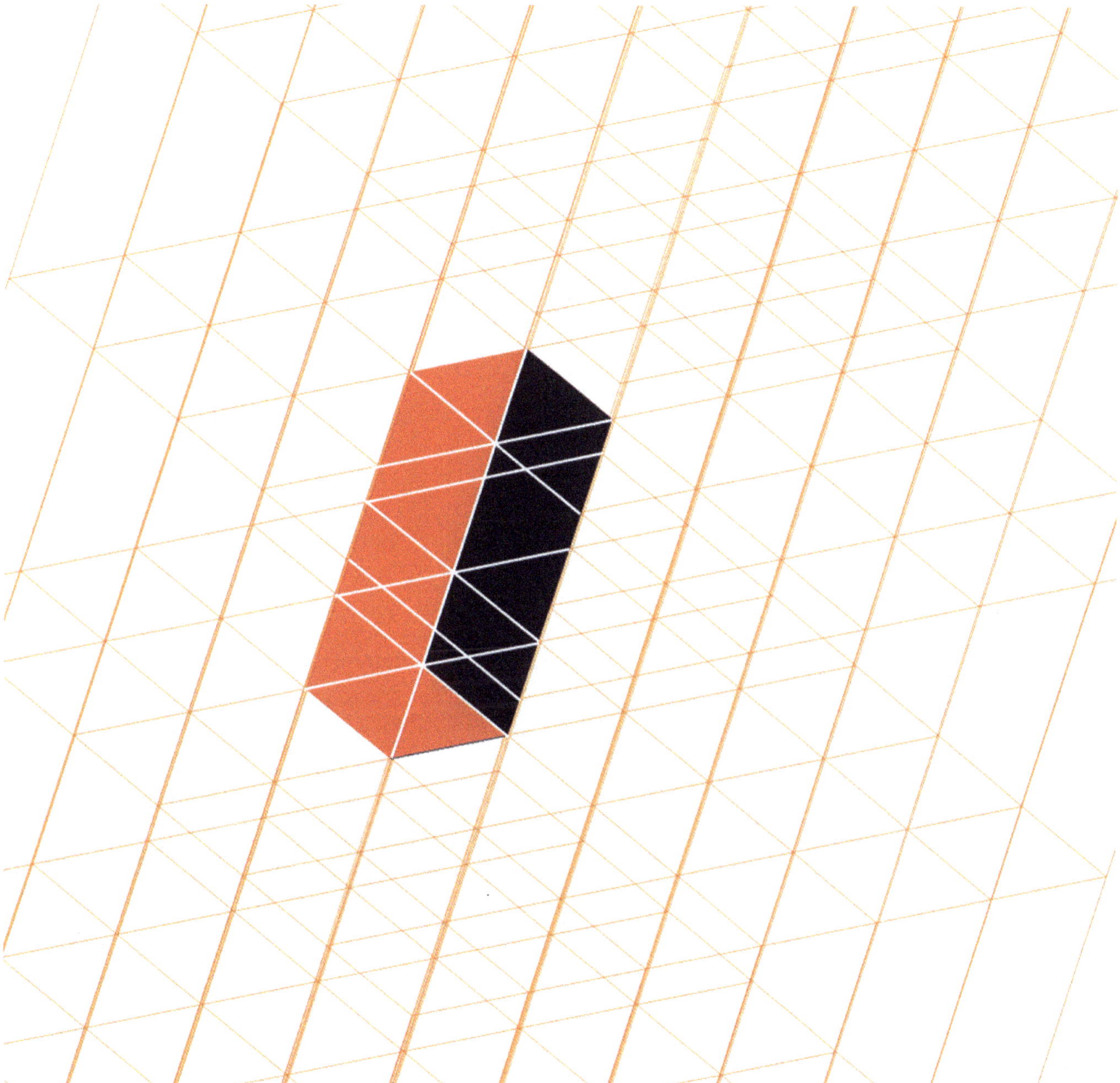

2.1.7 - Adventures in the Air

Starting with the six-by-six-by-fifteen basic unit that was, as it were, distilled out of the air of the NNG, a range of sizes can be generated as follows: (6,6,15); (12,12,30); (18,18,45); (24,24,60); (30,30,75); (36,36,90); (42,42,105) and (48,48,120). The system stops here because it seems inappropriate to extend the size of AIR Grid beyond the reach of the living being whose task it is to sew.

The metaphor of 'distilled air' can help to further understand the nature of AIR Grid? Reconsider the NNG, the space between the surface of the floor-slab and the underside of the roof-plate can be regarded to be a hall of air. The hall of air models the primal conditions of perception, the ambient light in the terrestrial environment, except, the primal difference of sky and earth is inverted. In the terrestrial environment what lies above is more massive than what lies below. A fundamental law of space is the law of strong light from above and weak light from below. The difference is usually coincident with the push and pull of gravity. In the hall of air that fundamental law is turned upside down, the earth is above and living being walks on air. The hypothetical emergence of AIR Grid out of the air disrupts the condition of primal difference. Here is a body, the body has boundaries. But the body has distilled out of the air, it conforms to the invisible order of the air, merely having converted that order into substance and light.

Being visible as AIR Grid the order of the air appears to carry information: material information is always about relationships. The living being looks to AIR Grid for information but finds very little; this is because the order of AIR Grid, being that of the air, is merely that of the primal difference of sky and earth. AIR Grid interrupts the air but it does so by materialising the air, not by displacing it. This feels strange, because the expectation of interruption is of a boundary, but here the effect is more that of coagulation: AIR Grid is heavier than air. In the inverted environment of the hall of air what is heavier must float upwards, AIR Grid must float upwards to meet the earth.

The logical trajectory of AIR Grid is up, not down. This leads us to conjecture that in order to invest AIR Grid with a maximum of energy it must be placed in the ground, not in the air.

DISTILLED AIR, electronic model, animation sequence 01

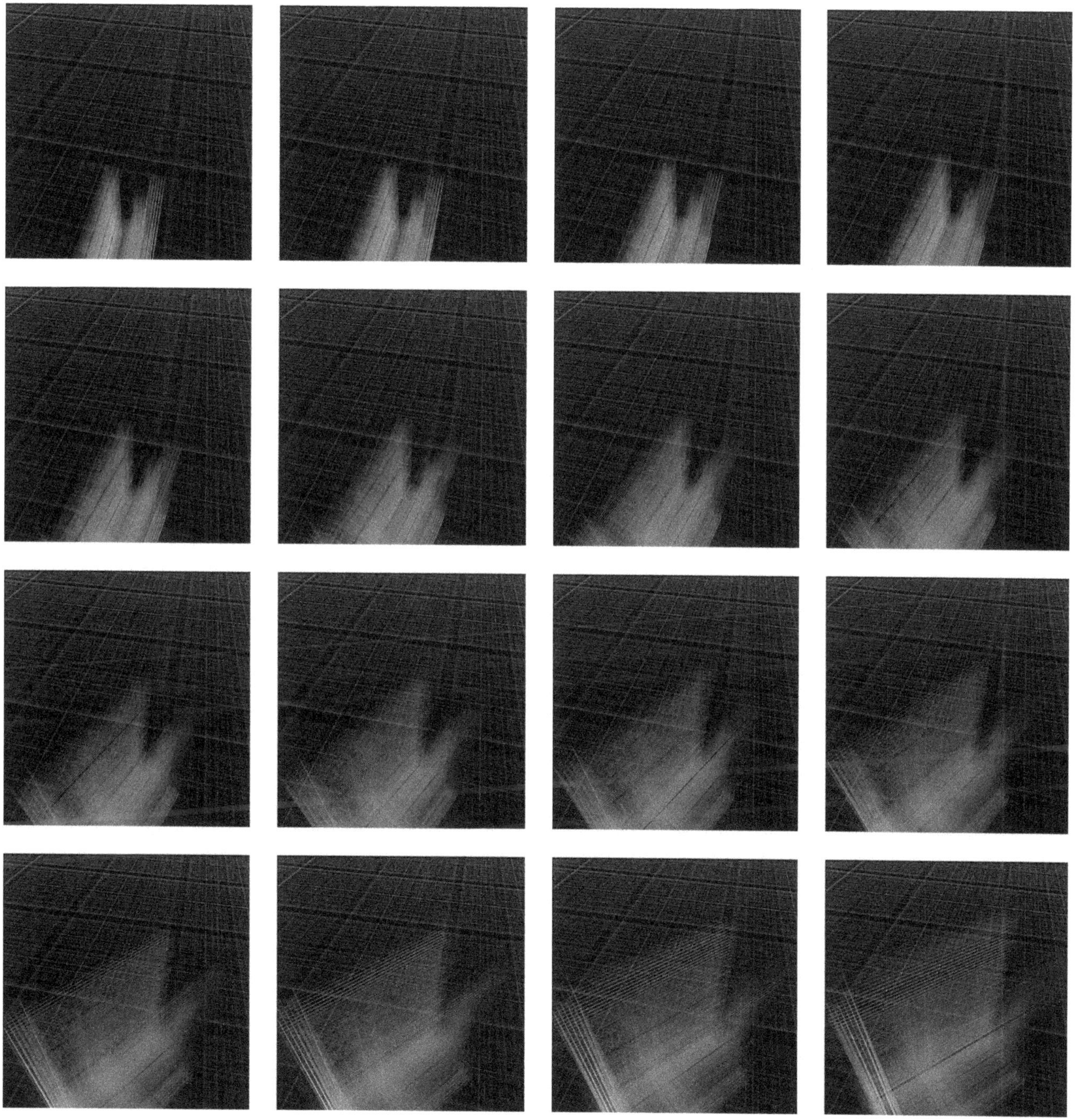

DISTILLED AIR, electronic model, animation sequence 02

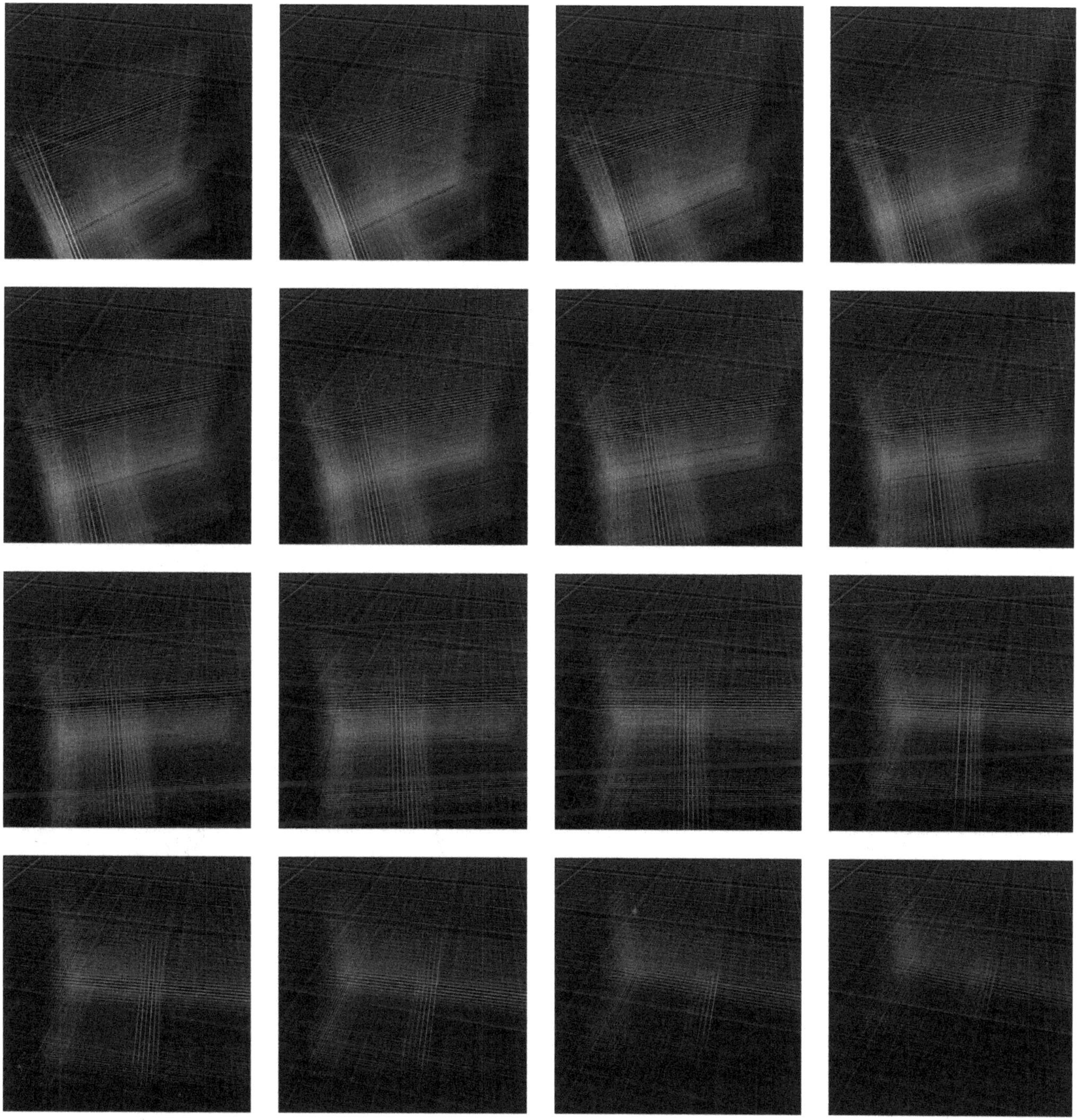

DISTILLED AIR: COAGULATION electronic model

EMERGENCE & FLIGHT, electronic model, animation sequence

EMERGENCE OUT OF THE AIR, electronic model, view

EARTH ABOVE, electronic model, view

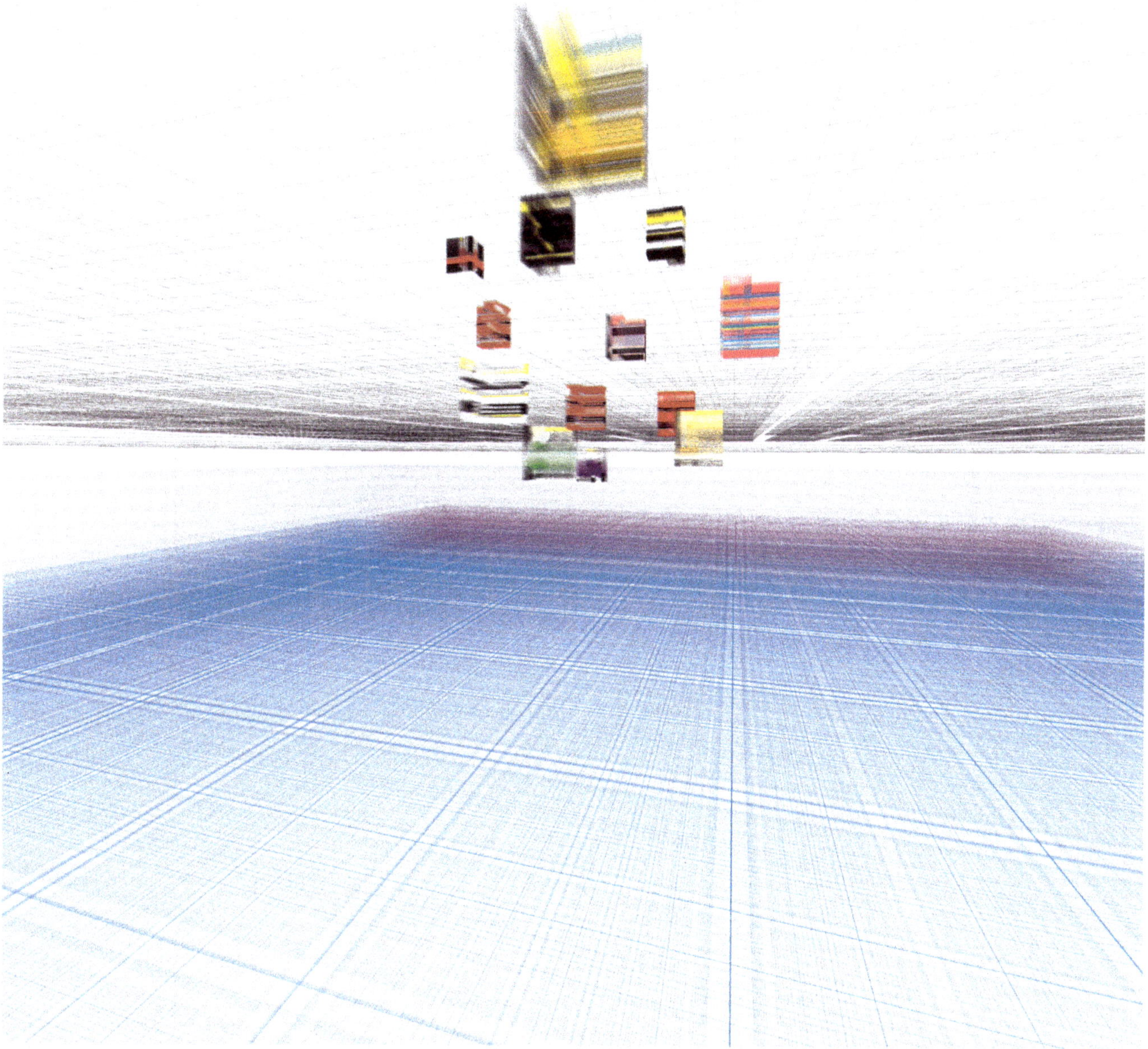

SINKING UPWARDS, electronic model, view

ASCEND DOWN, electronic model, view

THEY ARE FLOWN, electronic model, view

2.1.8 - A Small Inclination of the Support

Working with the dimensions derived from the NNG a number of trial units were been made. The problem of the support was greatly reduced by introduction of a small inclination of the support frame. The incline produced a gap between AIR Grid lattice and support, making it less likely that living being would read properties of the support into properties of the lattice. But it is impossible to achieve a one-hundred-percent separation of lattice and support, they are bound together in the nature of what an AIR Grid structure actually is, but the functional necessity of the bond depends on the laws of gravity rather than vision. Vertical alignment of grid and support is not essential to gravitational resistance. With the introduction of a slight incline into the AIR Grid support the vertical alignment of the AIR Grid lattice planes could now be identified as a property of the lattice, independently of the support.

A SMALL INCLINATION OF THE SUPPORT, foamboard, embroidery thread, approx., 54 x 54 x 60 cm

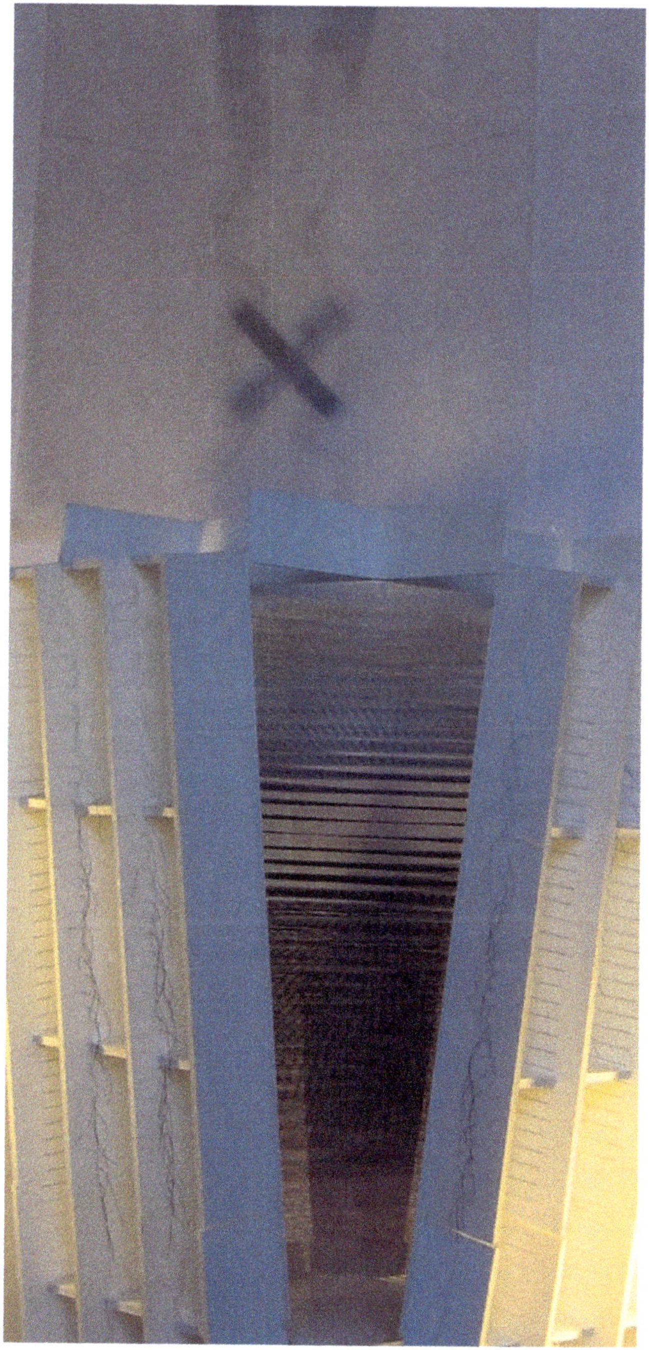

2.2: THE COTTON CAVES

Armed now with the confidence and understanding necessary to work with AIR Grid it was time to start using it. Of the two protagonists who had fuelled the thesis argument, Mies and Lefebvre, the former had so far played a more significant role in the invention of AIR Grid than the latter. However, with the question of how to use it, the thinking of the latter now came into play. Recollect Lefebvre's dismay as he looked down on the new town. He saw it as pure system, a place with no meaningful space of representation. Recollect his profound experience of the Sagrada Familia. In what follows Lefebvrian dismay is appropriated in an attempt to convey what was missing from the new town.

The sequence of research, intuition and experiment that led to the creation of AIR Grid was not the justification of AIR Grid. Although AIR Grid is inextricable from the circumstances of its discovery, it is not reducible to them. Irrespective of its Miesian origin, AIR Grid can be deployed independently as a means of activating space. AIR Grid has the potential to activate space thanks to its tendency to bifurcate between: 1. an array of parallel planes, 2. a volume of mist. There are moments when AIR Grid appears to be all planes and no mist and there are moments when it appears to be all mist. There are also moments where it appears to be both, at one and the same time.

The bifurcating of AIR Grid depends on the presence of living being. It is living being who switches AIR Grid back and forth between the two moments. This effect is due to living being's innate sense of the laws of space, which are not laws that have been learnt but immanent to all living bodies. In the switching of AIR Grid, living being senses something of itself, something that seems primal, fundamental and locked up inside.

To conclude this research it is proposed to deploy AIR Grid in the creation of a series of caves, which will be called Cotton Caves. The caves are to be located in the dells that circumscribe the new town of Stevenage. Stevenage was one of the eight new towns proposed by the Greater London Plan of 1944. The ambition for each new town was that it would each provide a community in which 60,000 people could live and work. The village of Stevenage became the first designated new town in 1946. Recollect Lefebvre's question as he looked down on the new town of Mourenx:

Will people be compliant and do what the plan expects them to do, shopping in the shopping centre, asking for advice in the advice bureau, doing everything the civic centre offices demand of them like good, reliable citizens?.....Can spontaneity be revitalized here, can a community be created?[1]

Some sixty years into the future, in the now not so new

town of Stevenage, the answer to Lefebvre's question is yes; people do shop in the shopping centre, they do tend to seek advice in the advice bureau and they do tend to comply to the demands of the civic centre offices, like good, reliable citizens. All of which, in itself, Lefebvre would have regarded in a positive light, functionalism does have its benefits. But, Lefebvre would want to know: does anything else ever happen?

The purpose of the Cotton Caves is to provide a place where the people of Stevenage and visitors to the town, can come to search for AIR Grid and enjoy the experience of AIR Grid when it is found. The search and experience will involve anticipation and delight, rather like searching for crystals, precious stones, gorgeously coloured species of birds and insects. It is envisioned that the Cotton Caves will have a fairy-tale effect on the minds and the imaginations of the people who visit them, in some cases prompting exhilaration and mild feelings of giddiness.

The extent of the caves is potentially endless since new chambers can be added at any time. However, it is necessary to start digging somewhere. It is proposed the first entry point and chamber will be built to the north of the new town, located under the chalk berm that cuts from east to west across a gently sloping field near Crow End, this will be called Cotton Cave 01.

Cotton Cave 01 will serve as the operational headquarters for the construction, maintenance and management of the Cotton Caves. For this reason, in addition to the grid chambers that will be common to all Cotton Caves (see below), Cotton Cave 01 will be equipped with all the facilities necessary to support the headquarter function. These will include: cooking and eating facilities, sleeping facilities, cleansing facilities, a drawing office, studio space, materials store, temporary storage for grid support units, lighting store.

A grid chamber is an ovoidal space into which an assembly of AIR Grid structures can be sewn, the inner surface is painted matt black. Grid support is facilitated by preformed, standard units of black polyurethane which come in a range of sizes designed to suit specific AIR Grid configurations, corresponding to the range of sizes distilled out of the ambience of the NNG (see above). The polyurethane unit is a single, seamless, entity presenting four identical surfaces, in parallel facing pairs, between which AIR Grid can be sewn. Each surface is marked by a raised panel (approximately five millimetres). The raised panel marks out and identifies the sewing field of a particular surface. The sewing field is coated in a fine layer of Cotton Cave Chalk Polymer (CCCP).

CCCP is an emulsion based artificial resin consisting of a fifty-to-fifty mixture of calcium carbonate and titanium oxide, which are cold mixed in a dilute solution of polyvinyl acetate fixative. The coating of CCCP is intended to give to the sewing field a matt white finish, making it appear as a floating white plain.

Located on the sewing field is the grid of holes, at one centimetre centres, through which AIR Grid will be sewn. The back of the grid support is profiled to provide vertical ribs. These are slit with fine incisions, at one centimetre centres, corresponding to the cadence of the grid of holes. The purpose of the slits is to grasp the ends of the threads and hold the lattice taut. The vertical ribs are spaced so as to deliver grids whose sizes correspond to the range distilled out of the ambience of the NNG. The support structure of the smallest grid (6, 6, 15) consists of one bay, it is determined by two ribs at seven centimetre centres, the next size up (12, 12, 30) has three ribs, two of the ribs comprise a seven centimetre bay, two of them comprise a bay of six centimetres. Further increments of six centimetre bays delivers all the required support sizes. Once the grid has been sewn into the support structure the total assembly can be fixed to the upper surface of the level portion of the ovoidal grid chamber.

It is intended that lighting will be directed from the outer layer of the grid chamber, onto the surface of the sewing field, however since it is likely that living being will want to experiment with the lighting arrangements the installed fittings will be easy to move and adjust, consisting of free-standing spot lamps and projectors on adjustable trolleys.

The schema for sewing AIR Grid structures into any particular grid chamber will be determined by living being. Four factors influence the range of possible sewing configurations. First, the grid sizes. Because the range of possible sizes corresponds to the range of sizes distilled out of the ambience of the NNG, so there are eight possible sizes of AIR Grid (6,6,15); (12,12,30); (18,18,45); (24,24,60); (30,30,75); (36,36,90); (42,42,105); (48,48,120).

Second, the grid colours. In the experimental AIR Grid work conducted by the researcher it has been shown that the greatest mist effect is achieved by sewing to a colour base. Sewing to a colour base does not mean that the entirety of the AIR Grid is sewn out of thread of a single colour. Sewing to a colour base involves the selection of a range of threads whose colour is closely related on the colour spectrum, for example a blue base might involve the selection of a range of threads from cyan to ultraviolet. Subsequent prioritization of the amount of cyan would give to this AIR Grid a distinct blueness which, had violet been prioritised, would be blueness of a very different kind.

Bold colour contrast is not recommended as a strategy

for determining AIR Grid colour, it tends to fragment the lattice; however; the introduction of small, barely perceptible areas of colour contrast can have a wonderful effect. Just as living being enjoys the feeling that it is they who are switching the AIR Grid back and forth so, when the subtle contrast of colour appears, they cannot be certain if it is a property of AIR Grid or if it is they who have made it appear (this is because colour is a relational property, the explanation of which is beyond the scope of this thesis).

Third, the angular and dimensional relationships between the different AIR Grid structures in a particular grid chamber. Clearly, the gathering of a variety of differently sized and differently coloured grids into a single chamber will produce extraordinary effects. Strategies for predicting particular effects due to angular and dimensional relationships can only be arrived at through empirical experimentation and observation, here there is scope for further research.

Fourth, the precise shape of any particular grid chamber. Although the generic module of the grid chamber is two-point-four metres and the radius of curvature is one-point-two metres, the precise number and configuration of modules will vary from one chamber to another. The extent and arrangement of modules of any particular chamber will influence the sewing strategy adopted for that chamber. What is more, differences between the extent and arrangement of modules of particular chambers will influence the sewing strategy adopted between chambers. The spatial logic of Cotton Caves is such that the grid chamber is best understood as a space, or a sequence of spaces, set inside the excavated space of the cave. This offers the potential for a wide range of different journeys and modes of occupancy of the Cotton Caves. In fact there is such a variety of possibilities built into the project of the Cotton Caves that it is hard to imagine ever exhausting the entire range.

SIGNAGE INDICATES THE WAY TO THE COTTON CAVES, electronicmontage, 15 x 15 x 80 dpi

Public Brid
Cotton
Caves
Cotton
Caves
Hertfordshire Way

ENVELOPED IN THE GREY MISTS OF A GREY DAY, view of Stevenage new town with hospital and pylons, digital photograph, 15 x 7.5 x 110 dpi

LOCATION OF COTTON CAVE 01, gently slopping field with chalk berm, Crow End, Stevenage, digital photograph, 15 x 7.5 x 110 dpi

COTTON CAVE 01, site plan, electronic drawing, 50 dpi @ scale 1:1000

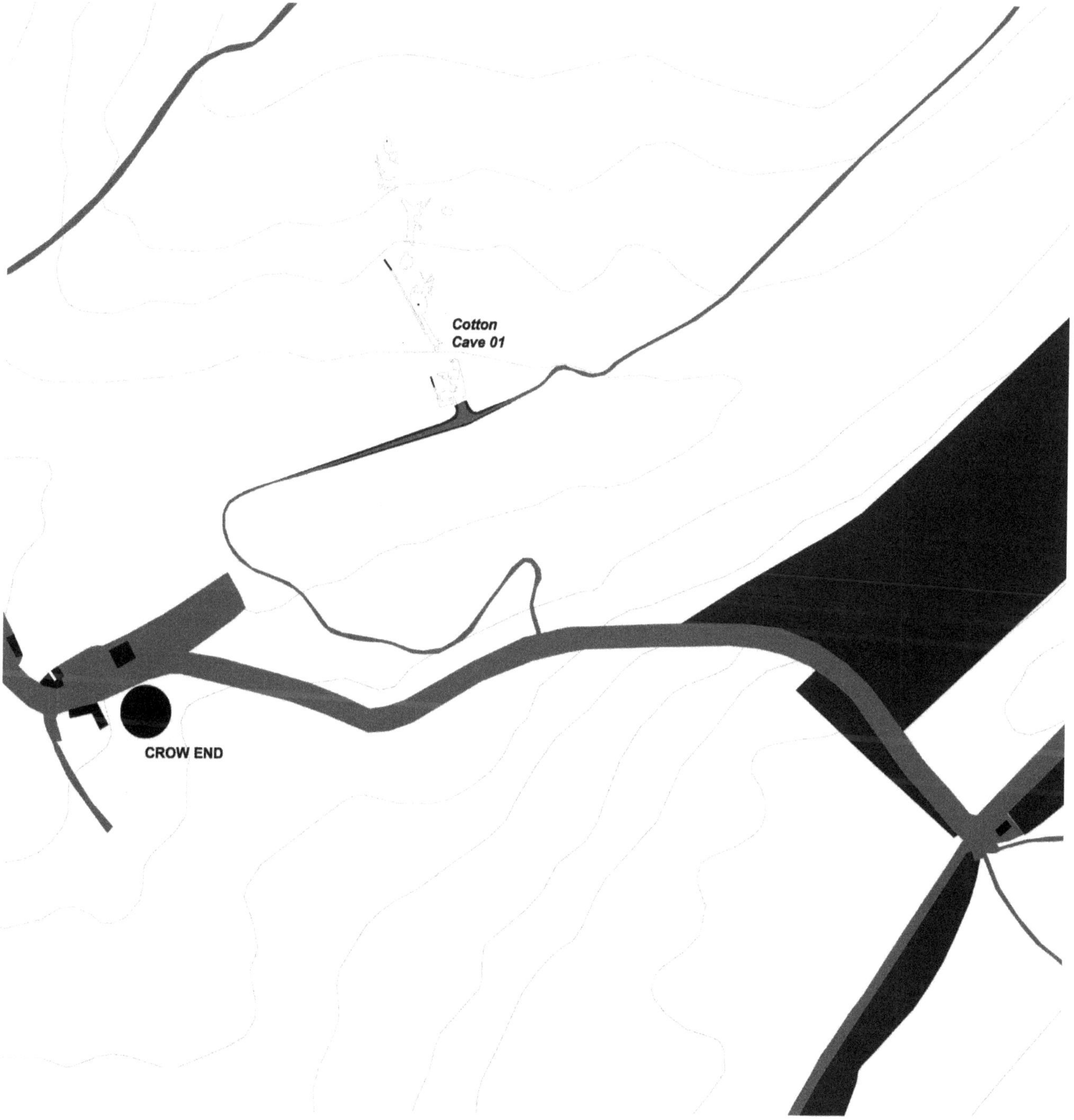
Cotton
Cave 01
CROW END

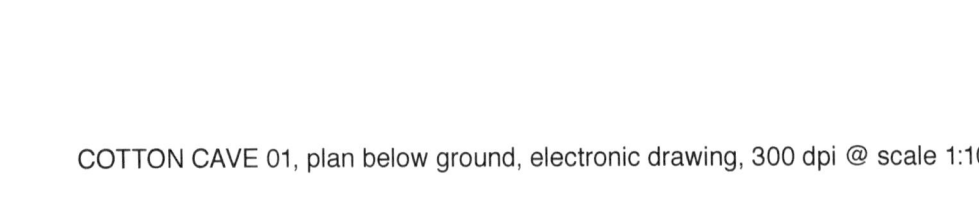

COTTON CAVE 01, plan below ground, electronic drawing, 300 dpi @ scale 1:100

A
A

COTTON CAVE 01, section AA, electronic drawing, 300 dpi @ scale 1:100

DETAIL, goods entrance and house of living being

DETAIL, sequence of grid chambers & anti-chamber

DETAIL, junction of two grid chamber sequences and tunnel

DETAIL, material & equipment store and experimentation cavern

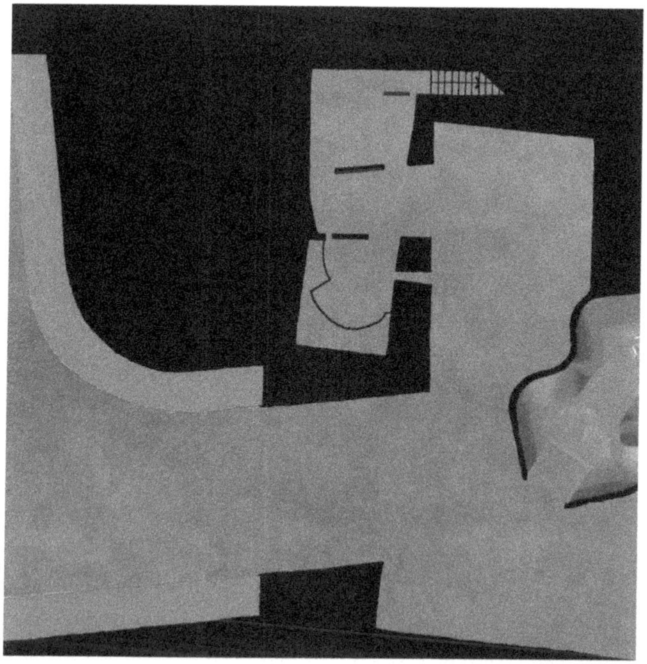

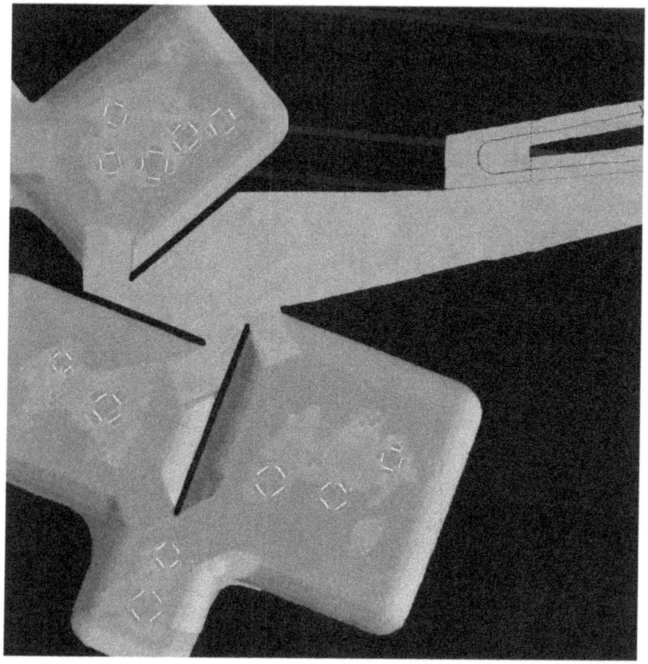
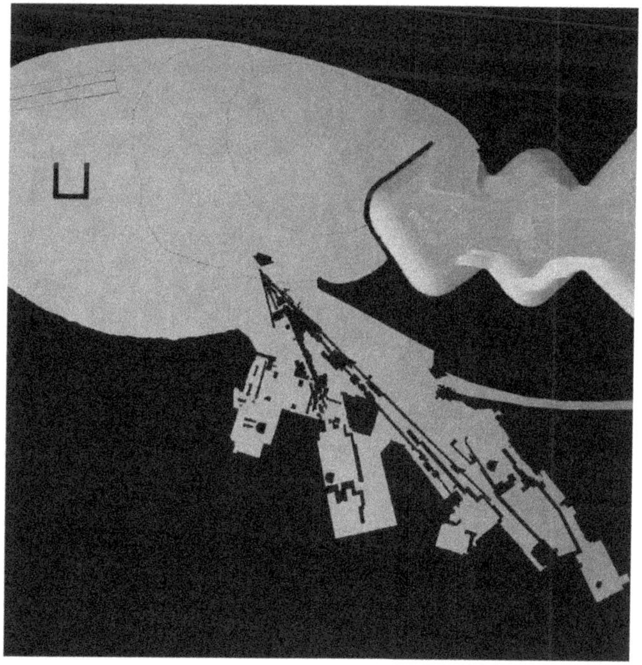

DETAIL, house of living being and underground goods yard

DETAIL, sequence of grid chambers & anti-chamber

DETAIL, tunnel and shaft to experimentation cavern

DETAIL, junction of experimentation cavern and grid chamber sequence

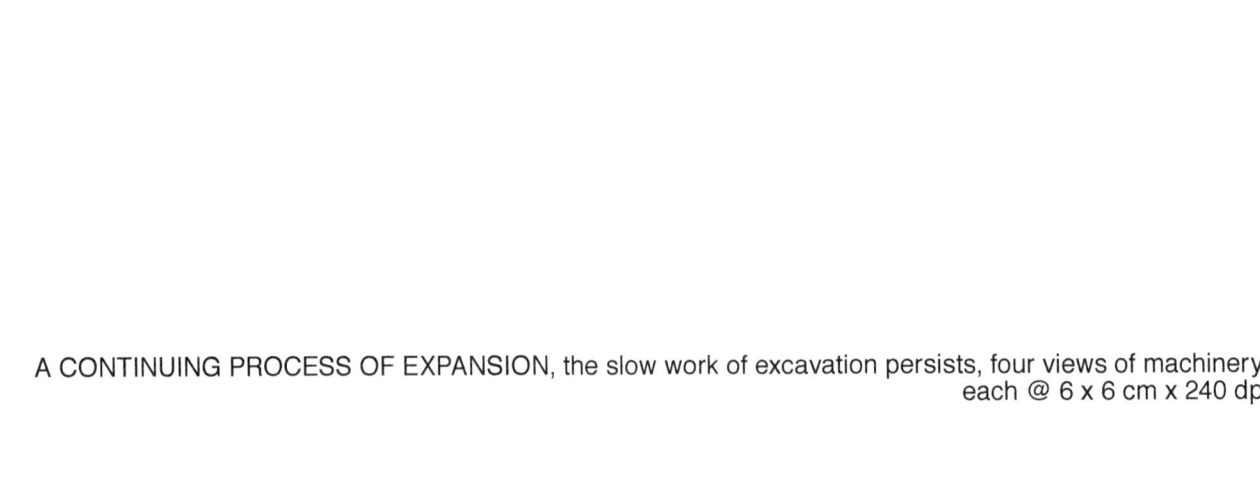

A CONTINUING PROCESS OF EXPANSION, the slow work of excavation persists, four views of machinery, each @ 6 x 6 cm x 240 dpi

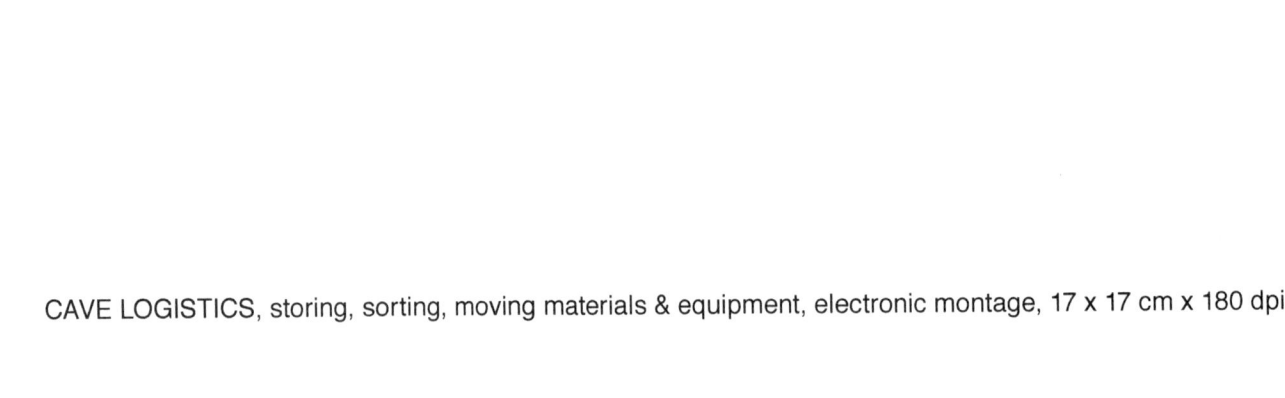

CAVE LOGISTICS, storing, sorting, moving materials & equipment, electronic montage, 17 x 17 cm x 180 dpi

BULK STORAGE, embroidery thread, calcium carbonate, grid support units, electronicmontage,
17 x 17 cm x 180 dpi

GRID CONSTRUCTION MANUAL, sample page, diagram A, electronic vector drawing

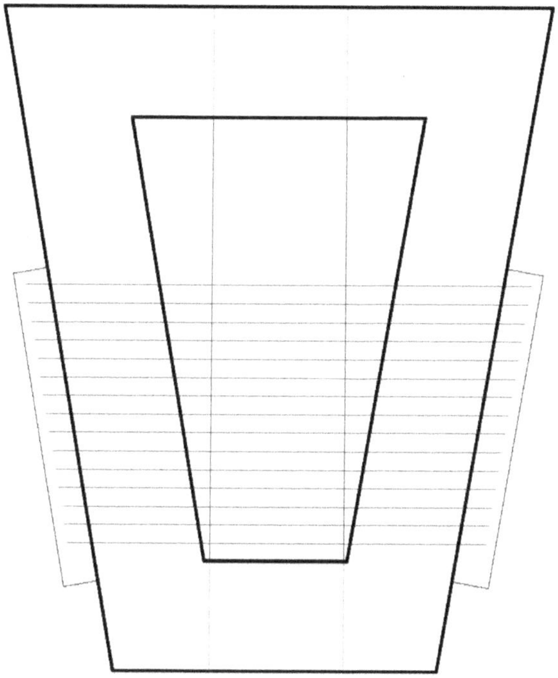

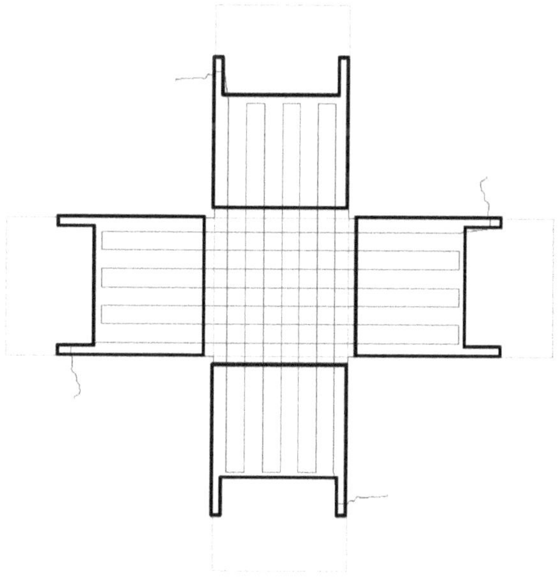

GRID CONSTRUCTION MANUAL, sample page, diagram O, electronic vector drawing

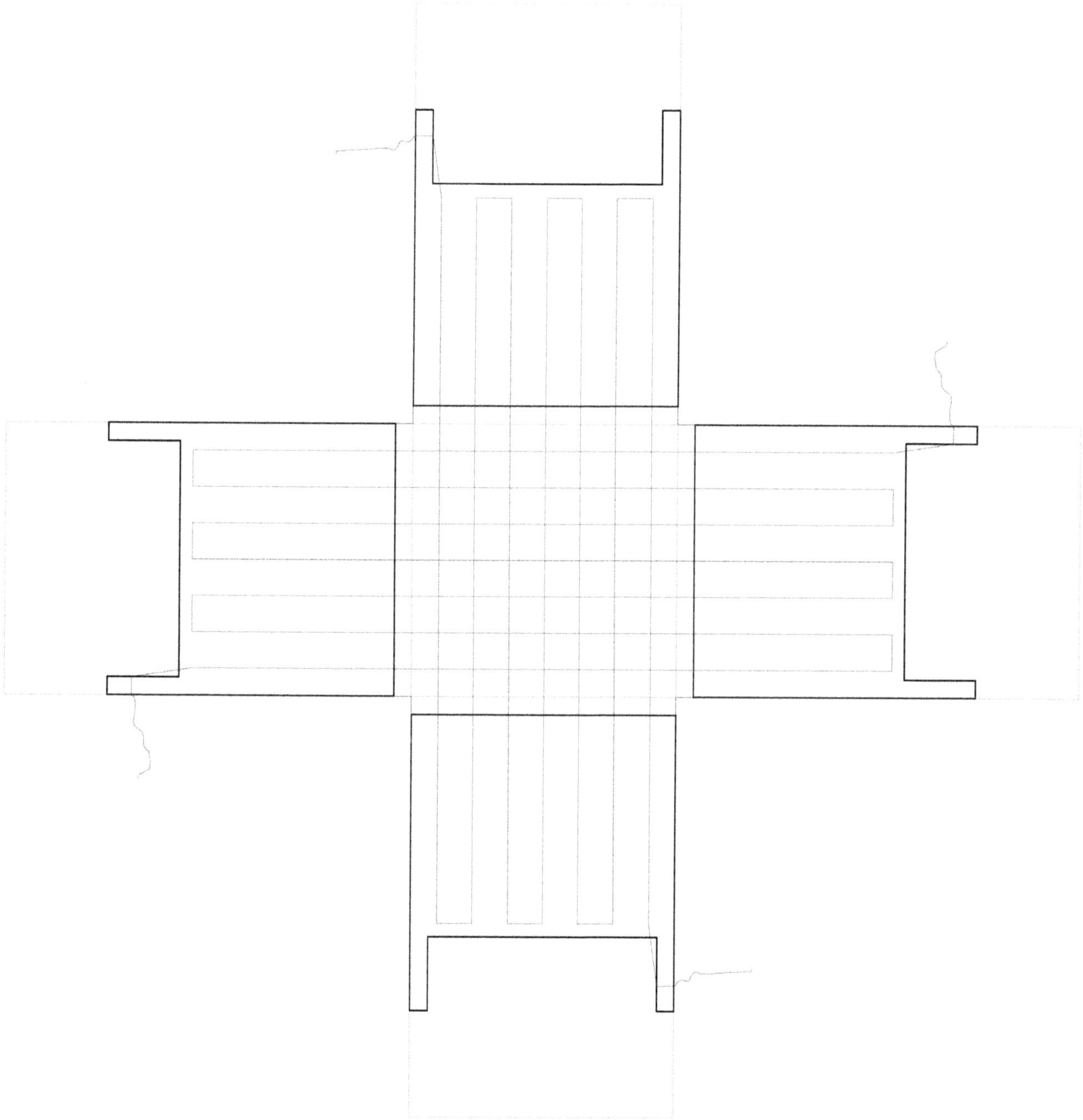

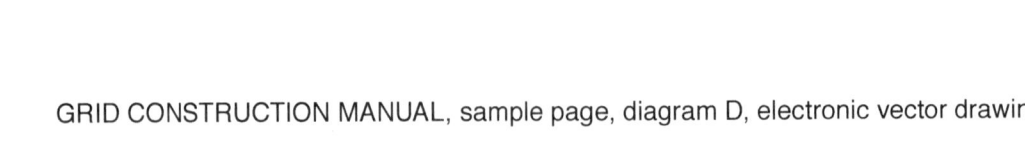

GRID CONSTRUCTION MANUAL, sample page, diagram D, electronic vector drawing

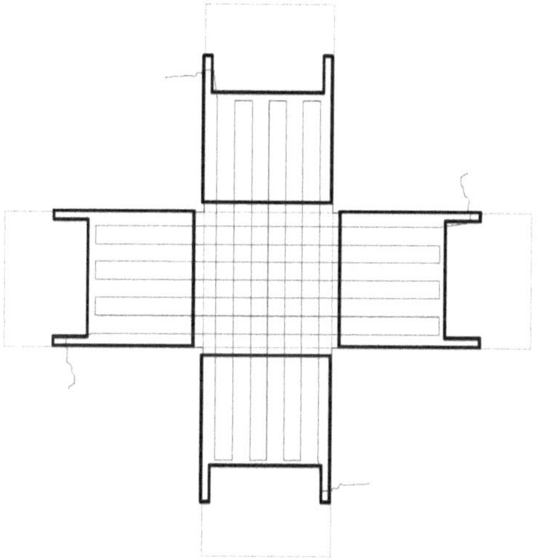

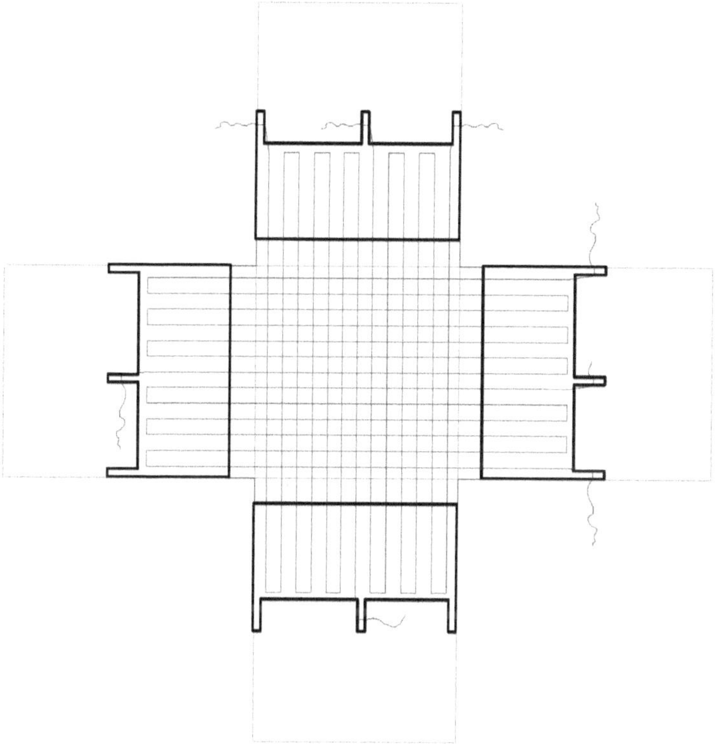

GRID CONSTRUCTION MANUAL, sample page, diagram G, electronic vector drawing

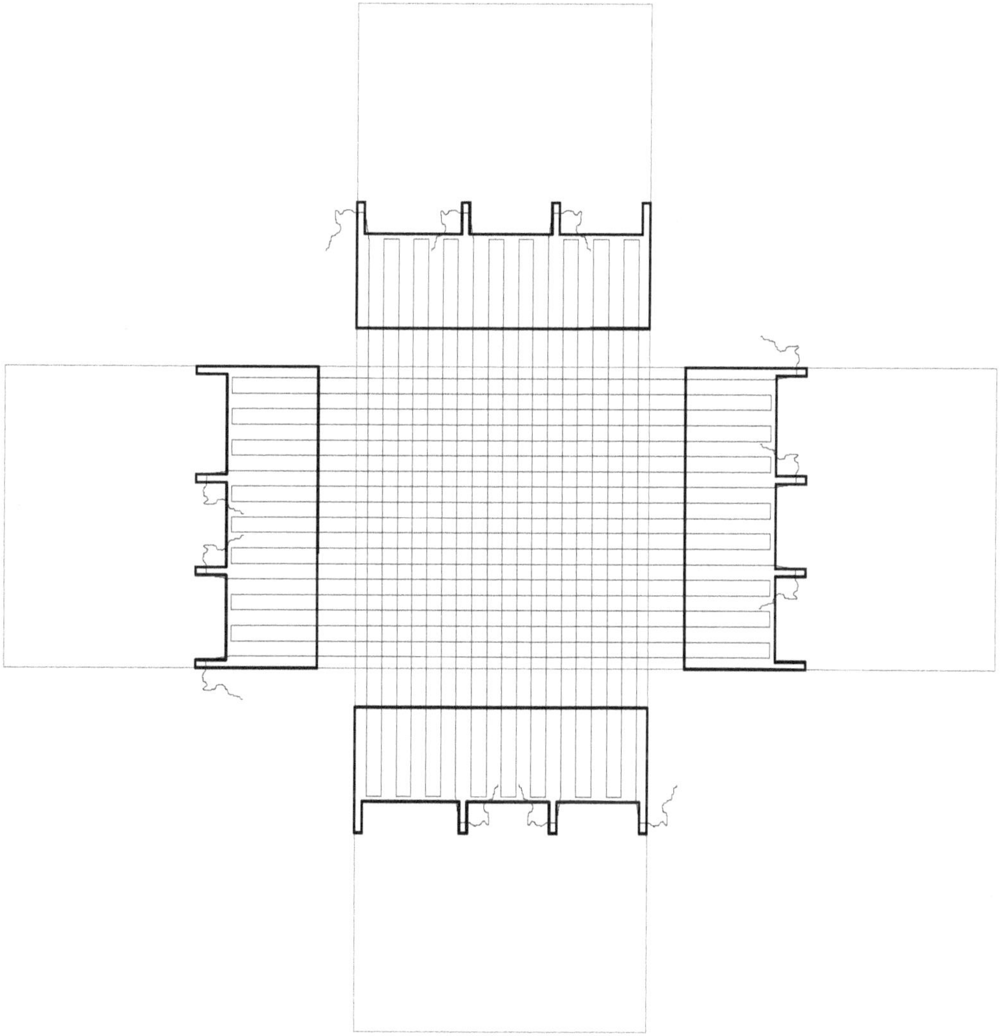

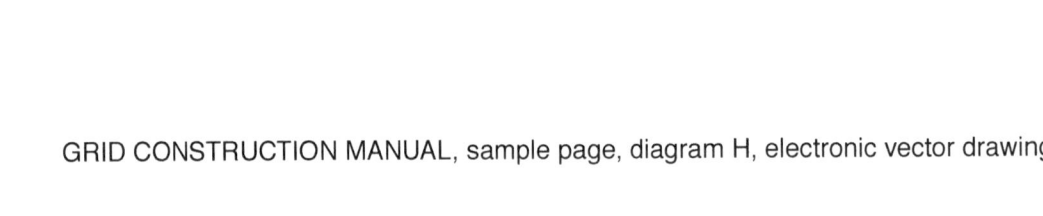

GRID CONSTRUCTION MANUAL, sample page, diagram H, electronic vector drawing

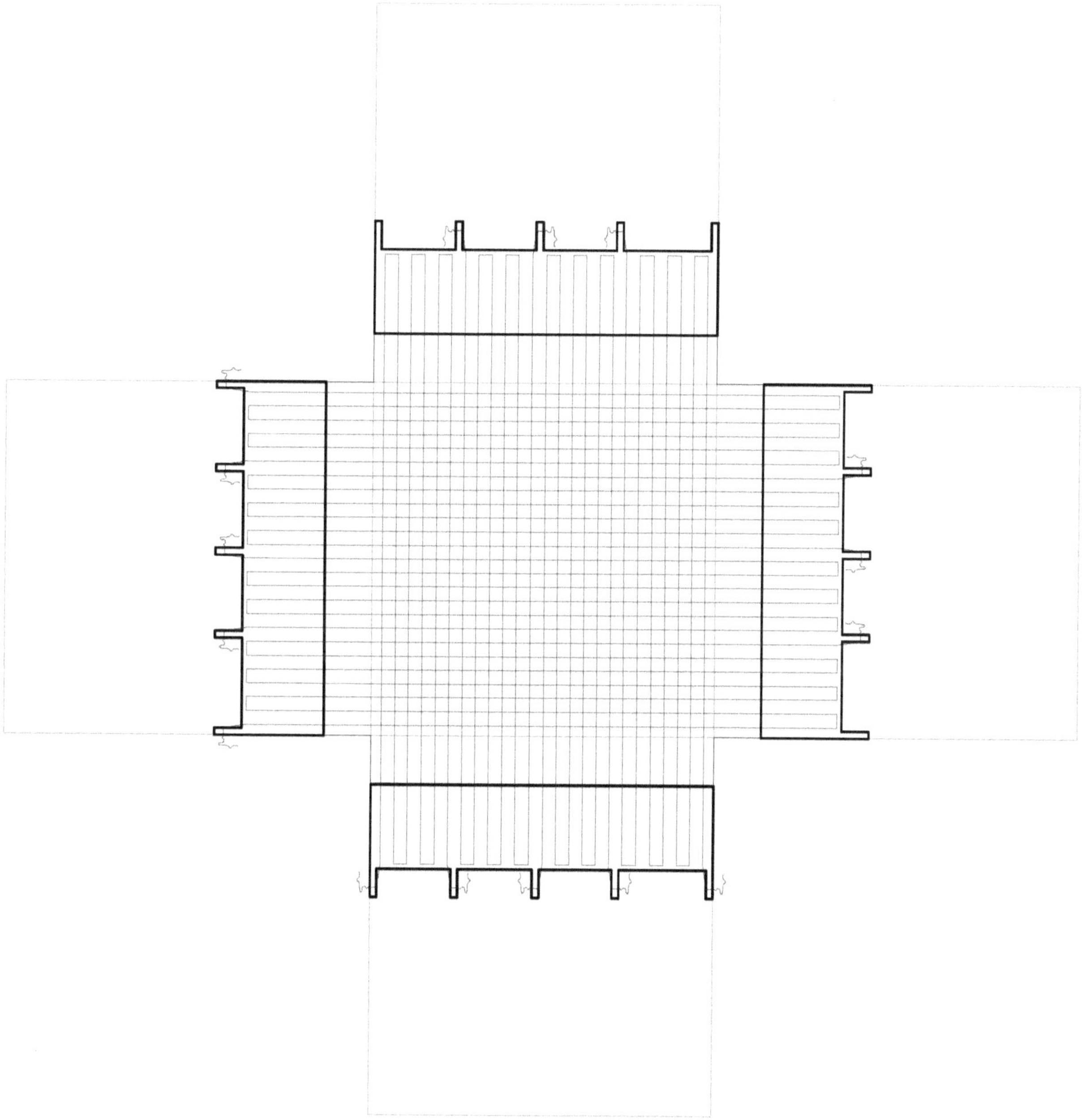

GRID CONSTRUCTION MANUAL, sample page, diagram P, electronic vector drawing

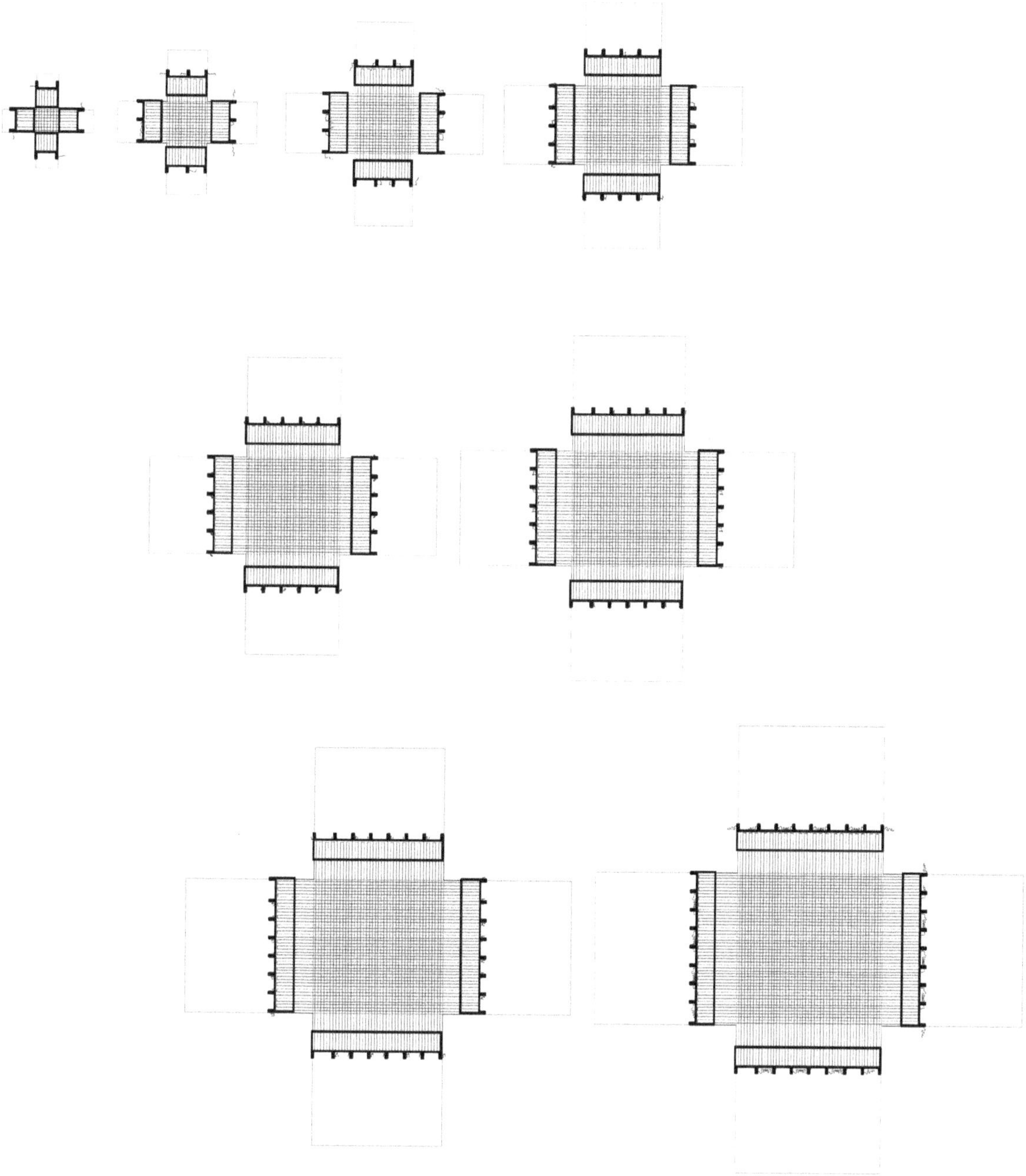

GRID CONSTRUCTION MANUAL, sample page, diagram W^1, electronic vector drawing

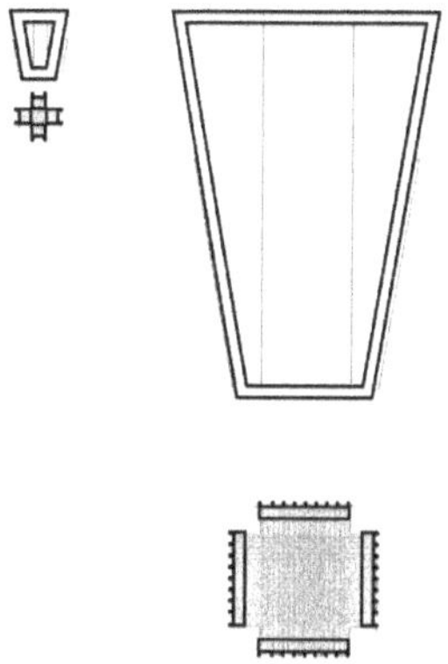

GRID CONSTRUCTION MANUAL, sample page, diagram W^5, electronic vector drawing

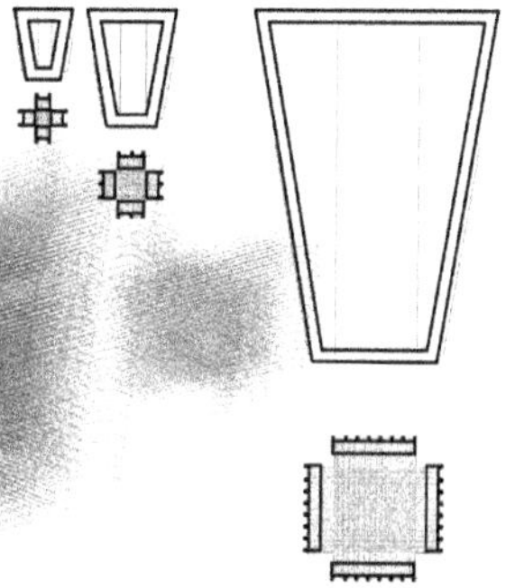

GRID CONSTRUCTION MANUAL, sample page, diagram W^7, electronic vector drawing

GRID CONSTRUCTION MANUAL, sample page, diagram W[8], electronic vector drawing

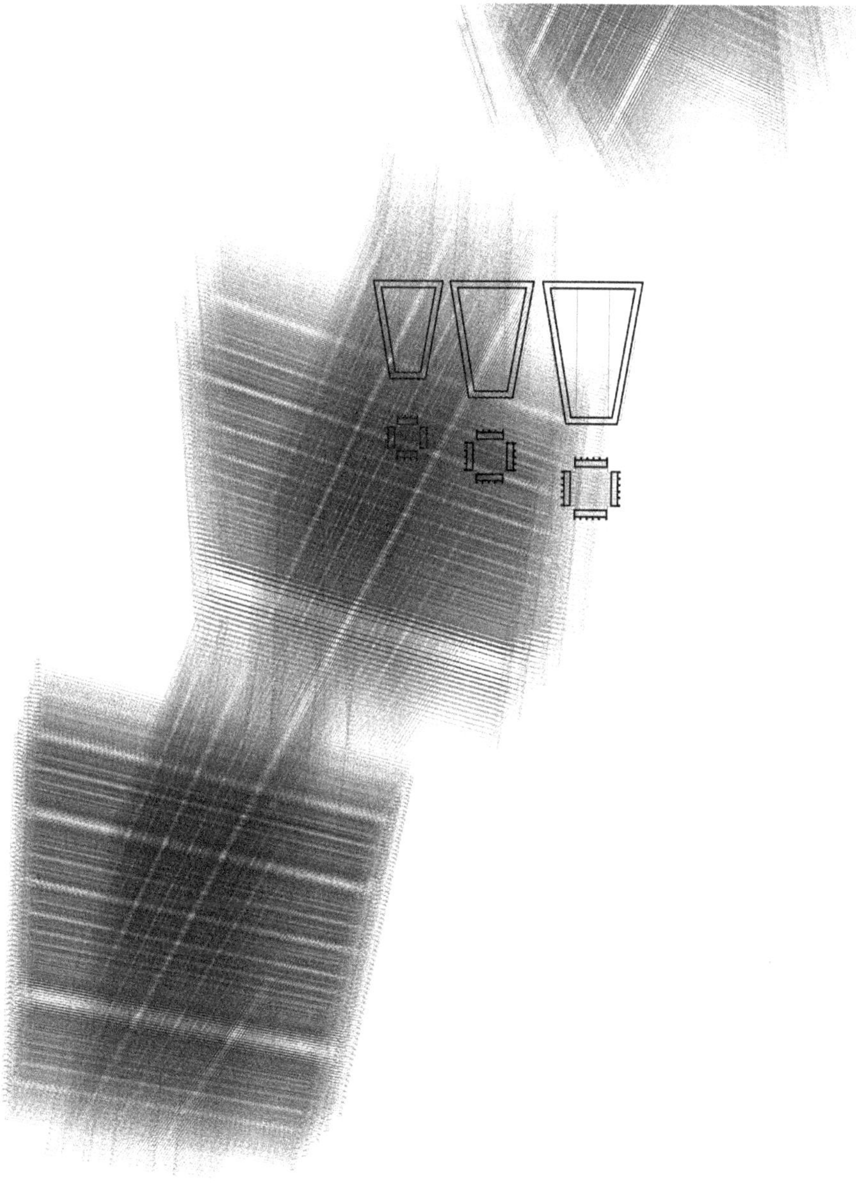

AIR (nee COTTON) GRID LIGHT, electronic model, views 01-04

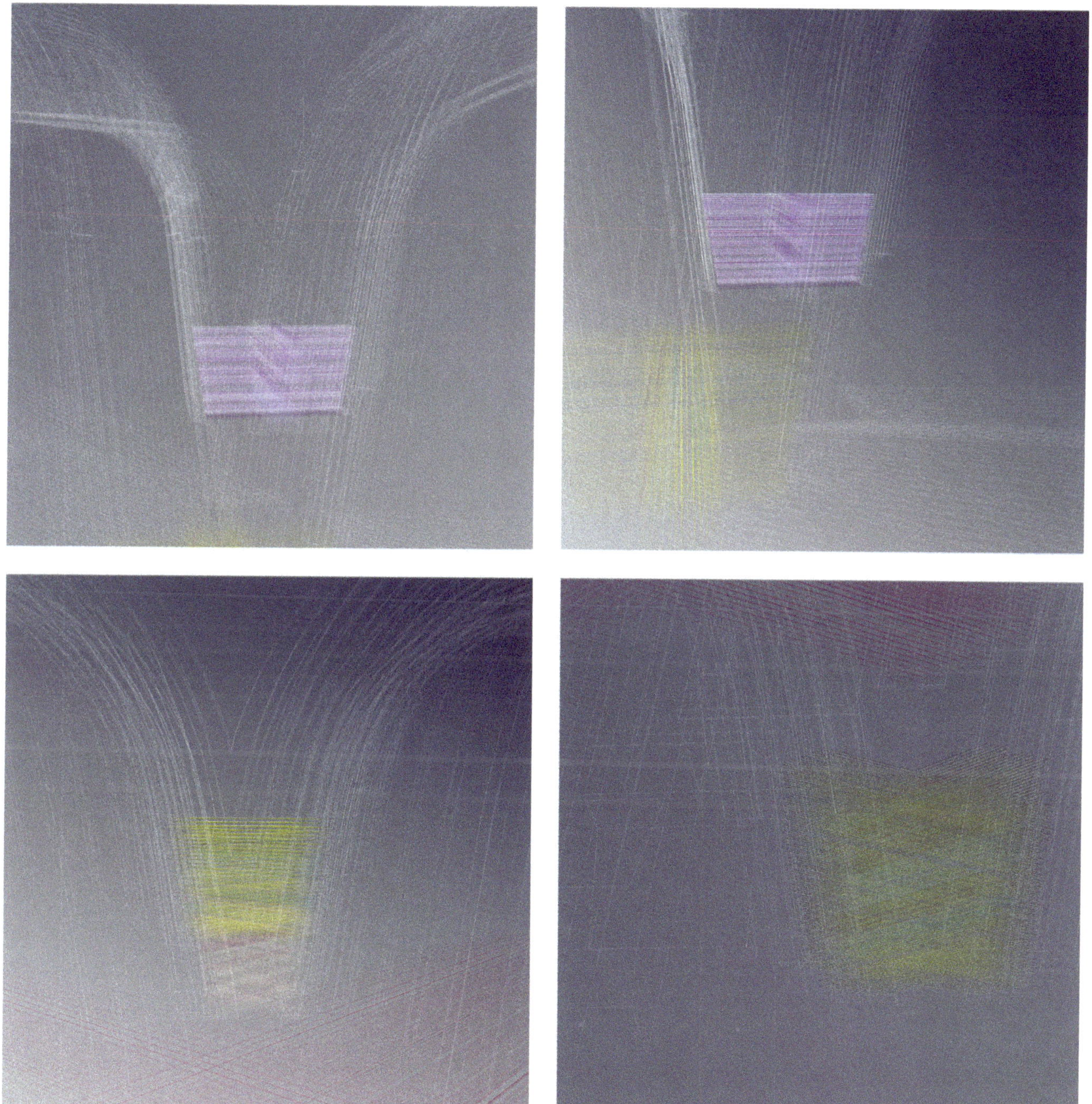

AIR (nee COTTON) GRID LIGHT, electronic model, views 05-08

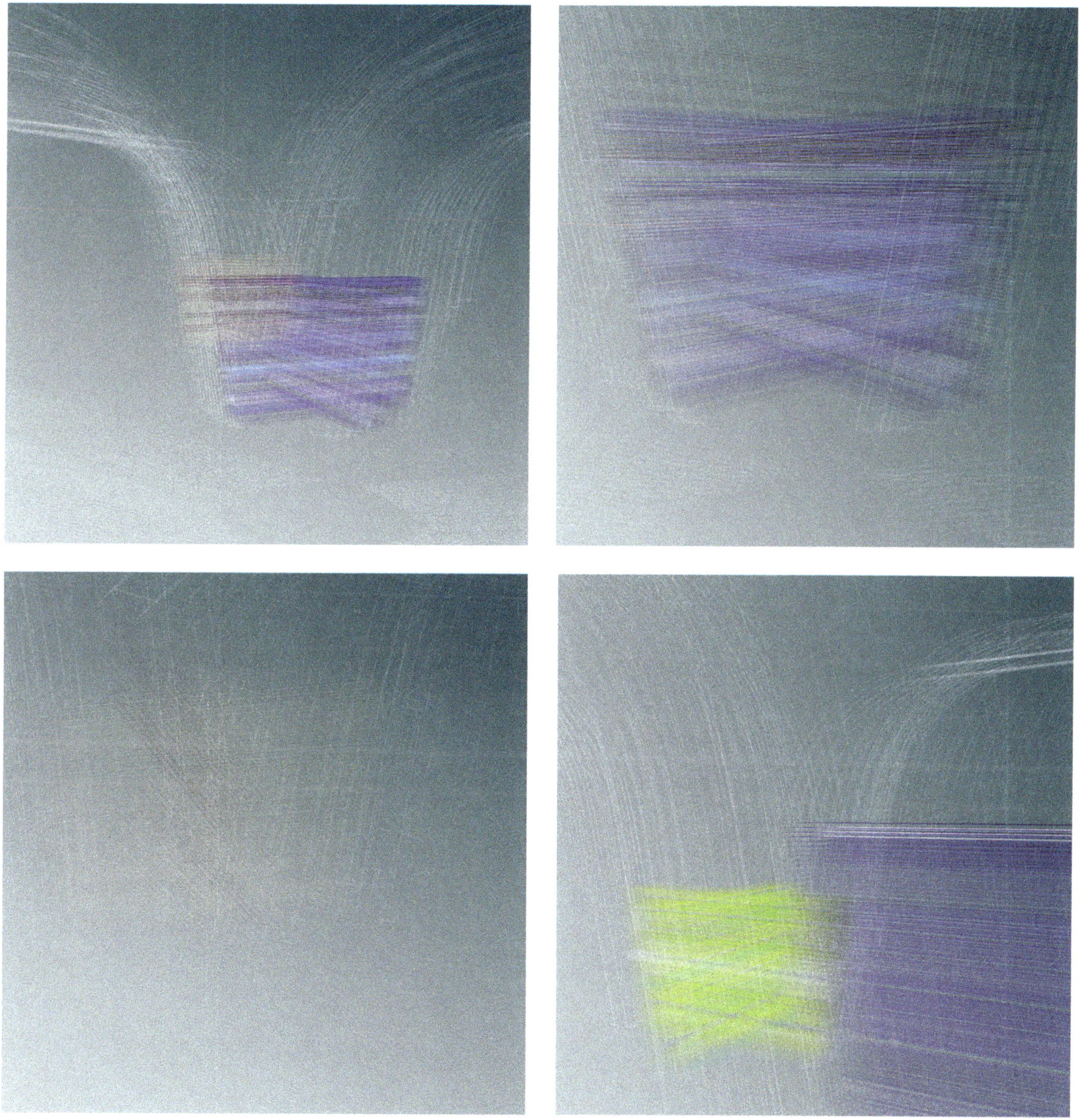

AIR (nee COTTON) GRID LIGHT, electronic model, views 09-12

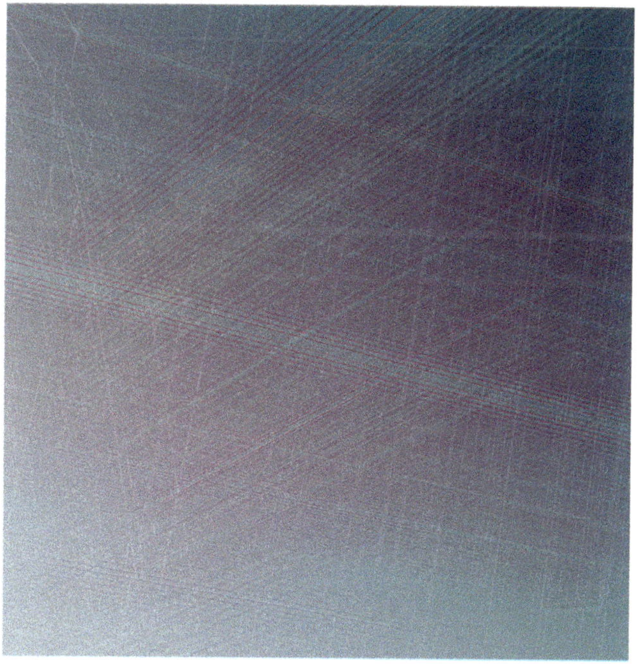

AIR (nee COTTON) GRID LIGHT, electronic model, views 13-16

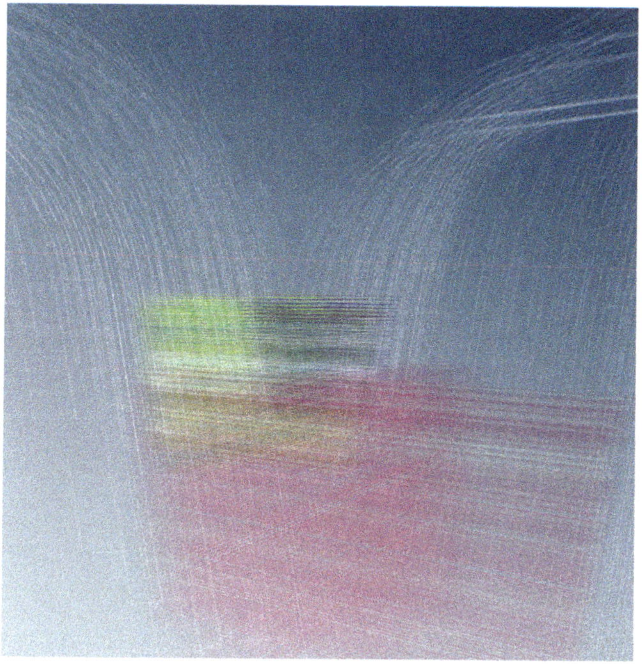

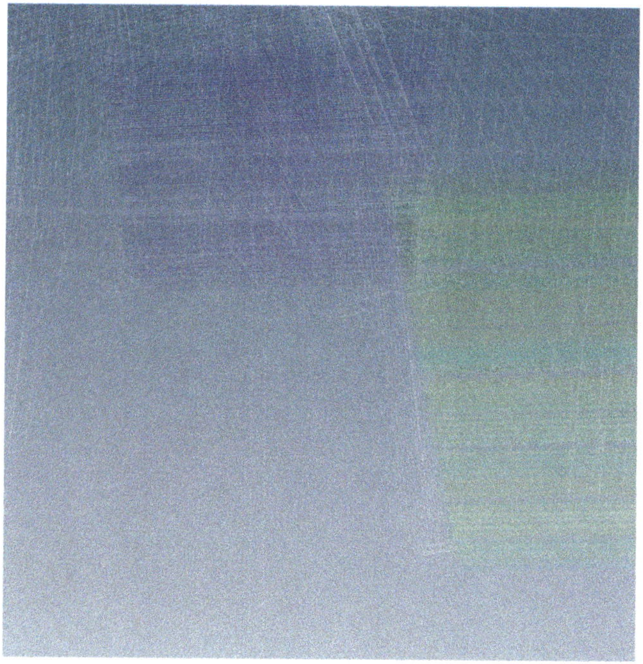
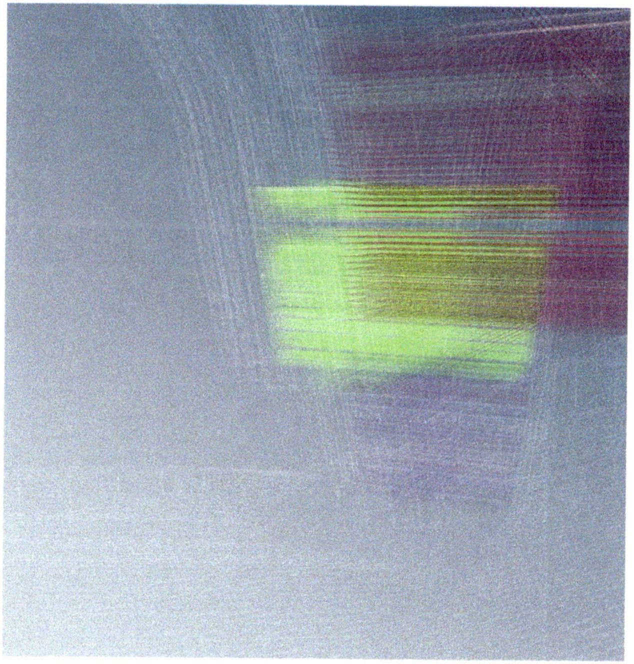

AIR (nee COTTON) GRID LIGHT, electronic model, views 17-20

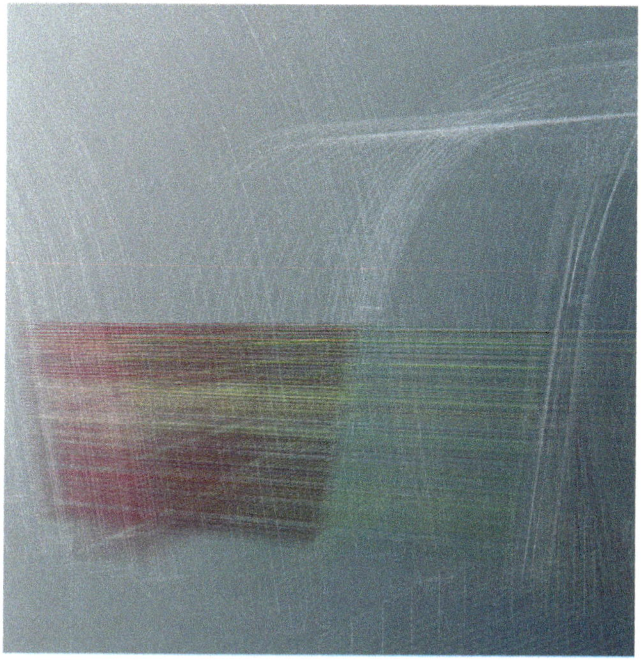

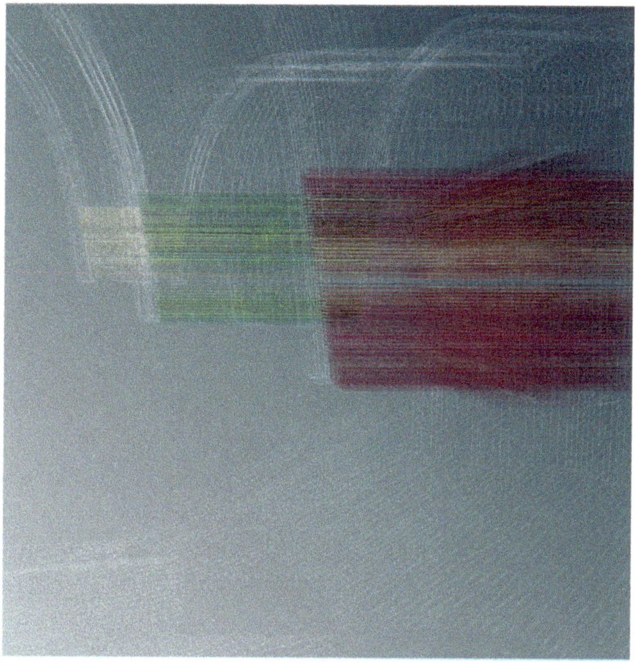

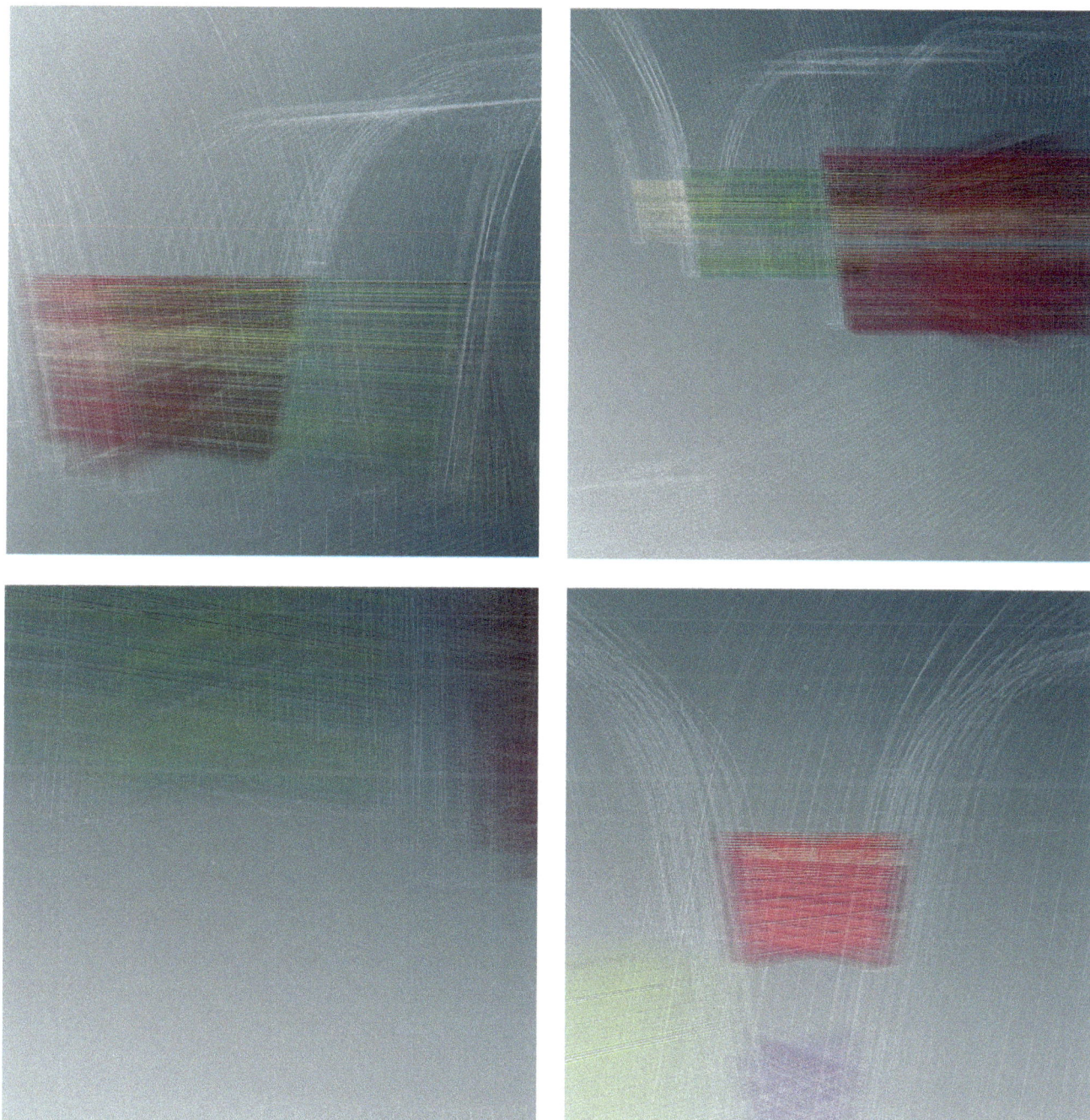

AIR (nee COTTON) GRID LIGHT, electronic model, views 21-24

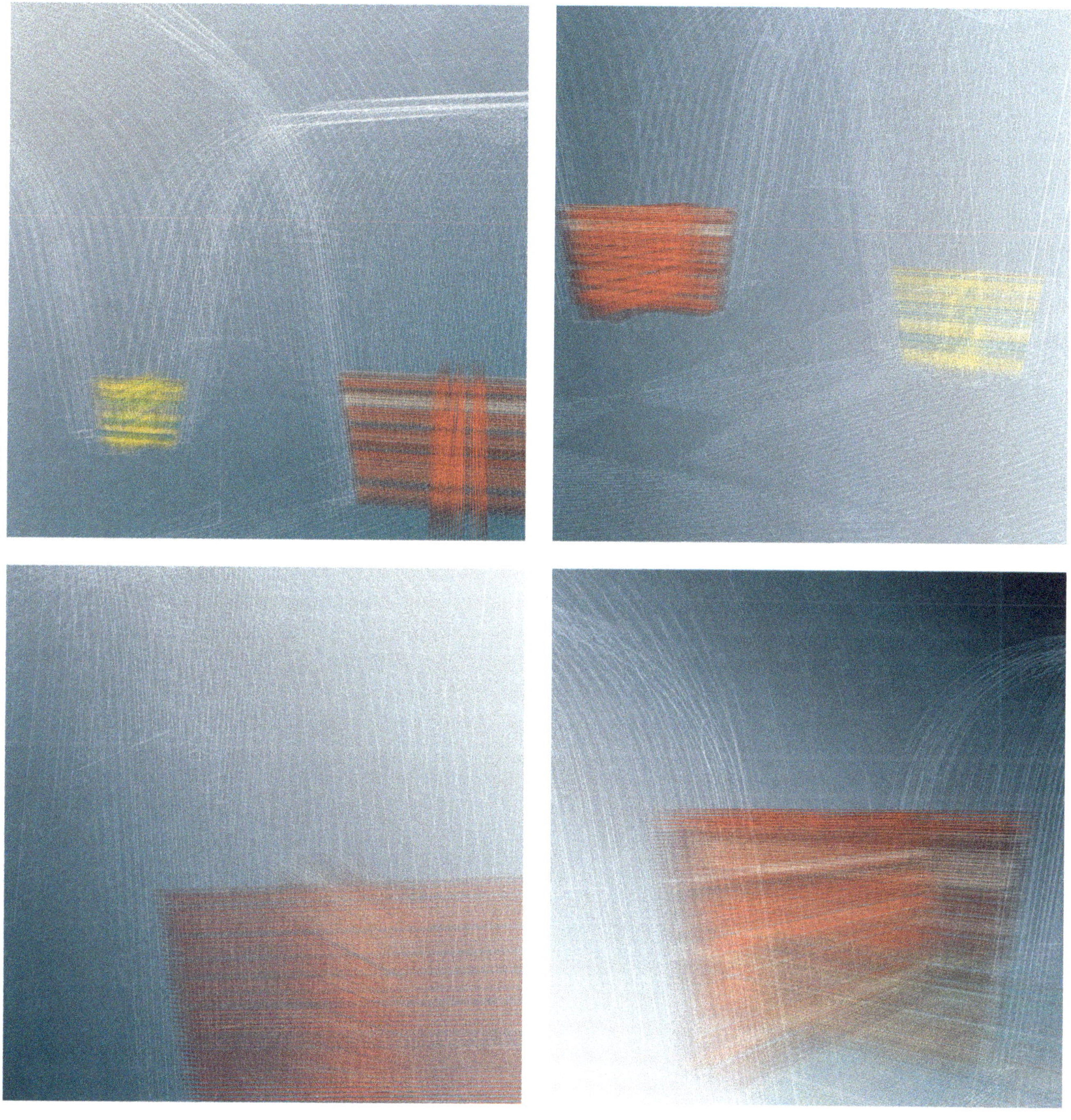

AIR (nee COTTON) GRID LIGHT, electronic model, views 25-28

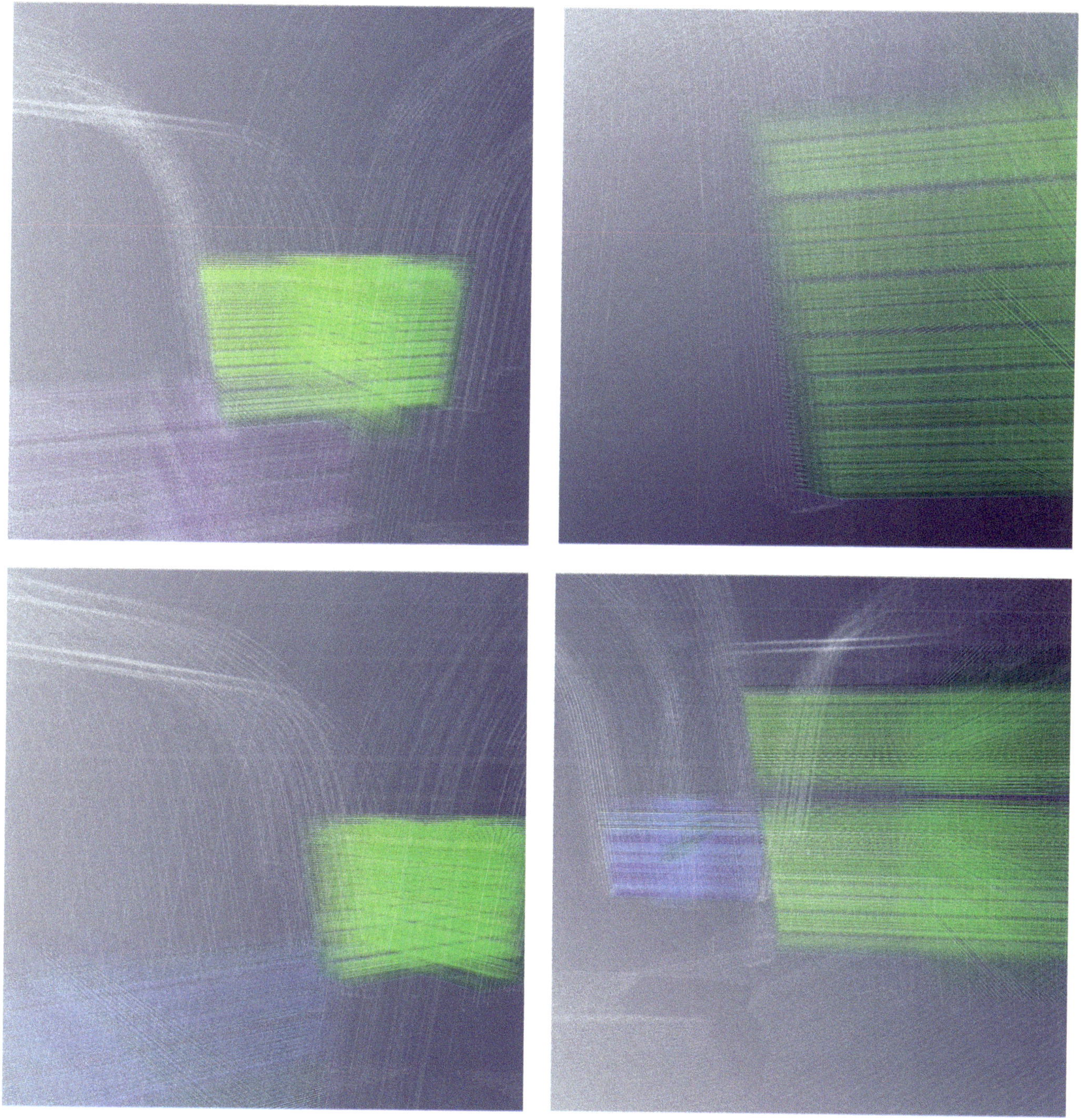

AIR (nee COTTON) GRID LIGHT, electronic model, views 29-32

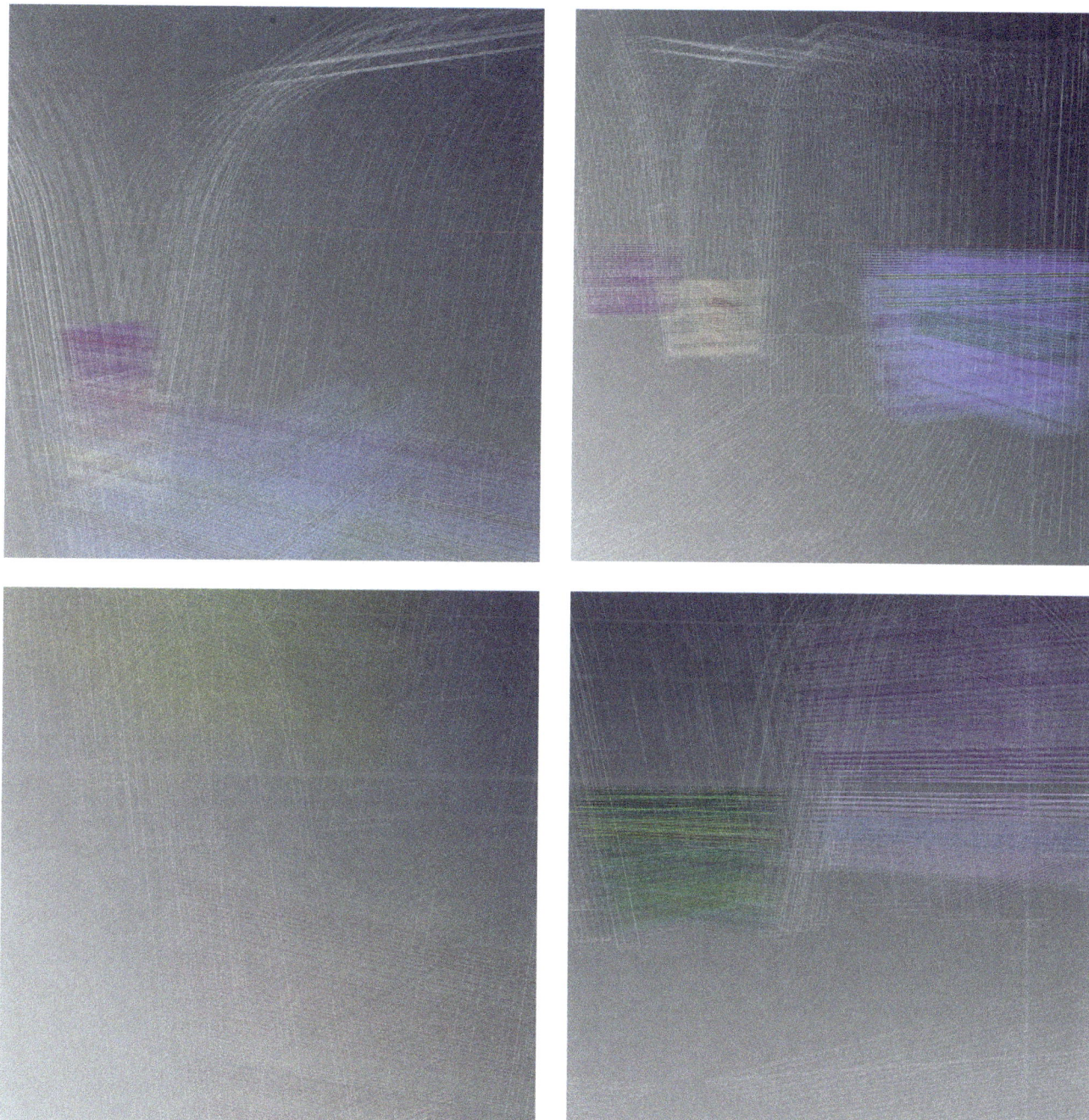

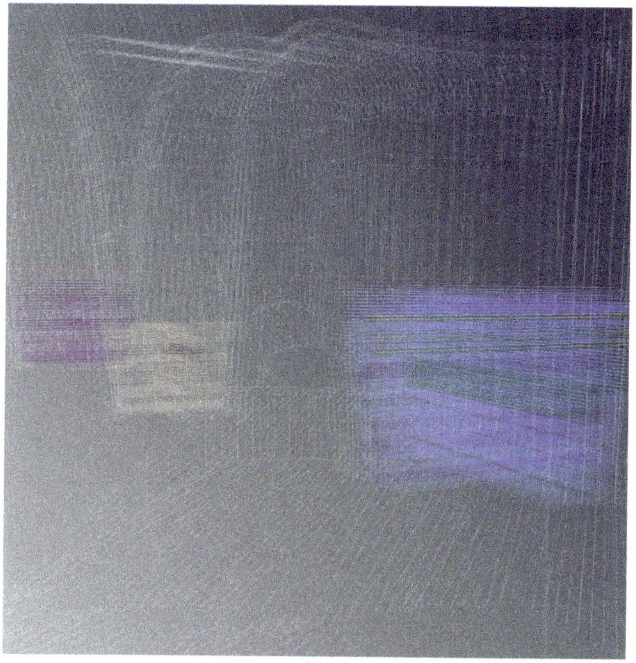

AIR (nee COTTON) GRID LIGHT, electronic model, views 33-36

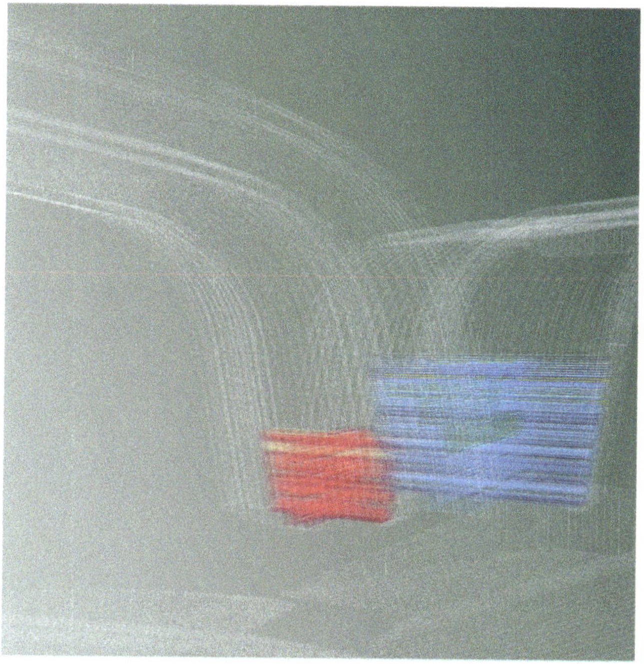
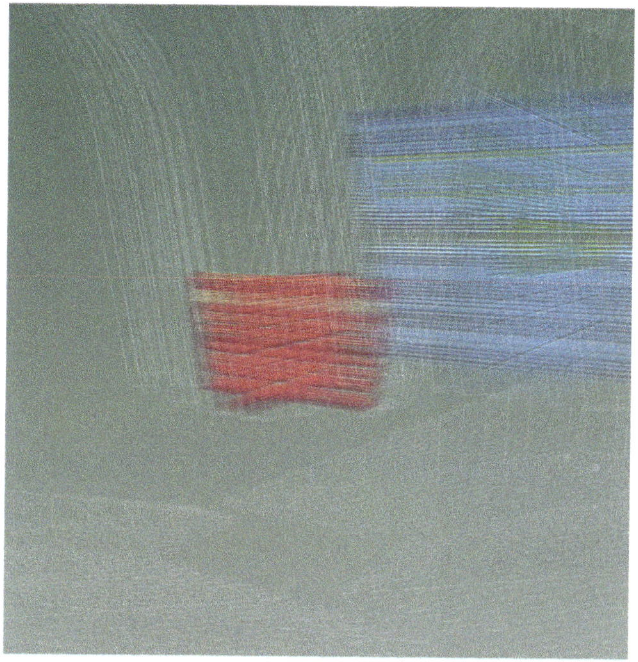
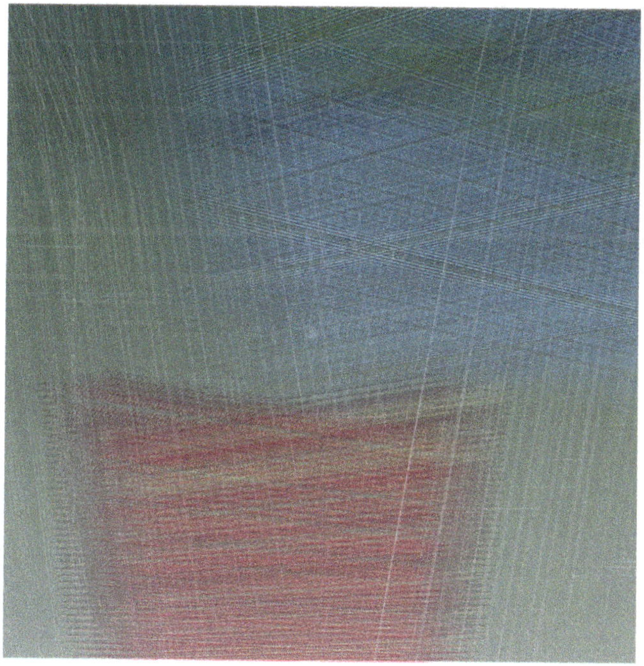
 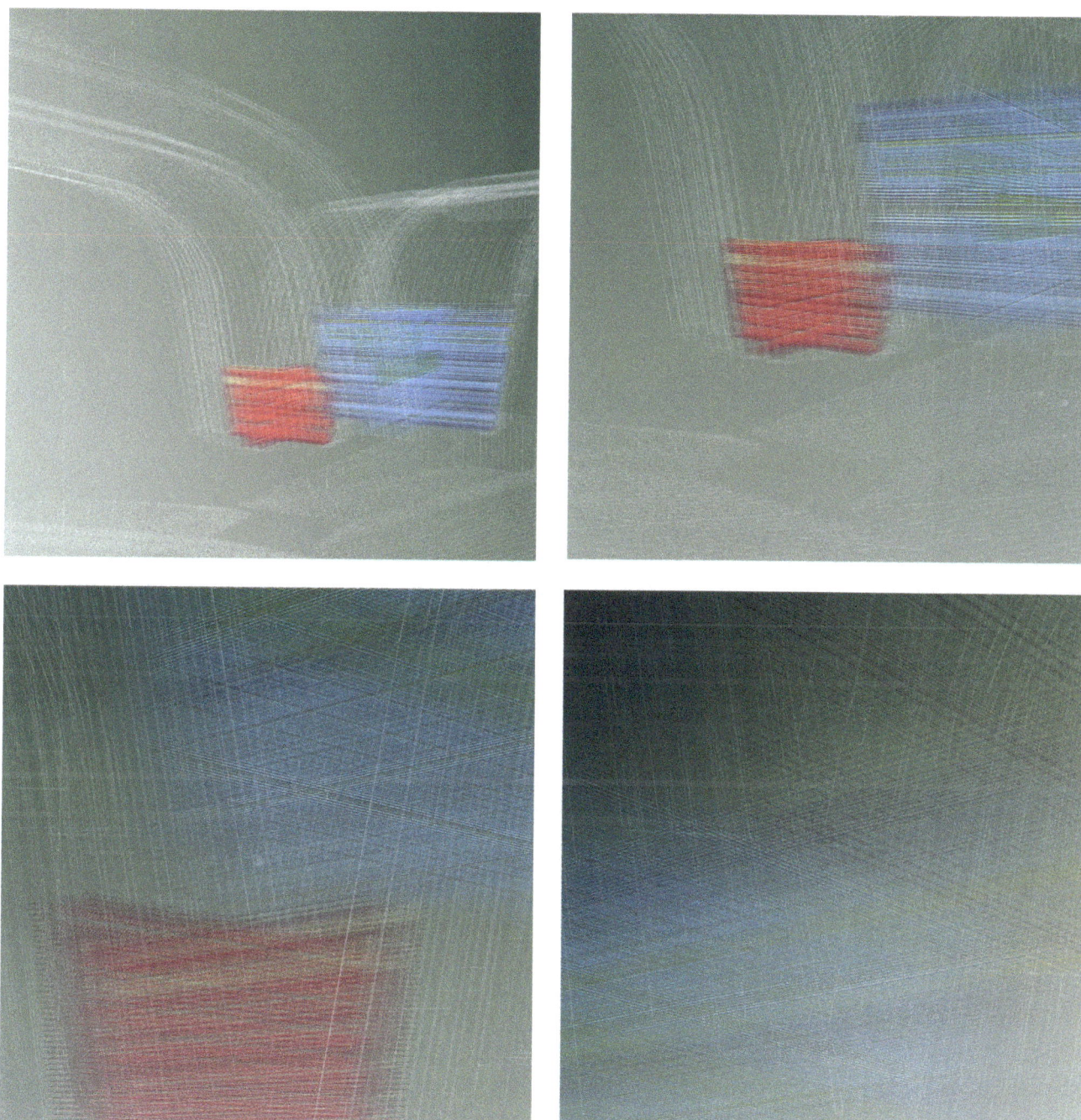

AIR (nee COTTON) GRID LIGHT, electronic model, views 37-40

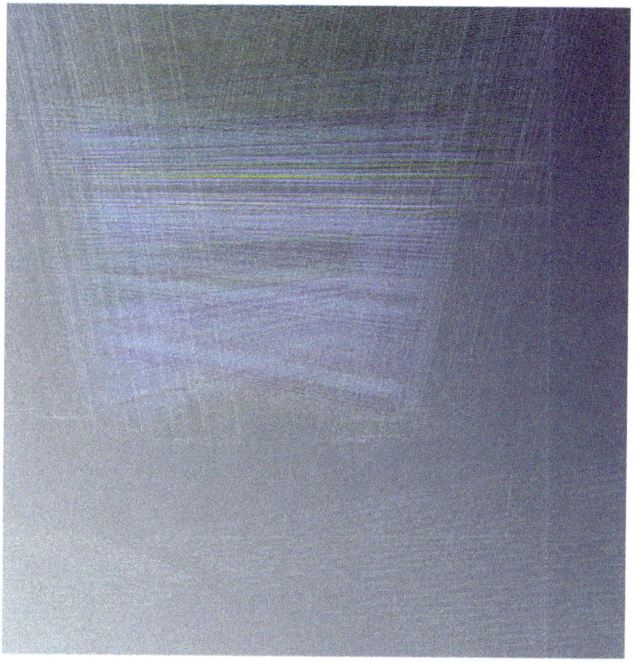

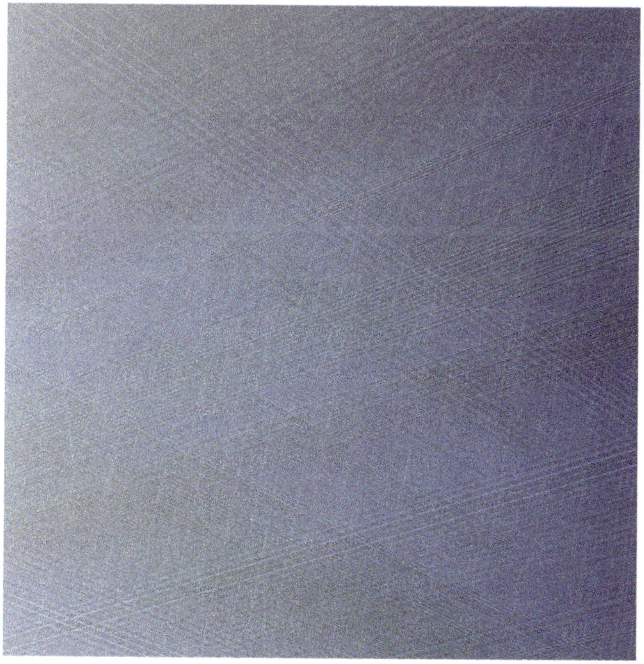

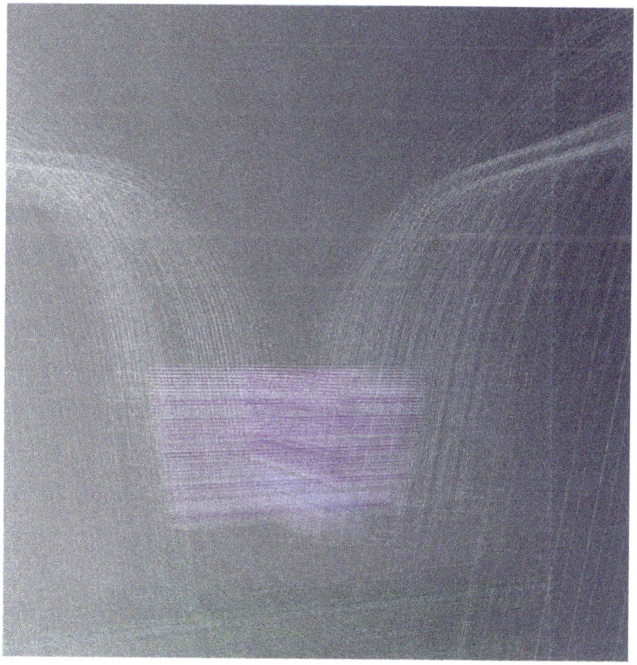

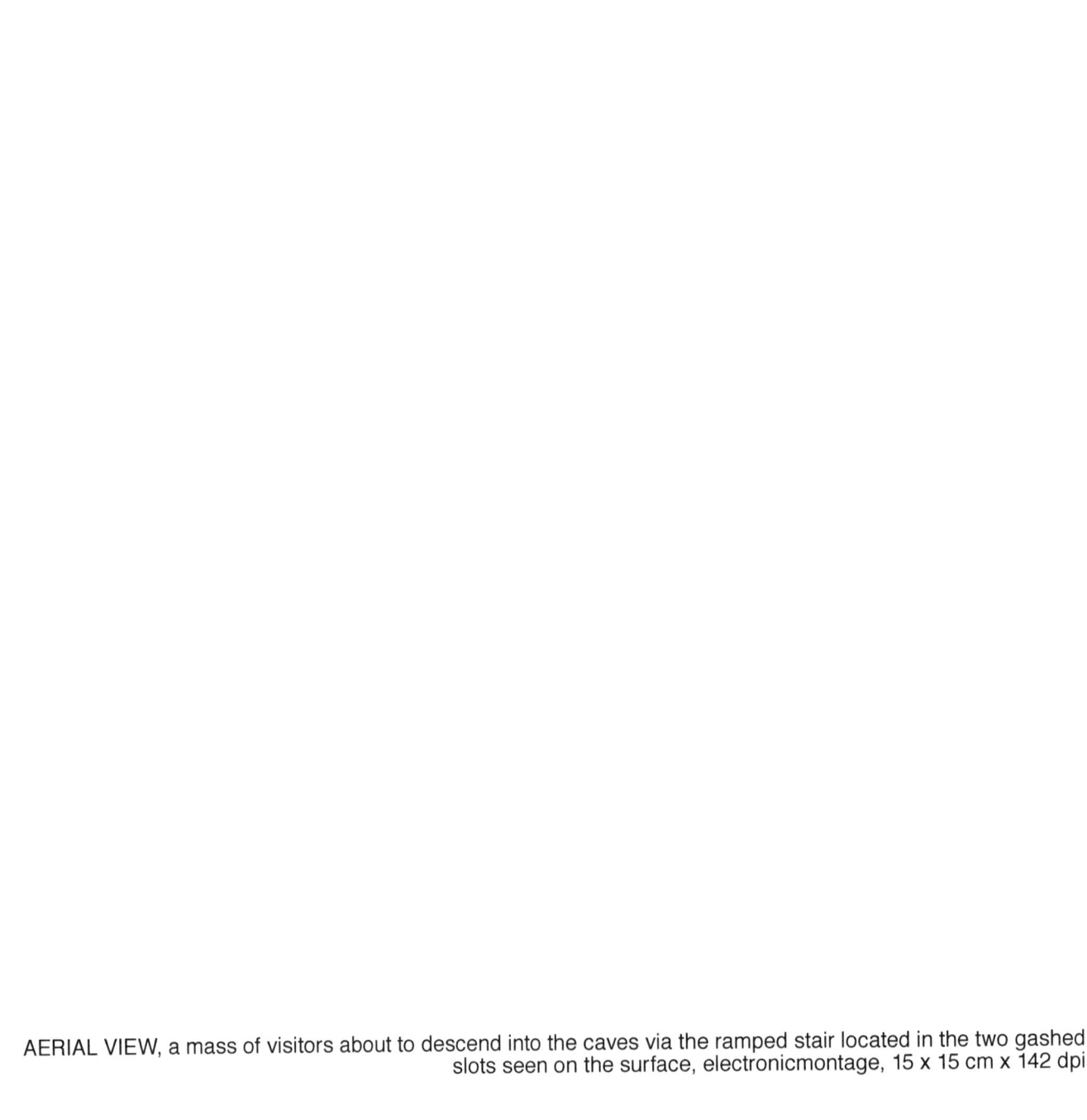

AERIAL VIEW, a mass of visitors about to descend into the caves via the ramped stair located in the two gashed slots seen on the surface, electronicmontage, 15 x 15 cm x 142 dpi

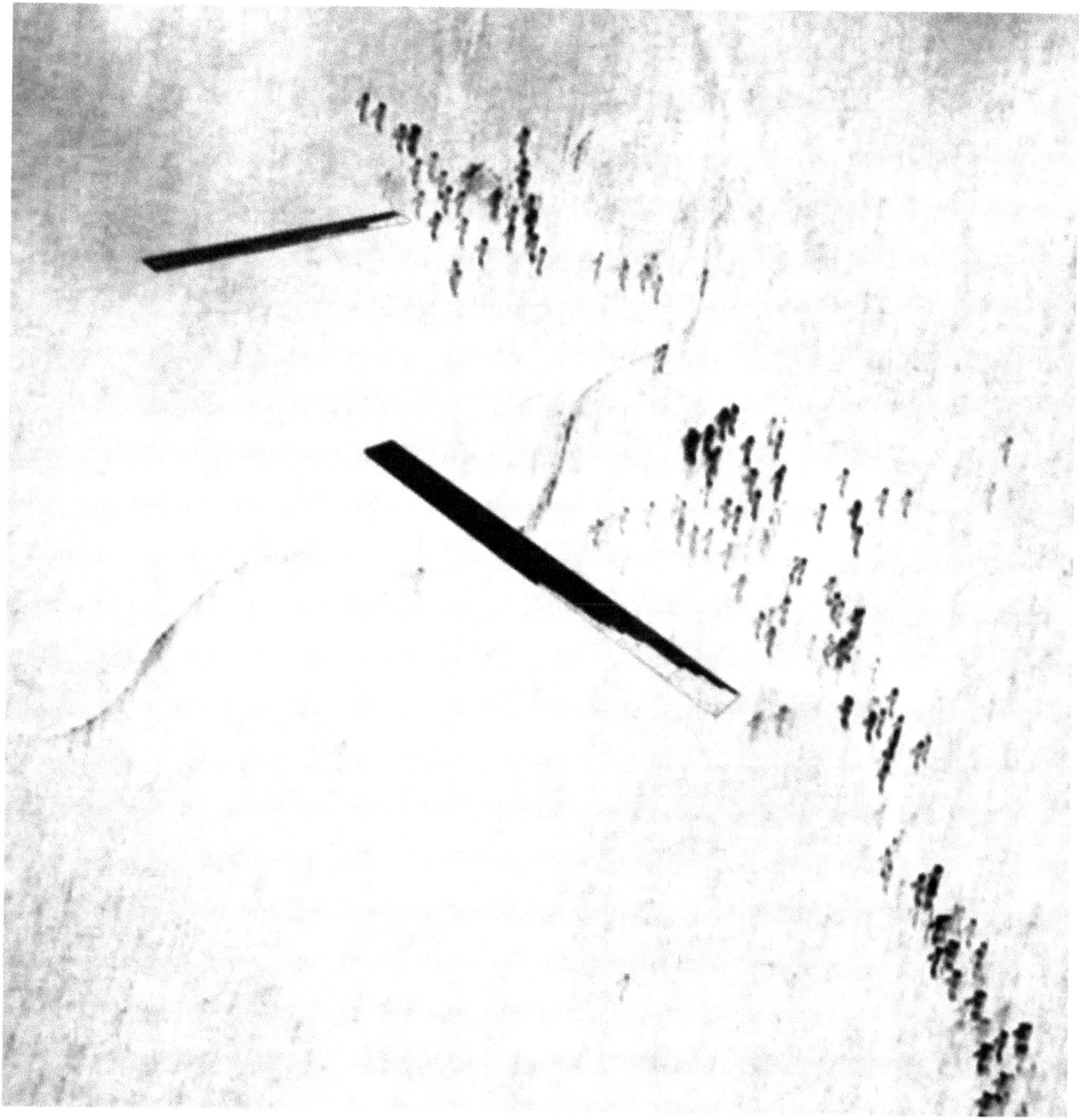

IN A CAVERN UNDERGROUND, a grid chamber is found, electronicmontage, 25 x 25 cm x 300 dpi

A LARGE GRID BECKONS ENTRY, electronicmontage, 19 x 19 cm x 300 dpi

INSIDE THE GRID CHAMBER, view 01, electronicmontage, 24 x 24 cm x 300 dpi

INSIDE THE GRID CHAMBER, view 02, electronicmontage, 24 x 24 cm x 300 dpi

INSIDE THE GRID CHAMBER, view 03, electronicmontage, 24 x 24 cm x 300 dpi

INSIDE THE GRID CHAMBER, view 04, electronicmontage, 24 x 24 cm x 300 dpi

INSIDE THE GRID CHAMBER, view 05, electronicmontage, 24 x 24 cm x 300 dpi

INSIDE THE GRID CHAMBER, view 06, electronicmontage, 24 x 24 cm x 300 dpi

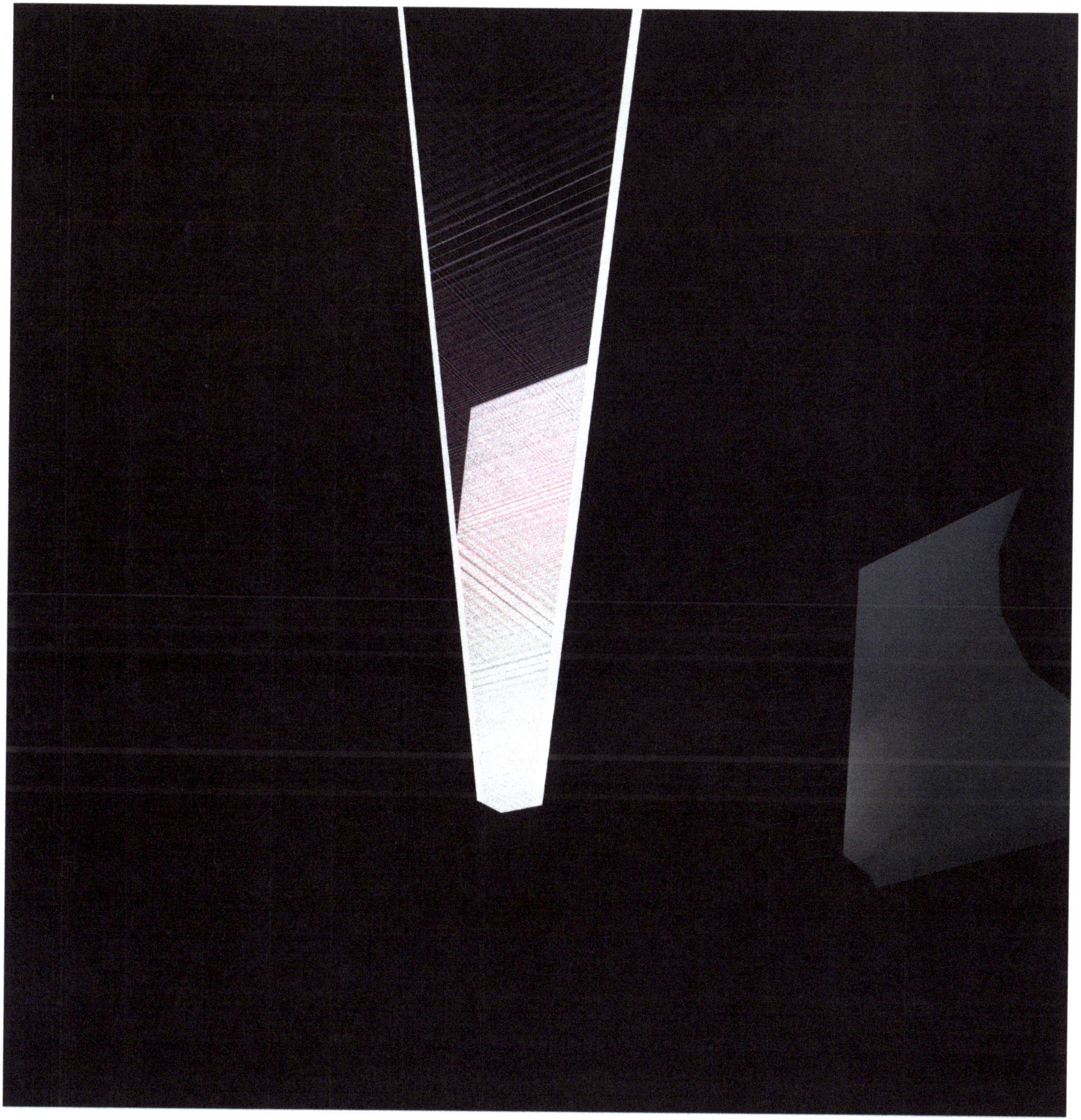

INSIDE THE GRID CHAMBER, view 07, electronicmontage, 24 x 24 cm x 300 dpi

INSIDE THE GRID CHAMBER, view 08, electronicmontage, 24 x 24 cm x 300 dpi

INSIDE THE GRID CHAMBER, view 09, electronicmontage, 24 x 24 cm x 300 dpi

INSIDE THE GRID CHAMBER, view 10, electronicmontage, 24 x 24 cm x 300 dpi

INSIDE THE GRID CHAMBER, view 11, electronicmontage, 24 x 24 cm x 300 dpi

INSIDE THE GRID CHAMBER, view 12, electronicmontage, 24 x 24 cm x 300 dpi

INSIDE THE GRID CHAMBER, view 13, electronicmontage, 24 x 24 cm x 300 dpi

INSIDE THE GRID CHAMBER, view 14, electronicmontage, 24 x 24 cm x 300 dpi

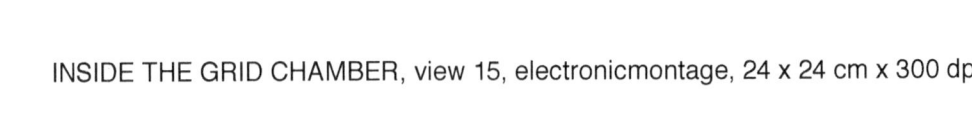

INSIDE THE GRID CHAMBER, view 15, electronicmontage, 24 x 24 cm x 300 dpi

INSIDE THE GRID CHAMBER, view 16, electronicmontage, 24 x 24 cm x 300 dpi

INSIDE THE GRID CHAMBER, view 17, electronicmontage, 24 x 24 cm x 300 dpi

INSIDE THE GRID CHAMBER, view 18, electronicmontage, 24 x 24 cm x 300 dpi

INSIDE THE GRID CHAMBER, view 19, electronicmontage, 24 x 24 cm x 300 dpi

INSIDE THE GRID CHAMBER, view 20, electronicmontage, 24 x 24 cm x 300 dpi

VISITORS MERGE WITH COLOURED LIGHT, prismagram 0^{Z}, 17 x 17 cm x 180 dpi

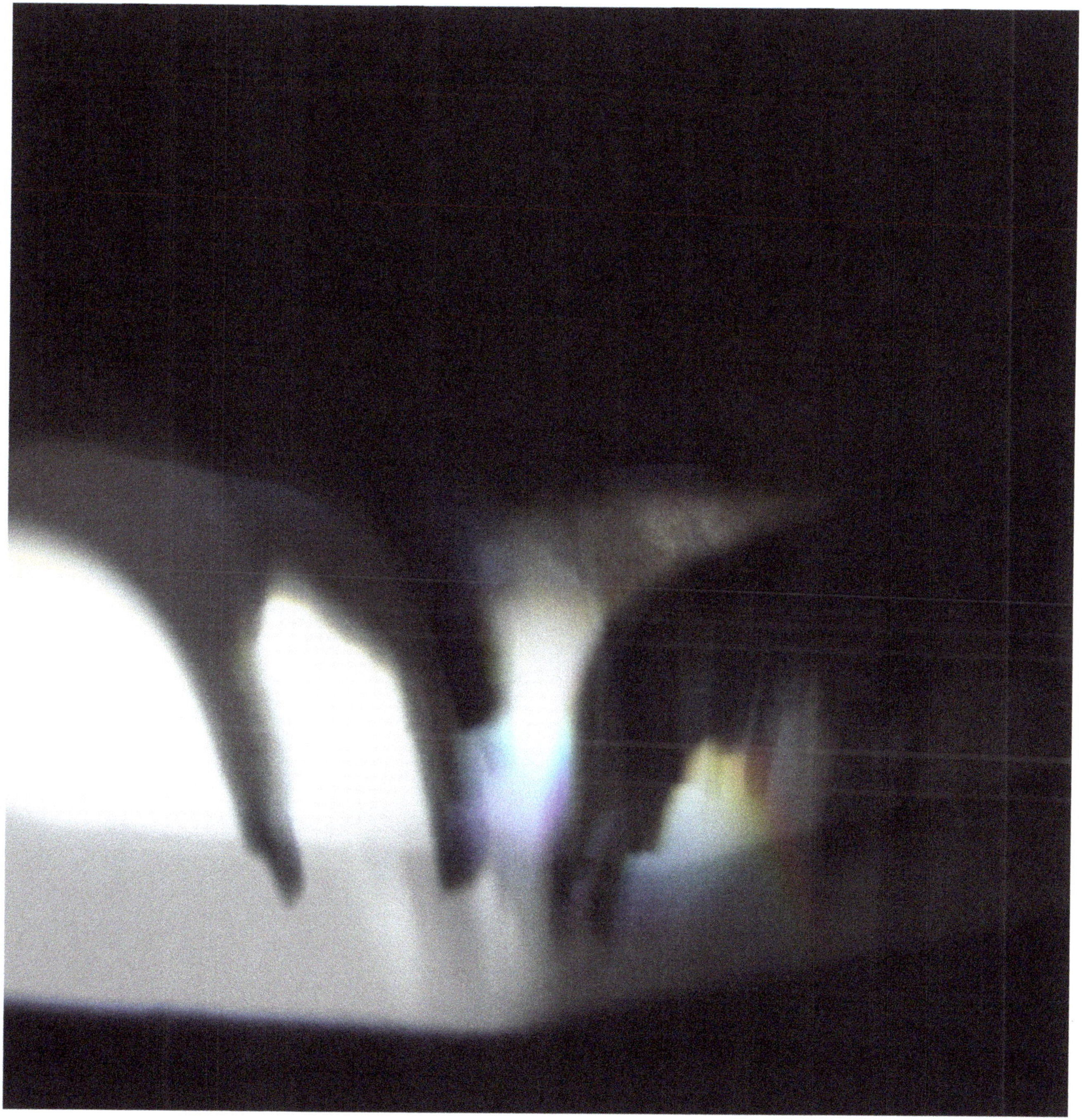

VISITORS MERGE WITH COLOURED LIGHT, prismagram 0^{Y}, 17 x 17 cm x 180 dpi

ANIMATION SEQUENCE, prismagrams

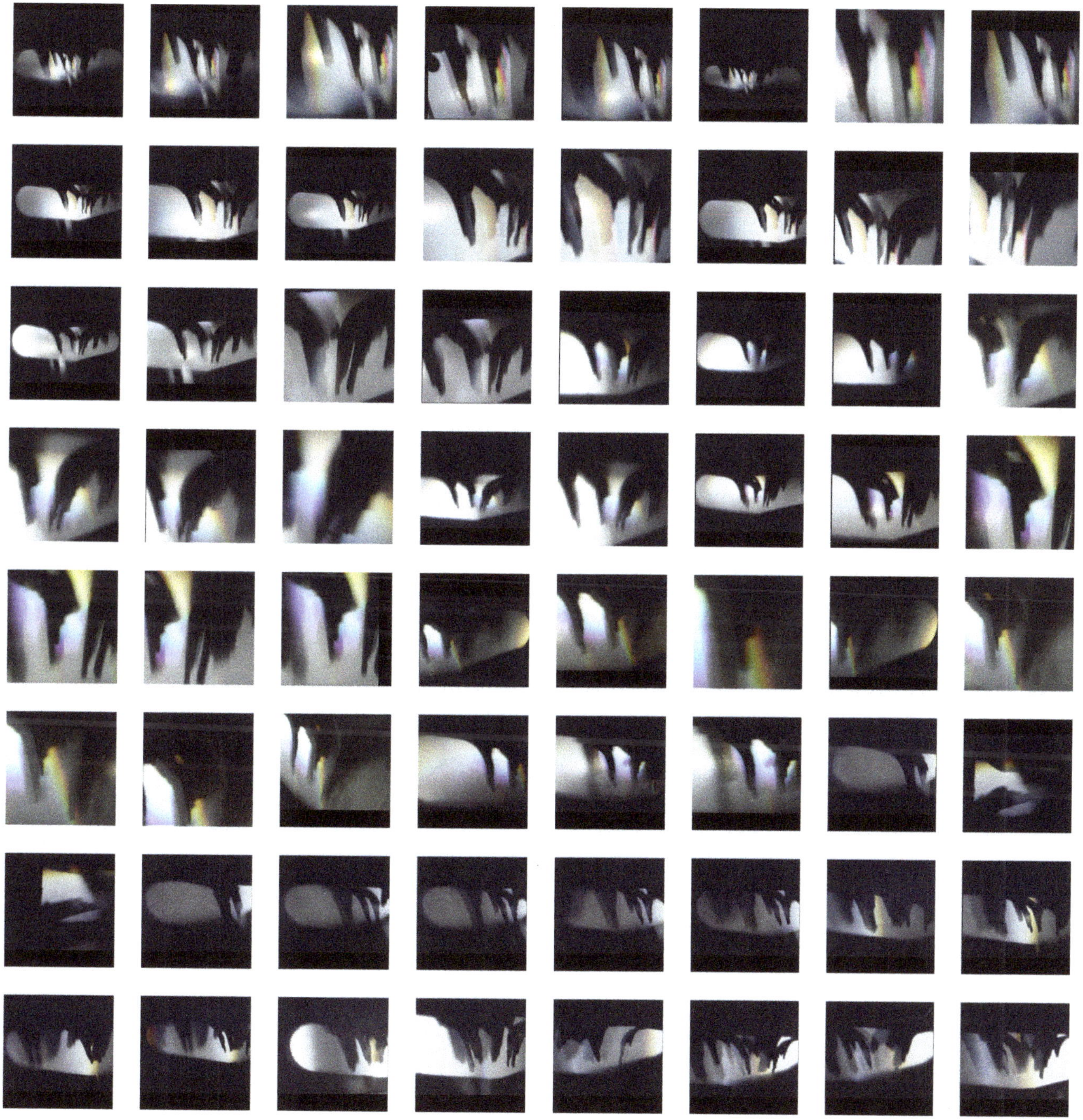

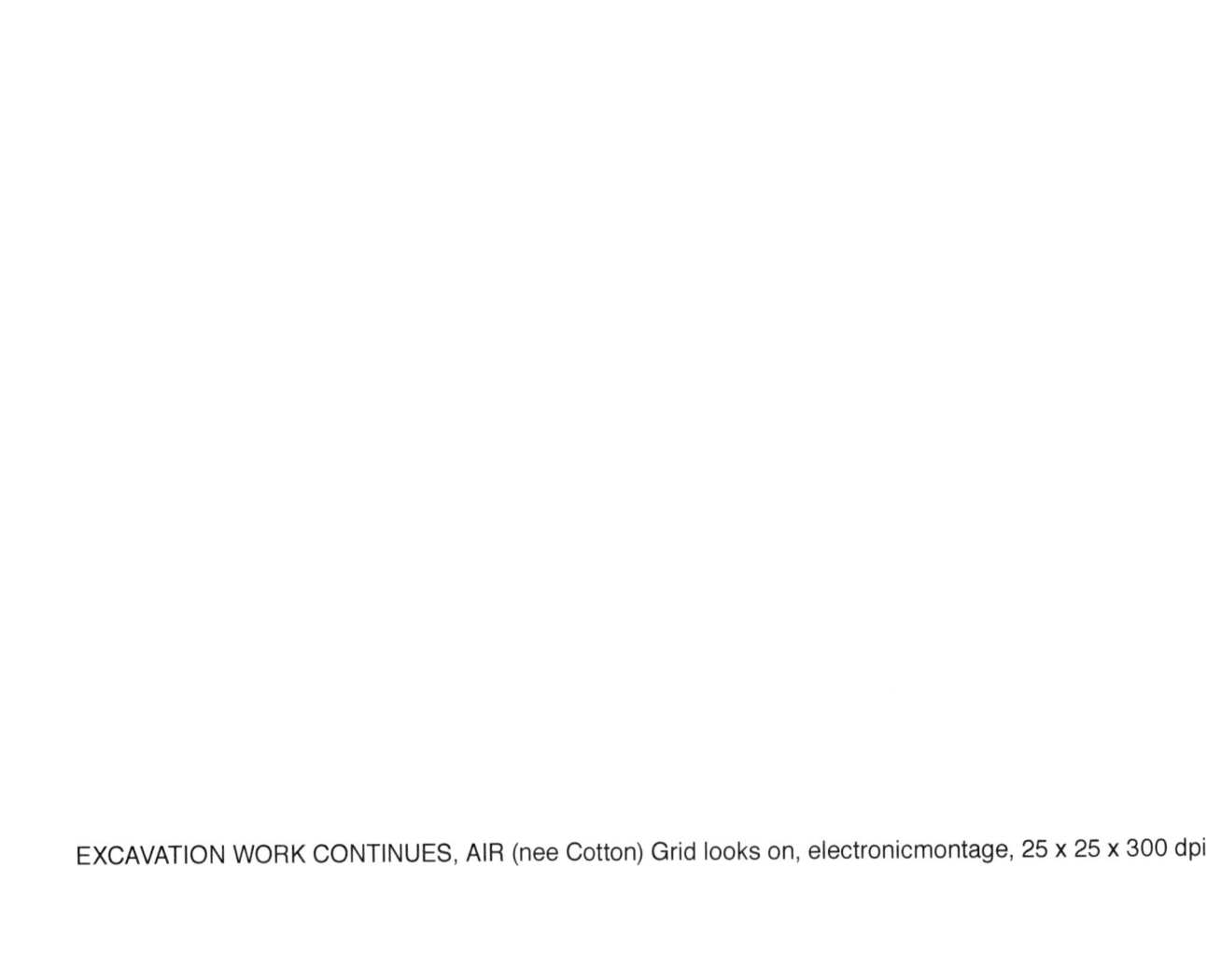

EXCAVATION WORK CONTINUES, AIR (nee Cotton) Grid looks on, electronicmontage, 25 x 25 x 300 dpi

CONCLUSION

This thesis is an exploration of the sensibility of modernity, focused through a dualistic study of the work of Mies, it has aimed to critique and revise post-modernist readings of the Modern Movement in Architecture. The work of the thesis has been conducted through discussion of analytical texts, including Mies' own writing, through making and through architectural propositioning. The choice of Mies as subject matter was a response to the suggestion that a new, post-modern, Mies had been discovered. The presence of the new Mies was very much in evidence at the conference, held in Toronto in 1992, to celebrate the twenty fifth anniversary of the Toronto Dominion Centre, 1967, designed by Mies. The conference was entitled The Presence of Mies, a title that also served for the collection of conference papers, published as a book in 1994.[1] As noted in the thesis introduction, one critic, Rosalind Krauss, had reservations about the post-modern Mies. She suggested there was still much about the old one that remained something of a mystery; she thought to rush hastily toward another kind of Mies, no matter how up-to-date he might seem, was likely to lead to the production of superficial readings.[2] Krauss followed up her warning with a fascinating reading of the grid paintings of Agnes Martin, suggesting that there was something to be learned from Martin's painterly grids about the architectural grids of Mies. To exemplify Mies' interest in the grid-form Krauss alluded to the 1000-ton plate of the roof of the New National Gallery in Berlin.

This thesis can be understood, then, as a response to Krauss's suggestion that by engaging with the grid form it may be possible to learn something new about something old. This thesis began by attempting to rediscover the old Mies, in doing so it examined a number of concepts that had been formulated in the body of literature, produced between 1920 and 1960, which not only marked, but was also instrumental in Mies' rise to the position of being deemed a leading practitioner of the Modern Movement in Architecture. The concepts are interesting because of the way in which they both can and cannot be seen to inhere in Mies' work. For example, Van Doesburg's related concepts of 'pure surface' and 'involuntary beauty' do seem to apply to Miesian architecture; and yet when Mies himself referred to materials he did so in a manner that was objective and matter of fact; certainly he never suggested, as did Van Doesburg, that materials are possessed of an energy-force, a will of their own. Similarly, when Mies referred to beauty he did not see it as something residing in the materials of which a particular architectural artifact had been made. For Mies beauty was a matter of relationships, it lay between things and was invested in artifacts through a process he termed 'form-giving.'

The anomalous relation between Miesian architecture and the critical concepts developed through discussion of that architecture is present in all the concepts discussed in the first section of the first part of this thesis. Concepts such as 'structural honesty,' 'metaphysical beauty,' 'universal space,' can be seen to come close but to miss their subject. It is interesting that Mies' own favourite concept, form-giving, was touched upon by one critic only: Ludwig Hilberseimer. Hilberseimer thought the beauty of Miesian architecture depended upon the relationship of the two dimensional plan to the three-dimensional appearance in space; surely it is to this moment of transformation that we should look if the Miesian concept of form-giving is to be understood?

There is one concept which seems to have preoccupied the American critics, Johnson, Hitchcock and Blake, far more than the Europeans: function. When Lefebvre entered the debate on modern architecture he complained about function as an inadequate basis for generating architectural form. Mies would have agreed with him about this, but while Lefebvre missed exuberance and excess in the functionalist approach, Mies thought it neglected beauty and form-giving.

The second section of the first part of the thesis consists in the attempt to reconcile Lefebvre's notion of excess, which he saw as a fundamental ingredient of space, with Mies' notion of form-giving. In order to do so it has been necessary to set out Lefebvre's concept of living being, that is his concept of an embodied consciousness which knows itself. In order to understand living being it is necessary to appreciate the terminology by which Lefebvre constructed the conceptual form of living being, these terms are: 'living body,' 'space,' 'structure,' 'energy,' 'real reflection,' 'imaginary reflection,' 'the generation of consciousness,' 'self-consciousness,' 'the laws of space.' Lefebvre was adamant about the vital role architecture plays in the sustenance of living being. Architecture engages with living being by two means, which are interconnected. Architecture engages with living being, first as the producer of living bodies, which embody the laws of space and which serve as a haven within which living being, itself produced out of the laws of space, can reconnect to those laws. Second, architecture engages with living being by contributing to the reflective process by which living being constitutes itself as knowledge, i.e., by which living being knows itself. Lefebvre called this process abstraction and he regarded it to be potentially dangerous for living being. Lefebvre tended to be more interested in the second moment of architecture's engagement with living being than he was in the first; his interest in the first tending toward the manifestation of his personal preference for an architecture of mass: Lefebvre liked the massive brick vaults and walls of roman and baroque architecture.

Through familiarity with the terms by which Lefebvre constructed his concept of the relation of architecture to living being it is possible to use those terms to put together a new reading of Miesian architecture, and perhaps, more generally of Modern Architecture. This reading is made, first, by looking carefully at Mies' statements about architecture, second, by looking at a number of theoretical and unbuilt projects, including the texts Mies wrote to accompany them, and third, by recounting the experience and analysis of a realised project, this being the project to which Krauss herself alluded at the Toronto conference, the New National Gallery, Berlin. The analysis revealed the extraordinary persistence of the grid presence in the Miesian work and suggested it be understood as a demonstration of form-giving, as a transformative process effected by the active engagement of living being with space.

In concluding the analysis of Miesian architecture the thesis returned to Krauss' suggested analogy between the grids of Agnes Martin and those of Mies. It suggested the three moments of experience, through which Krauss read Martin's paintings, were reproduced in the experience of Miesian architecture, but with one important difference. While the middle moment of the painterly sequence is the optical effect of the painting becoming like mist, in the architectural sequence it manifests in the gravitational effect of the architecture becoming weightless.

The second part of the thesis, Making and Using AIR Grid, sets out the process of research and development that led to the discovery of AIR Grid. The adventure began by attempting to model the weightlessness of Miesian architecture, in doing so it produced the three-dimensional grid made of thread, this type of grid was seen to produce effects similar to those of the three moments of Martin's paintings. The correspondence was taken as confirmation, first, that Krauss was correct and it is valid to read Miesian architecture, as she did Martin's paintings, in terms of the atmospheric signifier: /cloud/. Second, and following from the first, it was taken as confirmation that the reading of the New National Gallery, as set out in the second section of the first part of this thesis was also valid.

If the interest of AIR Grid lay with the fact it delivered an experience of /cloud/, then it became important to identify a location in which that experience might be valid and necessary. Turning to Lefebvre's reservations about Modern Architecture, particularly to his argument that function alone could not serve as the basis for architectural production. Lefebvre believed that when the built environment is over-prescriptive in terms of use then something important goes missing, namely excess. Like Nietzsche, Lefebvre believed the eruption of massive bursts of energy was vital for the sustenance of living being. For Lefebvre the problem of Modern Architecture was not simply that it failed to provide for festival, spontaneity and play, but it positively crushed the desire for such modes of expenditure. The reason for this, he suggested, was because the modern environment operated by means of signification, it was an environment that signals to the user what kind of behaviour is expected. The users in turn, once immersed in a signalling milieu, come to depend on messages to tell them what to do, they only respond to environmental signals. Lefebvre's answer to the problem of modernist environments was the introduction of symbolic form, his account of the Sagrada Familia revealed what he meant by this.

In so far as Lefebvre believed what was missing from modern society is symbolic form his thinking is entirely in line with the thinking of Mies. Lefebvre argued that architecture could participate in the production of symbolic form by creating living bodies. In the presence of massive walls and arches of brick and stone and in the abundance of surface decoration, Lefebvre saw evidence that architecture had produced a body. Although Mies would not have used Lefebvre's terminology, it seems that his notion of clear construction, of structure and of form-giving were all aimed toward the idea that the architectural work must, like any living body, be capable of being perceived as a form, that is as an entity whose identity can only be understood as arising from an inherent determination. Unlike Lefebvre, who was more interested in the activities of the living body, Mies was preoccupied with its coherent organisation, these are not mutually exclusive preoccupations but, as the case of Mies and Lefebvre demonstrates, there is a distinct shift of emphasis between the two. In his evocation of the Sagrada Familia Lefebvre presented this living body as one that is dense with meaning, as if the walls and the vaults were radiating meanings into the air. If, in the case of Miesian architecture, there is the density of anything then that is the density of the air itself, it is the presence of the atmospheric signifier, the /cloud/, produced in the three moments of experience of the grid. The atmospheric signifier has very little meaning, it is a signifier, but nothing very much is signified. The feeling prompted by the experience of the atmospheric signifier is a feeling that something is missing. It is not a feeling of loss, rather it is a feeling of potential, as if something is about to happen, or something is about to be done. It is this feeling of uncertain change that the project of the Cotton Caves aimed to arouse in the community of the new town of Stevenage.

Unfortunately it was beyond the scope of the thesis to measure the success of the project of the Cotton Caves. The thesis served merely to introduce the project, to reveal the theory which underpinned it and to set out some basic principles upon which a strategy of future research and development might be based.

ENDNOTES

INTRODUCTION

1. Krauss, 1994, 133.
2. For instance, Charles Jencks' essay, 'The Problem with Mies', Jencks.
3. Krauss, ibid.
4. Ibid., 136.
5. Lefebvre, 1991, 126.
6. Concinnitas is the idea that a work of architecture should be regulated by the use of a concept of the whole and that this concept is logically prior to the work and determines the position of the parts and their relations with each other and with the whole. The concept of concinnitas is concerned with issues of skill, of the distinction between that which is well made and that which is not. It draws attention to issues of planning and foresight, not with a view to predetermining the use of an architectural artifact but with a view to elegant manufacture.
7. For an excellent account of the philosophy and history of this tradition see Van Eck.
8. Krauss, 1994, 138.
9. Ibid., 140.
10. Ibid.
11. Ibid., 140-141.
12. Ibid., 141

PART ONE: SPECTERS OF MIES
1.1: A MODERN MOVEMENT MIES

1. Lefebvre, 1991, 126.
2. Van Doesburg, 'Ambiguous Mentality', 59.
3. Van Doesburg, 'Significance of Glass', 67.
4. Van Doesburg, 'Dwelling Machine', 100.
5. Van Doesburg, 'Spirit of Space', 91.
6. Ibid., 95.
7. Ibid.
8. Ibid., 94.
9. Van Doesburg, 'Weißenhof,' 165.
10. Ibid., 167.
11. Ibid.
12. ibid., 169.
13. McGrath, 30.
14. Ibid.
15. Ibid., 29.
16. Carroll, 173.
17. Ibid.
18. Mies, 'Mirror-Glass', 314
19. Mies, 'Build Beautifully', 307
20. Ibid.
21. Ibid.
22. To avoid confusion this text will refer to the publication as The International Style and to the style concept as *The International Style*
23. Hitchcock & Johnson, 81.
24. Ibid., 91-92.
25. Johnson, 16.
26. Ibid., 21-22.
27. Ibid., 35.
28. Ibid., 42.
29. Ibid., 43.
30. Ibid., 49.
31. Ibid.
32. Ibid.,131.
33. Ibid.,137.
34. Ibid.
35. Ibid., 138.
36. Ibid.
37. Berlage, 'Style', 136.
38. Berlage, 'Foundations', 238.
39. Carter, 1961, 97.
40. Two of Berlage's essays would have been available to Mies in German: 'Gedanken über den Stijl in der Baukunst' (Leipzig,1905) and 'Grundlagen und Entwicklung der Architektur' (Berlin, 1908). All quotes in this section are taken from the translations of these two essays in Berlage, 1996
41. Schulze, 281.
42. Hilberseimer, 16.
43. Ibid.

44. Ibid., 12.
45. Ibid.
46. Ibid.
47. Ibid., 36.
48. Ibid., 41.
49. Ibid.
50. Ibid.
51. Ibid., 40
52. Mies, 'Radio Address', 311.
53. Blake, 17.
54. Ibid., 139.
55. Ibid., 144.
56. Ibid., 180.
57. Norberg-Schulz, 338.
58. Ibid.
59. Ibid.
60. Ibid., 339.
61. Blake, 183.
62. Mies, 'Lecture', 1924, 250.
63. Lefebvre, 1995, 119.
64. Ibid.
65. Ibid.
66. Ibid.
67. Ibid., 125.
68. Ibid.
69. Ibid., 95.
70. Lefebvre, 1991, 123-4.
71. Ibid., 124.
72. Ibid., 126.

1.2: MIESIAN ARCHITECTURE & LEFEBVRIAN SPACE

1. Lefebvre, 1996, 116.
2. Lefebvre, 1991, 170.
3. Ibid., 171.
4. Ibid., 173.
5. Ibid.
6. Ibid., 174.
7. Ibid., 183 -184.
8. Ibid., 183.
9. Ibid., 185.
10. Ibid., 203.
11. Ibid., 178.
12. The influence of Nietzsche's thought in the circle of friends and mentors around Mies in his years in Berlin is documented in The Artless Word. See Neumeyer, 1991.
13. Nietzsche, 1967, 38.
14. Ibid., 35.
15. Ibid.
16. Ibid., 36.
17. Ibid., 37.
18. Ibid., 61.
19. Ibid., 62.
20. Ibid., 64.
21. Ibid., 40.
22. Lefebvre, 1991, 179.
23. Ibid., 177.
24. Ibid., 137.
25. Quoted in Evans, 1995, 333.
26. Lefebvre, 1991, 232.
27. Mies, 'Museum', 322.
28. Ibid.
29. Ibid.
30. Mies, 'The Adam Building', 305.
31. Ibid.
32. Ibid.
33. Ibid.
34. Ibid.
35. Mies, 'Radio Address', 311.
36. Mies, 'Regarding', 257.
37. Mies, 'Preconditions', 300.
38. Mies, 'Where do we go', 332.
39. Mies, 'On Form', 257.
40. Krauss, 1994, 146.

PART TWO: MAKING AND USING AIR GRID

2.1: GENESIS & EVOLUTION

1. Mies, Skyscrapers, 240
2. Mies, Office Buildings, 241

3. For instance, Robin Evans' essay, 'Mies van der Rohe's Paradoxical Symmetries', in: Evans, 1997; or see J.M. Richards' criticism of The New National Gallery, in Architectural Review, December, 1968.

2.2: THE COTTON CAVES

1. See above, A Modern Movement Mies, note 63

CONCLUSION

1. Mertins.
2. Krauss, 1994, 143.

BIBLIOGRAPHY

Abbott, E.A., *Flatland*, Princeton, New Jersey, Princeton University Press, 1991.

Adcock, C., *James Turrell, The Art of Light and Space*, Berkeley, Los Angeles, Oxford, University of California Press, 1990.

Alberro, A. (Ed), *Two-Way Mirror Power Selected Writings by Dan Graham on His Art*, Cambridge, Massachusetts, London, England, MIT Press, 1990.

Anon., 'Seagram's Bronze Tower,' *Architectural Forum, v109,* July, 1958, 67-77.

Anon., 'Mies Speaks', *Architectural Review, V144*, December, 1968, 451-452.

Anon.: 'The New National Gallery in Berlin by Ludwig Mies Van Der Rohe', *Architectural Record, November, 1968*, 115-122.

Anon., 'A Latterday Temple in Berlin', *Architectural Design, v39*, February 1969, 79-88.

Anon., 'A Mies Monument', *Progressive Architecture, v49*, November, 1968, 108-112.

Architectural Association, *Dan Graham Architecture*, London, 1997.

Art Institute of Chicago, *Mies Reconsidered: His Career, Legacy and Disciples*, New York, New York, The Art Institute of Chicago & Rizzoli, 1986.

Baal-Teshuva, J., *Mark Rothko 1903-1970 Pictures as Drama*, Köln, London, Los Angeles, Madrid, Paris, Tokyo, Taschen, 2003.

Bachelard, G., *Water and Dreams, an Essay on the Imagination of Matter*, trans., E.R. Farrell, Dallas, The Dallas Institute, 1983

Bachelard, G., *Air and Dreams, An Essay on the Imagination of Movement*, trans., E.R. & C.F. Farrell, Dallas, The Dallas Institute, 1988

Banham, R., 'Almost Nothing is too Much', *Architectural Review, v132*, September, 1962, 125-128.

Bataille, G., Theory of Religion, trans., R. Hurley, New York, Zone, 1992.

Baudrillard, J., *The System of Objects*, trans., J. Benedict, London & New York, Verso, 1996.

Baume, N. (Ed), *Sol Lewitt: Incomplete Open Cubes*, Hartford Connecticut, Wadsworth Atheneum Musuem of Art & Cambridge, Massachusetts, London, England, MIT Press, 2001.

Behne, A., *The Modern Functional Building*, trans., M. Robinson, Santa Monica, California, Getty Research Institute, 1996.

Berlage, H.P., *Thoughts on Style 1886-1908*, trans., I. Boyd Whyte & W. De Wit, Santa Monica, California, Getty Research Institute, 1996.

Berlage, H. P., 'Thoughts on Style in Architecture', trans, I. Boyd White & W. De Wit, Berlage, 1996, 122-156.

Berlage, H. P., 'The Foundations and Development of Architecture', trans, I. Boyd White & W. De Wit, Berlage, 1996, 185-257.

Blake, P., *The Master Builders*, London, Victor Gollancz, 1960.

Blaser, W., *Mies Van Der Rohe: The Art of Structure*, London, Thames & Hudson, 1965.

Blaser, W., *Mies van der Rohe*, Bologna, Zanichelli, 1977.

Blaser, W., *Mies van der Rohe, Farnsworth House Weekend House*, Basel, Boston, Berlin, Birkhäuser, 1999.

Bois, Y-A. & Krauss, R. E., *Formless, A Users Guide*, New York, Zone, 1997.

Borden, I., *Skateboarding, Space and the City*, Oxford & New York, Berg, 2001.

Callois, R., 'Mimicry and Legendary Psychasthenia', trans, Shepley, J., in: *October, no. 31, winter, 1984*, 16-32.

Calvino, I., *Cosmicomics*, trans., W. Weaver, London, Picador, 1965.

Calvino, I., *t zero*, trans., W. Weaver, San Diego, New York, London, Harcourt Brace & Company, 1967.

Calvino, I., *Invisible Cities*, trans., W. Weaver, London, Penguin, 1972.

Carroll, L., *Alice's Adventures in Wonderland and Through the Looking Glass*, London, Everyman, 1992.

Carter, P., 'Mies van der Rohe an Appreciation on the Occasion of his 75th Birthday', *Architectural Design, March, 1961*, 95-117.

Carter, P., *Mies Van Der Rohe at Work*, London, England, Phaidon, 1999.

Caumont, J. & Gough-Cooper, J. (Eds), *Yves Klein, 1928-1962, Selected Writings*, trans, B. Wright, Millbank, London, Tate Gallery, 1974.

Charlet, N., Yves Klein, Trans., M. Taylor, Paris, France,
Charlet, N., Yves Klein, Trans., M. Taylor, Paris, France,
Vilo, 2000.

Claxton, E., *The Hidden Stevenage*, Sussex, England, The Book Guild, 1992.

Damisch, H., *The Origin of Perspective*, Cambridge, trans., J. Goodman, Massachusetts & London, England, MIT Press, 1994.

Damisch, H., A Theory of /Cloud/: Towards a history of Painting, trans., J. Lloyd, Stanford, California, Stanford University Press, 2002.

Daza, R., *Looking for Mies*, Barcelona, ACTAR, Basel, Boston, Berlin, Birkhäuser, 2000

Deleuze, G., Nietzsche and Philiosophy, trans, H. Tomlinson, London & New York, Continuum, 1983.

Drexler, A., *Ludwig Mies Van Der Rohe*, New York, Braziller ,1960, 139-141.

Eco, U., *Art and Beauty in the Middle Ages*, trans., H. Bredin, New Haven & London, Yale, 1986.

Evans, R., *The Projective Cast*, Cambridge, Massachusetts & London, England, MIT Press, 1995.

Evans, R., 'Mies van der Rohe's Paradoxical Symmetries', Evans, 1997, 232-276.

Evans, R., *AA Documents 2: Translations From Drawing to Building and Other Essays*, London, Architectural Association, 1997.

Fer, B., *On Abstract Art*, New Haven & London, Yale, 1997.

Feynman, R. P., QED, *The Strange Theory of Light and Matter*, London, Penguin, 1990.

Flam, J., *Robert Smithson: The Collected Writings*, Berkeley, Los Angeles, London, University of California Press, 1996.

Forty, A., *Words and Buildings: A Vocabulary of Modern Architecture*, London, Thames & Hudson, 2000

Foster, S.C., Hans Richter: *Activism Modernism and the Avant-Garde*, Cambridge, Massachusetts & London, England, MIT Press, 1998.

Foster, H., *The Return of the Real*, Cambridge, Massachusetts & London, England, MIT Press, 1996.

Freud, S., *Civilization and its Discontents*, trans., J. Riviere, London, England, Hogarth, 1963.

Gage, J., *Colour and Meaning: Art, Science and Symbolism*, London, Thames & Hudson, 1999

Geary, J (ed), Goethe: *The Collected Works, Volume 3, Essays on art and Literature*, New Jersey, Princeton, 1986.

Gibson, J. J., *The Senses Considered as Perceptual Systems*, Boston, Houghton Mifflin, 1966.

Giedion, S., *Space Time and Architecture: The Growth of a New Tradition*, London, Oxford University Press, 1952.

Guilbaut, S., *Reconstructing Modernism: Art in New York, Paris, and Montreal 1945-1964*, Cambridge, Massachusetts & London, England, MIT Press, 1990.

Harrison & Woods (eds), *Art in Theory 1900-1990 an Anthology of Changing Ideas*, Oxford UK & Cambridge USA, Blackwell, 1992.

Haskell, A., *Agnes Martin*, New York, Whitney Museum of American Art, 1992.

Hayward Gallery & MACBA, *Force Fields: Phases of the Kinetic*, London & Barcelona, 2000.

Hays, K. M., 'Critical Architecture: Between Culture and Form', *Perspecta No 21*, 1984, 15-29.

Hearn, G. F. (Ed), *The Architectural Theory of Viollet-le-Duc Readings and Commentary*, Cambridge, Massachusetts & London, England, MIT Press, 1990.

Heynan, J., *A Place for Art, Ludwig Mies van der Rohe, Haus Lange-Haus Esters*, Krefelder Kunstmuseen, Verlag Gerd Hatje, 1995.

Hilberseimer, L., *Mies Van Der Rohe*, Chicago, Paul Theobold & Co., 1956

Hilberseimer, L., *Groszstadt Architektur L'Architettura della Grande Citta*, trans., Bianca Spagnuolo Vigorita, Naples, CLEAN, 1998.

Hill, J., *Actions of Architecture: Architects and Creative Users*, London & New York, Routledge, 2003.

Hilpert, T., *Mies in Postwar Germany, The Mannheim Theatre*, Leipzig, Seemann, 2001.

Hitchcock & Johnson., *The International Style*, New York, 1966.

Houston, Rice University, Institute for the Arts, *Yves Klein 1928-1962 a Retrospective*, New York, 1982.

Houston, Contemporary Arts Museum, *James Turrell, Spirit & Light*, Houston, Texas, 1998.

Irwin, R., *Being and Circumstance: Notes Toward a Conditional Art*, San Francisco, California, Lapis, 1985.

Jencks, C., *Modern Movements in Architecture*, Harmondsworth, Penguin Books, 1973.

Johnson, P., *Mies Van Der Rohe*, New York, The Museum of Modern Art, 1947.

Johnson, P., *Mies Van Der Rohe*, London, Secker & Warburg, 1978.

Jordy, W.H., 'Seagram Assessed', *Architectural Review, v124*, December, 1958, 375-382.

Koerner, J.L., *Caspar David Friedrich and the Subject of Landscape*, London, Reaktion, 1990.

Kopp, A., *Town and Revolution*, trans., T.E. Burton, New York, Braziller, 1970.

Kracauer, S., 'The Mass Ornament', Levin, T.Y. (ed): *The Mass Ornament Weimar Essays Siegfried Kracauer*, trans., T.Y. Levin, Cambridge, Massachusetts, London, England, Harvard University Press, 1995, 74-86.

Krauss, R., *Passages in Modern Sculpture*, Cambridge, Massachusetts & London, England, MIT Press, 1977.

Krauss, R., 'Death of a Hermeneutic Phantom: Materialization of the Sign in the Work of Peter Eisenman', *Architecture & Urbanism, January 1980*, 189-219.

Krauss, R., *The Originality of the Avant-Garde and Other Modernist Myths*, Cambridge, Massachusetts & London, England, MIT Press, 1985.

Krauss, R., *The Optical Unconscious*, Cambridge, Massachusetts & London, England, MIT Press, 1993.

Krauss, R., 'The Grid the /Cloud/ and the Detail', Mertins, 1994, 134-147.

Kühne, G., 'Pure Form', *Architectural Design, v39*, February 1969, 89-90.

Lacan, J., *The Four Fundamental Concepts of Psycho-anaysis*, London, New York, Victoria, Ontario & Auckland, Penguin Books, 1977.

Lacan, J., *Ecrits: a Selection*, trans, A. Sheridan, London, Tavistock, 1977.

Lambert, P (ed), *Mies in America*, Canadian Centre for Architecture, Montreal, Whitney Museum of American Art, New York, Harry N. Abrams, Inc., 2001.

Ledeur, J-P., *Yves Klein, Descriptive Catalogue of Editions and Sculptures*, trans., P. F. Ledeur, Guy Pieters, 1999.

Lefebvre, H., *The Production of Space*, trans., D. Nicholson-Smith, Oxford UK & Cambridge USA, Blackwell, 1991.

Lefebvre, H., 'Notes on a New Town', *Introduction to Modernity*, trans., J. Moore, London, New York, Verso, 1995, 116-126.

Linville, K., 'Agnes Martin: An Appreciation,' *Artforum 9*, June 1971, 72-73.

Loeb & Loeb (trans), *Theo van Doesburg On European Architecture: Complete Essays from Het Bouwbedrif 1924 - 1931*, Basel, Berlin, Boston, Birkhäuser, 1990.

London, Royal Academy of Arts, *Bauhaus, 50 Years*, London, 1968.

Loos, A., 'The Principle of Cladding', trans., Newman & Smith, Adolf Loos: *Spoken Into the Void Collected Essays 1897-1900*, Cambridge, Massachusetts & London, England, MIT Press, 1982, 66-69.

Loos, A.: 'Architecture', in: Arts Council, *The Architecture of Adolf Loos*, London, 1985, 104-109.

Madge, C., *Industry After The War Who is Going to Run It?*, London, Pilot Press, 1945.

Mallgrave, H. F., Gottfried Semper: *Architect of the Nineteenth Century*, New Haven & London, 1996.

März, R., & Schneider, A. (eds): *Neue Nationalgalerie Berlin, Museum Guide*, trans. J. W. Gabriel, Munich & New York, Prestel-Verlag, 1997.

McGrath, R., 'Looking into Glass', *Architectural Review, January, 1932*, pp29-35.

Mertins, D (ed), *The Presence of Mies*, New York, Princeton, 1994.

Mies van der Rohe, L., 'Skyscrapers', Neumeyer, 1991, 240.

Mies van der Rohe, L., 'Office Building', Neumeyer, 1991, pp241-242.

Mies van der Rohe, L., 'Building', Neumeyer, 1991, 241-242.

Mies van der Rohe, L., 'Building Art and the Will of the Epoch', Neumeyer, 1991, pp245-247.

Mies van der Rohe, L.,'Lecture' (1924), Neumeyer, 1991, 249-250.

Mies van der Rohe, L., 'Regarding the New Volume', Neumeyer, 1991, p257.

Mies van der Rohe, L., 'On Form in Architecture', Neumeyer, 1991, 257.

Mies van der Rohe, L., 'The Preconditions of Architectural Work', Neumeyer, 1991, 299-301.

Mies van der Rohe, L., 'The Adam Building', Neumeyer, 1991, 305.

Mies van der Rohe, L., 'Build Beautifully and Practically! Stop This Cold Fuctionality', Neumeyer,1991, 307.

Mies van der Rohe, L., 'On the Meaning and Task of Criticism', Neumeyer,1991, 308-309.

Mies van der Rohe, L., 'Radio Address', Neumeyer, 1991, 311.

Mies van der Rohe, L.: 'What Would Concrete, What Would Steel Be Without Mirror Glass?' in: Neumeyer, 1991, 314.

Mies van der Rohe, L., 'Was Wäre Beton, Was Stahl Ohne Spiegelglas?', Neumeyer, 1986, 378.

Mies van der Rohe, L., 'Inaugural Address as Director of Architecture at Armour Institute of Technology', Neumeyer, 1991, 316-317.

Mies van der Rohe, L., 'Museum for a Small City', Neumeyer, 1991, 322.

Mies van der Rohe, L., 'Architecture and Technology', Neumeyer', 1991, 324.

Mies van der Rohe, L., 'Lecture (Chicago)', Neumeyer, 1991, pp325-326.

Mies van der Rohe, L., 'Where Do We Go From Here', Neumeyer, 1991, 332.

Miller, D (ed), Goethe: *The Collected Works, Volume 12, Scientific Studies*, Princeton, New Jersey, Princeton University Press, 1988.

Morris, R., 'Notes on Sculpture 1-3', Harrison & Woods, p 813-822.

Neumeyer, F., *Mies van der Rohe, Das Kunstlose Wort: Gedanken zur Baukunst*, Berlin, Siedler, 1986.

Neumeyer, F., *The Artless Word: Mies van der Rohe on the Building Art*, trans., M. Zarzombek, Cambridge, Massachusetts & London, England, MIT Press, 1991.

Néret, G.: *Kazimir Malevich 1878-1935 and Suprematism*, London, Los Angeles, Madrid, Paris, Tokyo, Taschen, 2003.

Norberg-Schulz, C., 'A Talk With Mies van Der Rohe', Neumeyer, 1991, 338-339.

Nietzsche, F., 'The Birth of Tragedy', Nietzsche, 1967, 15-144.

Nietzsche, F., *The Birth of Tragedy and The Case of Wagner*, trans., W. Kaufmann, New York, Vintage Books, 1967.

Nietzsche, F., *Human, All too Human*, trans., M. Faber & S. Lehmann, London, New York, Victoria, Ontario, Auckland, Penguin Books, 1984.

Podro, M., *The Critical Historians of Art*, London, Yale, 1982.

Quetglas, J., 'Fear of Glass, The Barcelona Pavilion', Colmina, B. (Ed), *Architectureproduction*, New Jersey, Princeton, 1988, 123-151.

Richards, J.M., 'Mies in Berlin, Criticism', *Architectural Review, v144*, Dec 1968, 410.

Richardson, M (ed), *Georges Bataille Essential Writings*, London, Thousand Oaks, New Delhi, Sage Publications, 1998.

Riley and Bergdoll (eds), *Mies in Berlin*, New York, Museum of Modern Art, 2001.

Rossi, A., T*he Architecture of the City*, trans., D. Ghirardo & J. Ockman, Cambridge, Massachsetts & London, England, MIT press, 1982.

Rowe, C., *The Mathematics of the Ideal Villa and Other Essays*, Cambridge, Massachusetts & London, England, MIT press, 1976.

Russell, B., *History of Western Philosophy*, London, Routledge, 1961.

Saddler, S., *The Situationist City*, Cambridge, Massachusetts & London, England, MIT, 1998.

Saint-Exupery, A., *Southern Mail/Night Flight*, trans., C. Cate, London, New York, Victoria, Toronto, Auckland, Penguin Books, 1971.

Saint-Exupery, A., *Wind, Sand and Stars*, trans., W. Rees, London, New York, Victoria, Toronto, Auckland, Penguin Books, 1995.

Mallgrave & Ekonomos (eds), *Empathy Form and Space: Problems in German Aesthetics 1873 - 1893*, Santa Monica, 1994.

Schopenhauer, A., *The World as Will and Idea*, trans, Berman, J., London & Vermont, Everyman, 1995.

Schulz, F., *Mies van der Rohe A Critical Biography*, Chicago & London, University of Chicago Press, 1985.

Schulz, F., *Philip Johnson Life and Works*, New York, Knopf, 1994.

Schumann, W., *Collins Photo Guide To Rocks Minerals and Gemstones*, HarperCollins, 1992.

Schwarz, D. (Ed), *Agnes Martin: Writings/Schriften*, Winterthur, Kunstmuseum Winterthur, 1992.

Segal, W., 'Mies Van Der Rohe', *Architects Journal, v150*, n35, 27 August, 1969.

Semper, G., *The Four Elements of Architecture and Other Writings*, trans. & introduction, H. F. Mallgrave, & W. Herman, Cambridge University Press, 1989.

Smithson, A & P., *Ordinariness and Light*, London, Faber & Faber, 1970.

Stevenage Development Corporation, *The New Town of Stevenage*, London and Hertford, The Stevenage Development Corporation, 1949.

Tafuri & Dal Col., *Modern Architecture/1*, trans., E. Wolf, Milan, faber & faber/Electa, 1976.

Tafuri, M., *The Sphere and the Labyrinth*, trans: P. d'Acierno & R. Connolly, Cambridge, Massachusetts & London, England, MIT Press, 1997.

Thornber, N., *Pennine Underground*, Clapham, Lancaster, dalesman publishing company, 1959.

Tschumi, B., *Theoretical Projects: The Manhatten Transcripts*, London, Academy Editions, 1994.

Van Doesburg, T., 'The Ambiguous Mentality', Loeb & Loeb, pp57-63.

Van Doesburg, T., 'The Significance of Glass: Toward Transparent Structures', Loeb & Loeb, 63-70.

Van Doesburg, T., 'New Accomodation Standards: Designing the Dwelling Machine', Loeb & Loeb, 98-103.

Van Doesburg, T., 'Defending the Spirit of Space: Against a Dogmatic Functionalism', Loeb & Loeb, 88-95.

Van Doesburg, T., 'Stuttgart-Weißenhof 1927: Die Wohnung', Loeb & Loeb, 164-172.

Van Eck, C., *Organicism in Nineteenth-Century Architecture: An inquiry into its Theoretical and Philosophical Background*, Amsterdam, A & NP, 1994.

Winter, J., 'Misconceptions About Mies', *Architectural Review, v151*, February, 1972, 69.

www.ingramcontent.com/pod-product-compliance
Lightning Source LLC
Chambersburg PA
CBHW061752290426
44108CB00029B/2971
9780995589384